THE ABC OF BREAKING AND SCHOOLING HORSES

THE ABC OF BREAKING AND SCHOOLING HORSES

JOSEPHINE KNOWLES

J. A. ALLEN
LONDON

British Library Cataloguing in Publication Data
A catalogue record for this book is available from
the British Library.

ISBN 0.85131.559.3

Published in Great Britain by
J. A. Allen & Company Limited,
1, Lower Grosvenor Place, Buckingham Palace Road,
London, SW1W OEL.

© J. A. Allen & Co. Limited, 1993

Reprinted 1994

Text illustrations Diane Breeze
Design Nancy Lawrence

Printed in Hong Kong by Dah Hua Printing Co. Ltd.
Typeset in Hong Kong by Setrite Typesetters Ltd.

CONTENTS

v

INTRODUCTION

I have written this book because when visiting stables, clubs and competitions I have seen so many problems, disasters and accidents involving young horses and their owners. These problems could often have been avoided by a little knowledge of young horses and an understanding of their physical and mental abilities at different stages of growth. In many of these cases the owner/rider's ability to recognise and interpret fear, tension, pain, temper, pleasure, tiredness, aggression, frustration, boredom, affection and sheer naughtiness would have been a great help to both owner and horse.

Nowadays many people, who have very little real knowledge of horses at all, are buying foals or youngsters because they are cheaper than older 'made' horses or perhaps because they see these horses as a challenge. Often these new owners think everything will work out all right because their 'friend has had his/her own horse for three years and will help'.

This will not work. A young horse needs someone with years of experience with many different young horses to oversee its education. The owner of a young horse must be a capable rider, not in the least nervous, and know all about handling and riding many different and difficult horses of all temperaments. They must be calm, confident and thoughtful, not tense, loud-voiced or short-tempered. They will need patience, sympathy and understanding, and the ability to use their imagination to foresee dangers and problems and thus avoid them. If this does not describe you, then perhaps you are not yet ready to take on a youngster.

The owner/trainer of a young horse must be willing to learn and adapt and be able to concentrate completely on the horse and on what they are doing with it. They must be observant, quickly noticing any change in the horse's mental or physical state, and have the knowledge to work out the reason for such a change and, if necessary, the remedy.

Above all, they will need the imagination to put themselves in the horse's place. Would they understand what was being asked of them? Would they be happy, calm and confident under the same conditons if they were a horse? Would they enjoy the work they were being asked to do and do it willingly and cheerfully?

If you have never owned a horse before, your first horse should not be a youngster as you will almost certainly lack the practical working experience necessary to care for an unpredictable, difficult or nervous animal. You must be completely *au fait* with all areas of stable management and feeding so that you can spot problems the minute they arise. If you have never cared for any horse, you should take a course in stable management and then buy a mature, sensible horse for your first animal.

This book does not set out to teach stable management. I have assumed throughout that the reader already knows how to run a yard and care for horses, and so have only explained stable management techniques where they relate to dealing with young stock in particular.

Section One covers the education of the young horse from foal to four or five. All horses are individuals and all individuals mature, both mentally and physically, at different rates. Just because your horse is three years old, this does not mean it *must* be doing the work covered under the chapter on the three-year-old. If your horse is a slow learner or a slow developer, it may well need to take much longer than another youngster to cover the work I have suggested for the yearling or two-year-old and so may still be covering this work well into its third year. There is no point in rushing through the syllabus so that your horse learns nothing properly and ends up confused. You must work at the pace your youngster needs to work at because the object is to produce a horse that is obedient to the aids, has confidence in its rider, enjoys its work, has absorbed a firm foundation in school work and jumping, is sensible to hack out, loads and travels well and is well behaved with vets and farriers − in short, a well-mannered youngster that is ready to go on and will be a credit to you.

Section Two covers various aspects of dealing with youngsters that apply to any age and I suggest that, no matter what age your youngster is, you should read this section carefully.

I hope that in this book you will find practical, helpful advice that is easy to understand and, contained in this, the answers to most of your questions.

AUTHOR'S NOTE

The photographs in this book are of people working their horses as they normally do. Many people are not wearing hats or gloves and unfortunately probably will not do so until they have had an accident. A lot of the horses are being worked without boots. Their owners know their own horses and are obviously prepared to take the risk of injury. There are too many accidents to horses and those who work with them. Think ahead, take precautions to protect yourself and your horse from accidents caused by lack of care.

SECTION ONE

Educating the Young Horse

1 FOAL TO YEARLING

A newborn foal must be handled with care and given the peace and quiet and plenty of sleep required by all baby animals. Do not allow visitors to enter the box in case they upset the foal or the mare. This is especially important if the foal is the mare's first foal because some mares are a little frightened of their new foal, which may even be the first foal they have ever seen. The mare and foal need time to get to know each other and to form a bond.

You must be very observant at this early stage in the foal's life. Make sure it gets the all-important first milk as soon as possible. This milk contains colostrum which carries antibodies that will protect the foal from infections. Colostrum also has a slightly laxative effect and should cause the foal to expel meconium (dark brown, sticky, first dung formed inside the foal before its birth).

Most foals find their mothers' milk quite quickly but some need to be guided gently in the right direction by pushing their hindquarters and supporting them so that their heads can reach the mares' udders. If you try to guide the foal by holding its neck or head it will only run backwards and both mare and foal will become upset.

If the foal is seen to be straining and produces no dung, a vet must be consulted as there may be a blockage.

As soon as the foal begins to drink milk regularly, its dung will change to a bright yellow colour. This is quite normal in all milk-fed young animals.

Watch the foal to make sure it is passing urine (staling) normally. Again, if there is any sign of straining or discomfort, you must call the vet. If noticed early enough, such problems can usually be overcome, but if they go on unobserved, they can prove fatal.

Your foal should gain in strength every day. If you notice it becoming more wobbly and less co-ordinated, perhaps having more difficulty than previously in getting up on its feet, call the vet.

Your vet should check the foal sometime in its first 24 hours. At this time he will give the foal protection against tetanus and may give antibiotics.

Provided the mare is happy and confident when you are in the box, you can begin to handle the foal within the first 48 hours of birth. The foal will feel safer with something its own height or smaller, so crouch down low and keep still. The mare will probably come up to you, followed by the foal who will sniff you all over and be very inquisitive. A foal tends to copy its mother's reactions, so a calm, sensible, friendly mare is a great asset.

Some foals are bold from the start and will allow you to rub and scratch them all over. Others are more timid, so you might need an assistant to hold the mare near the wall of the box, but leaving space for the foal to fit between its mother and the wall. Manoeuvre the foal into the gap with your assistant in front to prevent the foal from going forward. With the mare on one side of it and the wall on the other, you can then come up quietly behind it to rub its hindquarters gently, gradually working towards its head and neck. Do not pat it or try to touch its face, and move very slowly because any sudden movements may frighten it.

Once the foal is accustomed to this, you can introduce it to a foal slip. Allow the foal to sniff this new object and then, while you rub around the head and ears, gently ease the foal slip on and do it up, being careful not to pull on the foal's head. If a foal, or any youngster, is afraid to put its nose into a head collar, use one with an adjustable noseband and completely undo this. Put the foal slip or head collar on round the foal's neck first, move it up gently towards its ears and do it up. Do up the noseband afterwards.

Leave the lead rope slack, allowing your hand to follow the foal's movements at first, then gradually take up a contact and begin to control it a little, still maintaining an 'allowing' hand, otherwise the foal may throw itself over backwards and get hurt. After a few minutes, remove the foal slip gently. Repeat this twice a day until the foal is quite calm about it.

It is not safe to turn a foal out in a head collar. Many foals have been badly injured by catching a hind foot in a head collar while scratching their ears. They can also get caught up when rubbing on fences and gates and will then panic.

If the weather is mild and the foal strong and healthy, it should be able to go out in the field in the daytime when it is two days old. Bring the mare and foal in at night until the weather is really warm and settled. In hot weather they will be happier out at night and in by day, away from the flies.

Even if they are kept out both day and night, bring them in frequently so that you can begin to handle and educate the foal while it is not too strong. At first you may need three people to get the foal in and out if it is not yet accustomed to a foal slip. One person leads the mare and the other two link arms around the foal's chest and hindquarters to control and guide it.

Sometimes the mare is reluctant to leave the box because she is afraid of being separated from the foal, so you may need to push the foal out of the door first so that the mare will follow. Once she realises that the foal is with her, the mare will probably be quite willing to go on ahead and the foal will wish to follow her.

In the first few days of life a foal will often gallop very fast indeed without thinking where it is going. For this reason, well-constructed, solid, easily seen fences are essential in the mare and foal's field. Barbed wire or wire guard rails are highly dangerous during the foal's first weeks, even if the wire has strips of plastic tied to it to make it more obvious. Fields with deep, unfenced ditches or streams should also be avoided.

If the mare does not know the field in which you are putting her, lead her round the boundary and show her where the water is.

At first, the mare and foal will be safest in a field by themselves. Once they have settled into their routine, a second mare and foal could be introduced. Do not turn the mare and foal out with geldings, boisterous youngsters or with a mare who does not have a foal herself. Such a mare may try to take the foal away from its mother, causing the mother to gallop about in an attempt to protect her foal which may get hurt in the melée. Horses in a group are often very curious. They may mob and chase a foal, with disastrous consequences.

TYING UP

Before tying a foal up, remove all buckets from the box. Tie up the mare and put a strong foal slip on the foal, with a long, strong lead rope. Pass the rope through a metal ring set high enough up on the wall for the foal to be unable to get a foreleg over the rope. Do not tie the rope; keep the end of it in your hand and stand behind the foal with your other hand on its quarters to encourage it to move forward again each time it leans back on the rope. By this time the foal will be quite accustomed to your presence and touch and should not be afraid when you stand behind it. The foal will soon learn that a step forward takes the pressure off its head. Do not allow the foal to

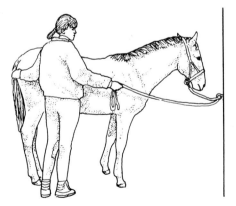

Figure 1.1 *Teaching a foal to tie up by passing a long lead rope through a strong loop or ring, and holding the loose end in the right hand. The left hand on the hindquarters encourages the foal forward if it should pull back.*

Figure 1.2 *This foal is being taught to tie up using the same method as in Fig. 1.1. Note that the trainer wears gloves to protect the hands against rope burns.*

pull and struggle against the rope. A very strong pull on the head collar can permanently damage a foal's head or neck at this age.

Next, using a quick-release knot, tie the foal up to a loop of baling string attached to the ring. Have a sharp knife handy so that you can cut the baling string if the foal goes down. Stand behind the foal and encourage it forward as soon as it pulls back.

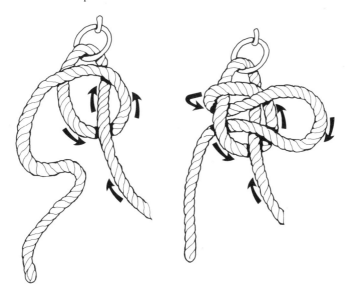

Figure 1.3 *How to tie a quick-release knot.*

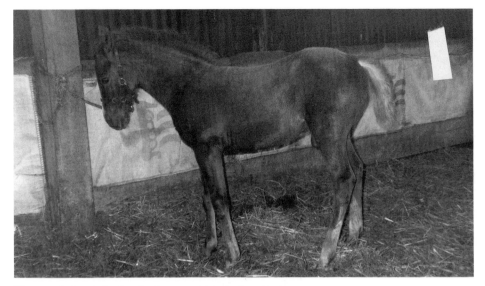

Figure 1.4 *A foal calmly accepting being tied up.*

Leaving the foal tied up for a few minutes every day is sufficient. At first, stay with it all the time, then, when the foal seems completely calm and quite content, leave it, but remain within hearing in case there is a problem.

After you have untied the foal, make it stand still for a minute, then it will not develop the habit of trying to whip off the second it is loose. Sometimes turn the foal towards the door, sometimes away from it. Push it backwards for a few steps, with one hand on its nose and the other on its chest, and say 'Back' in the same tone each time you do it. Sometimes lead the foal from the near side, sometimes from the off side, so that it will not become 'one-sided'. Make it stand still and wait before it goes out of the stable door or through a gateway and then it will not form the habit of barging.

Figure 1.5 *Two people controlling a foal by linking arms around the chest and hindquarters.*

If you have to control the foal before it is halter-broken, you will need two people to link arms around the foal's chest and hindquarters. With a big foal, you may need to run a length of strong, wide, soft material (like a scarf) round behind the foal to enable them to reach. Using this method, the foal can be practically carried in the direction you wish to go.

LEADING

If you are only going a short distance on a safe route, the foal can follow loose, but you should begin to practise leading it as soon as possible.

When leading a young horse, hold the lead rope so that your knuckles face upwards and your thumb is also above the rope. If your thumb is below the rope, it would easily be sprained if the youngster pulls back suddenly.

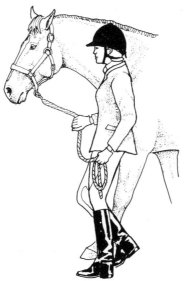

Figure 1.6 *The correct way to lead a young horse.*

Have an assistant to lead the mare, and put a foal slip and lunge line on the foal. Do not pull the foal or try to hold it back; just walk well behind it and allow it to follow the mare on a very light contact. If you hold it tightly, the foal may throw itself down on a hard surface or hurt itself on doorways or gateways. Not until you are safely in a field, and well away from fences, should you begin to take up a contact, gradually controlling the foal while still allowing it to move. Never pull or tug, because the foal's head and neck are easily damaged. Once this has been accepted, ask the foal to stand still while the mare walks on for a few yards. All of this will be made easier if the mare remains calm and unflustered. This, in turn, is more likely to be the case if the foal does not panic, so do not rush things.

If there are only two people to lead the mare and the foal, and the foal braces, not wanting to follow the mare, you may have a problem. The easiest way for one person to encourage the foal to go forward is to lead it with a very long lead rope. With your left hand hold the lead rope about nine inches from the head collar. Hold the end of the lead rope in your right hand and pass the rope over to the off side near the foal's withers allowing the rope to fall down and round its hindquarters resting just above its hocks, gently take up the slack with your right hand. Encourage the foal forward with the rope near the head collar in your left hand and, if it does not go forward, tweak on the rope round its hocks, gently at first but, if necessary, quite strongly. The rope round the hindquarters also helps to control them and keep the foal going straight. Before attempting this outside, handle the foal's hind legs well, then get it used to the feel of the rope above its hocks in the stable.

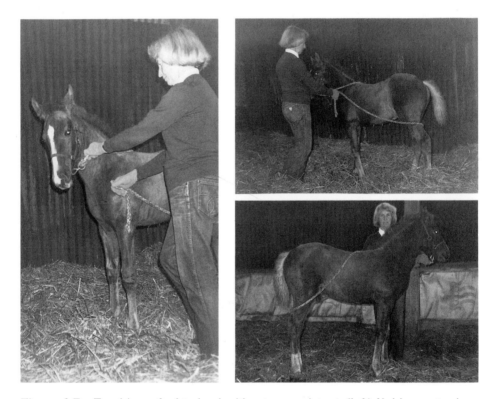

Figure 1.7 *Teaching a foal to lead without an assistant. (left) Hold an extra long lead rope in the left hand about 15 cm (6 in) from the foal's head collar. Pass the free end of the rope over the withers, round the hindquarters, above the hocks, and back to the right hand on the near side. (right above) Lead the foal forward with the left hand. If it does not respond, tweak the rope in the right hand. The movement of the rope above the hocks will encourage the foal to go forward. (right below) How the rope should lie on the offside of the foal.*

If you approach anything of which the foal may be very frightened, remember to place yourself between the frightening thing and the foal so that if it shies violently it will not jump on top of you, possibly knocking you over. If you are between it and the 'terror', it will shy away from you. In any case, if you are closer to the frightening object, this should give the foal more confidence.

If you intend to release the mare and foal in the field, remember to release the foal just before the mare in case the mare gallops off, causing the foal to panic. *Never* turn a foal out in a foal slip or head collar. Turn the mare and foal towards the gate (but well away from it) before letting them go. Then, when turning round before going off, they will be further away from you and you are less likely to be kicked if they are feeling lively.

Over the next few days, teach the foal to lead away from the mare. Have an assistant follow behind to encourage it forward with a hand on its quarters, because, if you go in front and pull on the head collar, the foal will run backwards.

If you are alone, have the lunge line in your left hand and place your right hand on the foal's quarters so that you are almost driving it in the direction you wish to go. Be very careful when you do this because you can easily be kicked in this position.

As you progress with this early training, you can walk level with the foal's shoulder, carrying the lunge line in your right hand and a stick in your left. By touching the foal lightly with the stick behind your back you can drive the foal forward if it does not respond to your vocal aids.

When you feel you have good control of the foal, lead it out with the mare to see the world; take it near to traffic (but not actually onto the road itself) and let it see other horses. Give it a short journey in a box or trailer. In a trailer, travel the mare and foal loose, or cross-tie the mare in the trailer and put the foal in front of her, under her nose, with a safe solid division to keep it there. Do not tie it up.

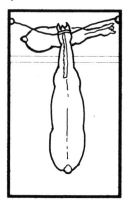

Figure 1.8 *Travelling the mare and a small foal in a trailer: the mare is cross-tied, and the foal is loose in front of the mare, under her nose.*

In a horse box it is safest to travel the mare and foal loose, with all partitions out. Before loading, check that the gap between the ramp and the floor of the vehicle is not wide enough for the foal's small foot and leg to slip through. Legs have been broken in this way.

If the mare is unwilling to load first because she is worried about the foal, it may be necessary to lift and push the foal gently into the vehicle first. Once the foal is even a little in front of her, the mare will usually follow.

GOOD MANNERS

From the first few days of life, and consistently from then on, practise firm but gentle discipline, always making sure that the youngster understands exactly what you want it to do. Avoid shouting, hitting or being rough, but quietly insist on obedience. If you begin when the foal is small, you should rear a calm, well-mannered horse that respects you but is not afraid of you. This will make the horse easy to handle by prospective owners, vets and farriers. There is nothing worse than a grown horse that will not stand still or barges through doorways and pulls when it is being led. Teaching your youngster good manners will make life more pleasant for both of you.

Handle the foal in the stable every day, rubbing, scratching and stroking every part of it. Do not pat it; young horses do not like it and it is not a normal caressing action. Gently pick up its feet, only for a very little way and for a very short time. Remember to run your hand down from the shoulder or quarters to the foot before asking the foal to pick it up. Use the

Figure 1.9 *Teaching the foal to pick up its feet. Gently but firmly hold the foot just a little way off the ground.*

command 'Up' or 'Lift' as you pick up the foot. If the foal struggles, hold on gently but firmly without lifting the foot too high. When it ceases to struggle, wait for a second and then slowly release the foot. As the foal gradually allows you to keep the foot up for longer, pick its feet out carefully and begin to tap gently on the walls of the foot with the hoof pick as a preliminary introduction to shoeing and hoof trimming.

Teach the foal to move over to the left or right by standing on one side of it, turning its head a little towards you with the head collar and, with your other hand just behind the girth area, pushing its quarters away from you, saying 'Over' as you do so.

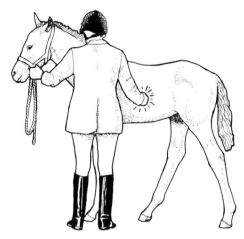

Figure 1.10 *Teaching a foal to move over.*

SAFETY MEASURES

Make sure that your foal is always in a safe environment, both indoors and out. In the loose box, remove handles from buckets and set the buckets in tyres to prevent spills. Check that there are no sharp edges for the foal to cut itself on. Feed hay from the floor. Never use a haynet in a stable or field containing a foal. In play the foal will prance about on its hind legs and may easily get a foreleg caught in a haynet. Many foals have been injured in this way. Have the loose box bedded down all over, day and night. A playful foal can slip and fall on a bare floor.

If the weather is warm, you can turn the new foal and its mother out on the second day after birth. Make sure your paddock is secure and that there is nothing for the foal to hurt itself on. Field companions should be mares with young foals. Do not turn a mare and foal out with a mare that has no foal or with geldings or large youngsters who could prove too rough. When turning out, always release the foal just a second before the mare in case she goes galloping off.

EXERCISING THE MARE

If you wish to ride the mare once the foal is three months old, you will not do any harm as long as she is ridden quietly. If you only intend to ride in the field, the foal can come along loose or be led by an assistant. If the foal has to be left behind in a loose box, remove all dangerous fittings, water buckets and haynets and make sure it cannot reach an unprotected window, even when standing up on its hind legs. All windows should be covered by strong metal grids, with the bars so close together that the foal could not get a foot between them. Close the top door of the box or put a strong, safe grid over it. If you have a very quiet pony to leave with the foal as a 'nanny', this is ideal. Alternatively, a small hole through which it can see a companion in the box next door is helpful. Ask a responsible person to stay with or near the foal the first few times you leave it.

Do not keep the mare away from the foal for too long. Half an hour is enough at first and one and a half hours is the maximum time. If the mare is very upset and becomes difficult to control when separated from her foal, wait until weaning the foal before you start to ride her.

INOCULATIONS

It is a good idea to ask your vet to check the foal within 24 hours of its birth. The vet will give it an injection to protect it against tetanus, and may give antibiotics.

The foal should begin its regular course of (two) injections against influenza and tetanus at the age of twelve weeks. The second of the two injections that make up the primary vaccination should be given no sooner than 21 days and no later than 92 days after the first injection. From then on a yearly booster should be sufficient.

You should have kept up to date with the mare's injections so that the foal may benefit from the antibodies that it will receive via its mother's blood while in the womb.

WORMING

The foal should be wormed as soon as it begins to graze properly (probably around six to eight weeks) because it is from grass that it will pick up worm infection. From then on worm every six weeks. Make sure you use a wormer that is suitable for a foal and that you give only the dose recommended for its weight and age. Check with your vet if you are unsure because an overdose of some wormers could be dangerous for a foal.

The syringe type of wormer is the easiest to administer. Put a foal slip on the foal and stand it with its hindquarters in one corner of the loose box so that it cannot run backwards. Gently insert the syringe nozzle into the corner of its mouth and press the contents out gradually.

SCOURING

At a week to ten days old, the foal may start to scour. This is usually because the mare has come into season and a change has taken place in the milk. The scouring should clear up in a few days. If scouring occurs at any other time, or if it does not clear up, call the vet.

FOOT TRIMMING

A good farrier will observe how the foal stands and moves before he trims its feet. A foot that is turned in will cause the foal to 'dish' (swing a foreleg outwards in a half circle). A foot that is turned out may cause 'brushing' (knocking the fetlock joint of the opposite leg; both fore and hind legs can be affected). If begun early enough and done regularly (every six weeks), corrective trimming can have really good results. The feet of a young horse must never be neglected.

CASTRATING

Colts are sometimes 'cut' as foals but more often this is done between a year and eighteen months old, according to the maturity of the animal. It is not a good idea to castrate in hot weather because flies can cause an infection. In very cold weather the youngster may stand about feeling stiff and uncomfortable, and catch a chill, so spring or autumn are the best times to choose. Some vets prefer to castrate foals before weaning as they feel the foal will do better if it can still receive milk and comfort from the mare.

WEANING

Normally, foals are weaned at about six months old, but if the mare is in good condition and is not in foal again, the foal can be left on her all winter. Before weaning, make sure the foal is eating hard food, then it will not lose too much weight. It will soon learn to eat this if you feed the mare from a container big enough for them to share. If the mare is jealous of the food, let the foal have a feed bowl of its own or install a foal creep. If you have two mares and foals, there is no problem about weaning. You can put both foals in a loose box and turn the two mares out together in a field well out of earshot, preferably without too much grass so that their milk will dry up quickly. One foal alone can be put in a box with a quiet companion or in a box where it can see and sniff its neighbour, who is later to be turned out with it. Turn them out in a small, well-fenced field out of hearing of the mare.

Most foals are born in the spring and weaning time is most likely to be autumn, so unless the foal is a hardy pony type, it is probably best to bring it in at night during its first winter. This also gives you the opportunity for regular handling. If foals have to live out, the field must be sheltered and the foals will require two or three visits each day.

FEEDING

A small pony foal will need approximately 900 g (2 lb) of oats, coarse mix or nuts a day; a horse foal will need up to 3.6 kg (8 lb). These amounts should be divided into three or four feeds per day. Both will need as much good hay as they can eat.

GROWTH AND CHANGE DURING THE FIRST YEAR

A foal is long in the leg in proportion to its body. To graze, it may have to splay its forelegs or place one foreleg forward and one back with a bent knee.

Figure 1.11   *The difference in development between a foal and yearling.*

The foal's bulgy forehead contains its brain. The brain, and the area of skull encasing it, are quite large at birth and do not grow very much more. The rest of the skull grows around this area.

The feet, which are soft and narrow at birth, will soon harden and gradually broaden.

The soft, fluffy foal coat will fall out and be replaced by a normal coat which will give you more of an idea of what the final coat colour will be. The soft, short, curly mane and tail will gradually grow longer and straighten out. Slight curls and waves can often still be seen in a three-year-old's tail if it has never been banged (trimmed level). Black-tailed youngsters often have reddish-brown hairs in their tails until three or four years of age.

The horse is at its most gawky stage as a yearling. It may look as if its head is too big for its body and it seems to have little control over its long, gangling legs. Don't be too disappointed. Time should bring about a dramatic improvement.

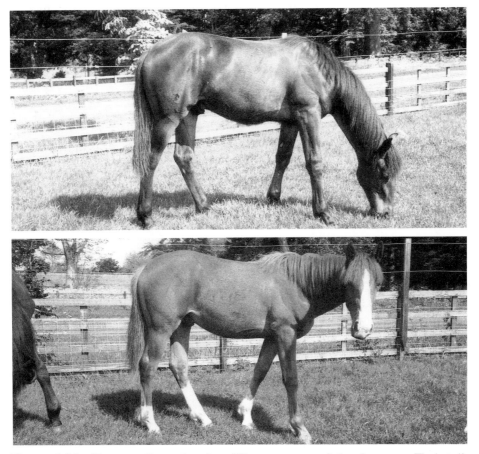

Figure 1.12 *Two yearlings showing different stages of development. Their tails still show traces of foal-like curls.*

⟦2⟧ THE YEARLING

LEADING IN HAND

When leading a youngster, hold the lunge line or long lead rope with your knuckles facing upwards and your thumb also above the rope. Never try to lead a young horse in just a head collar without a rope. You may injure your hand or pull a muscle and you are very likely to let go of the horse if it pulls back or rears.

Never, never wrap the spare loops around your hand where they could tighten and break your fingers or cause you to be trapped and dragged along the ground behind a panicking horse. Never put your hand, fingers or thumb where they can get caught up in the Ds or buckles of a head collar or cavesson if the horse rears or shoots off.

Hold the spare length of the lunge line in loops, each about 46 cm (18 in) long, and lying in the correct sequence for release across the hand that is further from the horse. The nearer hand controls the horse.

If something causes the horse to panic, do not shout at it. This will only convince the horse that you are frightened too and make things far worse. Use a calm, firm voice to reassure the youngster.

Whenever you are leading a youngster, always remain calm and relaxed but never allow your concentration to wander. Watch the horse's eye and ears and try to anticipate its thoughts and behaviour. Young horses react to things very quickly and they can be unpredictable. If the horse attempts to rear, raise the hand nearer to it really high to prevent the horse from getting a foot over the rope if it strikes out. It is safest to use a really long lead rope so that you have some length to play with in a crisis.

As a yearling the horse should be led about regularly, taken close to traffic and then along quiet roads with a sensible companion. The youngster should know and obey your chosen words of command for halt, walk and trot in hand, both towards and away from other horses.

By the time it is a year old, your youngster should lead well and calmly and be well mannered under all normal circumstances. Never stand or walk in front of a young horse. A frightened horse will leap or shoot forward without thinking and may knock you over or jump on your feet. If you are leading through a doorway or gateway, or up a narrow passage, stay well to

16

one side and level with the horse's head so that you will not get knocked over or find yourself level with the hind legs if it suddenly takes fright.

If you are passing something that the horse may spook at, you must place yourself nearer to the object so that the horse will shy away from you and not onto you.

If you use a normal length of lead rope, you could easily be pulled forward close to the horse's heels if it suddenly shoots forward in fright. On seeing you so close behind it or even feeling you accidentally touch its hindquarters, the horse could well kick out at you. Because a young horse's reactions are so quick, it will usually kick first and think afterwards, so you must concentrate on what you are doing and think ahead for both of you. If you use a long lead rope or lunge line, you will not end up quite so close to the horse if it does shoot past you and you are also less likely to let go of it in an emergency.

Always lead the horse in a well-fitting head collar or cavesson. Wear gloves to protect your hands against rope burns and strong shoes with a heel so that you will not slip easily. It is also sensible to wear a hard hat.

You should make a point of handling the youngster each day and it should be taught to stand quietly when tied up. Even so, someone should always remain within earshot of any young horse that has been left tied up in case it pulls back and slips.

During its first winter your youngster will probably have been brought in at night and should have had a companion with it or within sight and sound of it. At the end of its first winter it should be able to live out if the weather remains fair, but do not leave it unhandled to run wild for weeks. It should be out with one or more companions, because a youngster on its own will often get into trouble in its attempts to join horses in another field or even a group of horses being ridden past on the road. Remember that horses are herd animals, and it is a good thing for youngsters to learn to live together and accept their place in the natural 'pecking order' that all herd animals establish.

FOR EXTRA OR EMERGENCY CONTROL

If you have difficulty controlling a young horse in a head collar (and it has not yet worn a bridle, which would otherwise be the obvious solution, you can gain more control by passing the lead rope from the back D of the head collar anti-clockwise round the horse's nose, just above the nostrils, and through the back D of the head collar again to your hand. Pressure on the gristly part of the nose is more uncomfortable for the horse than pressure higher up, so your control will be greater and the horse may become more obedient. Remember to adjust the front loop on the nose so that it does not interfere with the horse's breathing.

Figure 2.1 *Extra control in a head collar. a) Pass the lead rope through the back D of the head collar anti-clockwise round the horse's nose, then through the back D of the head collar again to the right hand. b) Pass the lead rope through the offside D of the head collar, then through the horse's mouth (like a bit) over the tongue, and out through the nearside D to the hand.*

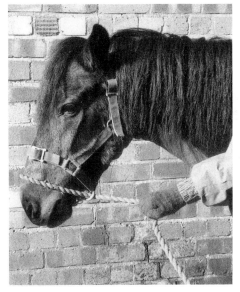

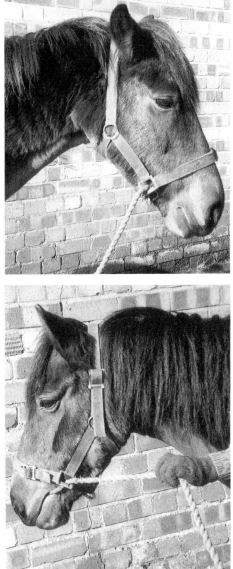

Figure 2.2 *Extra control: (left) The rope is passed round the horse's nose. (right above) The rope through the offside D prior to being passed through the horse's mouth. (right below) The rope emerging from the mouth and passing through the nearside D to the hand.*

Even more control can be gained by passing the lead rope through the offside D of the head collar, then through the horse's mouth (like a bit) and out through the nearside D to your hand. Make sure the rope passes over, not under, the horse's tongue, or else it might cause damage. If the lead rope is too thick to pass through the head collar D, pass it in front of the head collar cheekpiece on the off side, then through the mouth and out in front of the cheekpiece on the near side to your hand. This method can also be very useful when loading an awkward horse, but do not be rough or you could damage the mouth, lips or tongue.

CATCHING

As the young horse grows it will become stronger and fitter and will try out various manoeuvres in play, such as kicking, rearing, biting, pulling back and galloping off. Some of these games will be tried out on you when you go to catch it to bring it in. Do not allow your youngster to play games with you even when it is a small foal. What is sweet or funny when done by a tiny foal can be very alarming when performed by a large, strong youngster. From the very beginning, try to teach the young horse to obey and respect you at all times.

If you offer a piece of carrot or a handful of nuts when catching the horse, you will find that it is less likely to think of running off and will therefore become easier to catch. Do not take a bucket of food into the field as a catching device or all the other horses will mob you and probably kick out at each other.

Never grab at a horse when catching it or try to hold on to it by its mane. Be patient and wait until the animal is relaxed and confident. If there are other horses milling around, get someone to hold on to them or distract them to keep them away from the youngster.

Figure 2.3   *Offering a titbit to a young horse when catching it to encourage co-operation.*

Hold a titbit in your hand and encourage the horse to bring its head and neck across in front of you to reach this. You can then slowly and gently pass your right hand, with the rope in it, over the horse's neck. Your left hand moves slowly under the neck to take the end of the rope. Slide the rope a little closer to its ears and let the horse feel that you are holding it and that it has been caught before you attempt to put the head collar on. Say 'Whoa' or 'Stand' as you do this so that you train the horse to stand still while its head collar is put on. Do not put the head collar on until you feel the horse has accepted your control.

Practise this first in a yard or other small enclosure. Make sure the horse is confident and will accept this method of catching in the small enclosure before you try it in an open field. Once the horse has learnt that it can get away from you in the field and thus avoid being caught, it will remember and may turn this into a great game, so put in lots of practice and plan ahead to avoid this situation.

A fresh youngster will often try to get away from you as you lead it out to the field or from its field towards the gate, especially if other horses remain in the field. It is vital that you do not let go of the horse. It will never forget winning this battle and this can prove to be one of the biggest problems you will encounter with a young horse.

Watch its eyes and ears and learn to work out what it is thinking of doing next. Concentrate and be ready to anticipate its every move. If you are worried, ask someone to lead another horse to or from the field with your youngster so that it will have less excuse to misbehave. Remember that you *must not* let go of a youngster, so plan carefully to avoid this possibility.

Accustom your youngster to being in for a little while each day to have its feet looked at and to have a gentle grooming. This should not be so thorough that it removes the grease from the coat in rainy weather. It is more of an exercise in handling and checking for injuries rather than for cleaning the horse.

STABLE VICES

If, when first stabled, the youngster becomes excitable and rears up to get a foreleg over the box door, put up a bar across the space above the door on the inside of the box, making sure that it cannot get its head through the gap between the bar and door. If you have a metal grid to fit above the lower door, use this.

Most horses settle better when they can look out and see other horses, because youngsters feel trapped when they are first stabled. Make sure there is some hay to occupy it and that all fittings are safe. Visit the youngster often to talk to it and soothe it, do not yell and bang on the door if the youngster kicks at it, and do not leave the youngster in day and night or it will become bored and may develop stable vices.

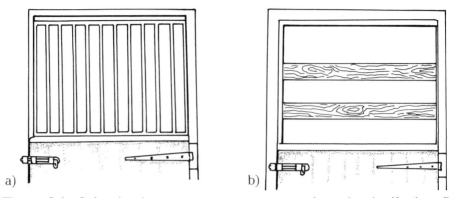

Figure 2.4 *Safety barriers to prevent a youngster damaging itself when first stabled. a) A metal grid. b) Wooden bars correctly spaced to prevent a youngster putting its head through the gaps.*

Crib-biting and Wind-sucking

Chewing the top of the stable door can lead to crib-biting. The horse does this by taking hold of the door or manger with its teeth and swallowing air while arching and stiffening its neck. Once learnt, this habit is very difficult to prevent and almost impossible to cure. It often gives the horse indigestion and a potbellied appearance. Other horses watching a crib-biter will quickly learn to copy the habit, so do not stable your youngster near a crib-biter.

Figure 2.5 *Crib-biting.*

Wind-sucking is one step on from crib-biting; the horse learns to swallow air without having to hold on to anything with its teeth.

Weaving

Weaving is another vice brought on by boredom or tension. The horse swings its neck and head from side to side in a ceaseless rhythm, at the same time lifting alternate forelegs. It is also another habit that is all too easily copied by other horses.

Figure 2.6 *Weaving.*

Banging the Stable Door

Constantly banging on a stable door can give a horse a big knee, so, if necessary, put a thick rubber panel on the inside of the door, or an old piece of carpet with hay behind it. (Ignore people who suggest that you use bundles of gorse; this is cruel because, besides being painful, sharp prickle heads in the horse's skin can cause festering sores.) A wire grill or bar to prevent the horse getting its head out over the door will also prevent the habit of banging.

At the slightest sign of these or other stable vices, turn the youngster out more and, when it is in, give it something to play with, such as a sturdy plastic bottle hanging in the doorway on a strong piece of string.

Turn the youngster out as much as possible. All of these bad habits are caused by keeping a young, active animal shut in a stable for too long. The horse has to do something to relieve its boredom!

STABLE DOOR HEIGHT

An important point, often overlooked, is the height of the stable door. If it is too high, the young horse cannot see over it comfortably, and may develop a bulge of muscle under its neck through continually raising its head to see over the door. This will also make the horse hollow its back and stand with its hind legs thrust out behind it. This is exactly the opposite posture to that which you hope your young horse will adopt when ridden. You have only to think how many hours a horse spends looking out over the stable door to realise how much this could affect it as it grows.

HANDLING THE YEARLING

Get your young horse used to strange sights and sounds and being touched all over its body. Once it will accept your hand and a soft brush anywhere on its body and legs, put your hand inside a rustly plastic bag and gradually rub it all over with that. Gradually progress to larger and noisier plastic bags, macintoshes, etc. until the horse is quite unconcerned when you pass these things between its forelegs and hind legs, under its tummy and all along its neck and back.

Hold these things really high above the horse's back in the position a rider would occupy, and move them about. Be careful not to frighten the horse. You must proceed gradually to gain its confidence and may need to do this sort of thing daily for several weeks before your youngster is completely unworried about your actions.

Figure 2.7 *Acclimatising the youngster to all kinds of sights and sounds by using a 'police horse' type of training, using plastic bags.*

This 'police horse' type of training will prepare the horse for lunge reins dangling round its legs, things flapping on a windy day and the sight of a rider on its back. If you persevere with this way of training you will produce a much calmer, safer horse.

Continue this training two or three times a week right up to the time you begin to ride the horse regularly.

GROWTH AND CHANGE BETWEEN THE AGES OF ONE AND TWO

The two-year-old should grow into its neck and body so that its head and legs look more in proportion with the rest of it. The withers may still be round and flat, although the wither of a Thoroughbred may be more pronounced. A smaller, shorter-coupled type of horse will become better balanced at this stage of growth and will have more control of its limbs, but very big late-maturing youngsters may still be as gawky and unbalanced as they were as yearlings.

Most two-year-olds are mentally immature. They are only able to concentrate for a few minutes and so can take in only a little training at any one time.

Your two-year-old will still have all its milk teeth. The first permanent teeth will appear in the centre front of both jaws at two and a half years of age.

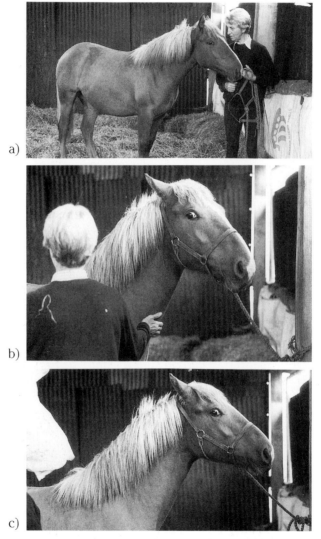

a)

b)

c)

Figure 2.8 *A two-year-old receives 'police horse' training. a) The youngster is curious and should be allowed to approach the handler. b) The horse is securely, but safely, tied, and the handler starts to work with the plastic bags; the youngster is apprehensive. c) and d) There is still some apprehension as work progresses; the animal's attention is directed back at the bags. e) Less worried; the ears and eyes are more relaxed. f) and g) Totally unconcerned; the youngster has learnt its lesson, and its attention is on other things.*

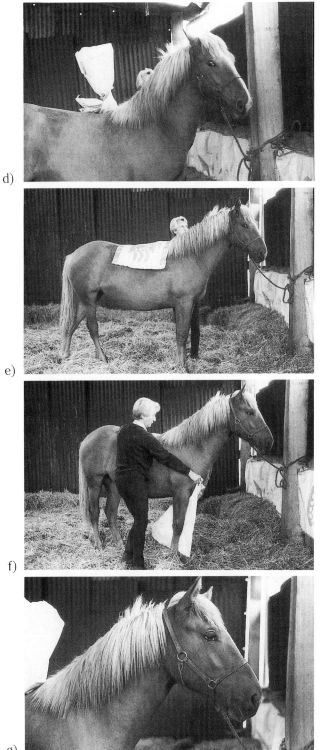

d)

e)

f)

g)

3   THE TWO-YEAR-OLD

If the young horse is one that you have bred yourself, then it should be accustomed to all the training covered in the chapters on the foal and yearling. If you have bought the youngster, you may have to begin at the beginning in order to teach it good manners and to lead. Even with a home-bred horse, you should now quickly revise the work done as a yearling before you accustom it to a roller. When you progress to saddling and bridling the youngster, see the chapter on Fitting Tack in Section Two.

FITTING A ROLLER

You must do this in a safe, enclosed area because some horses really do panic when first feeling something tight round their middles. The horse's own stable is the best place to introduce anything new, but be aware of the fact that, if it gets into a blind panic, the horse might attempt to jump out over the stable door and could very easily knock you over if it bucks round the box. There is no way that anyone can hold on to a horse that is bucking in terror, so you may need to climb into the manger or slip out of the door and leave the horse to settle.

When you intend to introduce it to a roller for the first time, have a head collar and lead rope on the horse but, if it has not totally accepted being tied, do not tie it up in case it bucks and plunges at the feel of the roller. At first just encircle the girth area with your arms and squeeze a little, then let the horse smell the roller. Now slide the roller into place, using a wither pad if necessary to avoid pressure on the spine. Hold the buckle in one hand and the strap in the other and gently pull them together to let the horse get the feel of something round its middle.

When the horse seems unafraid, do the buckles up, just tight enough to keep the roller in place. Fit a breast plate (or improvise with a tail bandage) round the chest to prevent the roller from slipping back. Stand to one side in case the horse leaps forward, bucking.

If the horse stands absolutely still, stiff and rigid, this is a sign that it is probably going to 'explode'.

When the horse is relaxed, lead it round the box in both directions and gradually tighten the roller. Some animals do not seem to mind this at all; others hold their breath and then plunge about. For this reason, always turn your youngster in both directions in the box, to let it feel the roller tighten against both of its sides, before leading it out, and do not take the horse out of the box wearing a roller until it is completely unconcerned by the object. Leave the roller on in the stable for half an hour or so every day to let the horse become accustomed to it.

TYING UP

If there is a strong, safe ring, level with the horse's head, to which you can tie it and where there is nothing in which it can get a leg caught, you can use this throughout the horse's training. Tie the horse up short with about 90 cm (2 ft) of rope between the knot and a very strong, well-fitting head collar. The horse must be able to stand with its head at a normal angle; the head must not be pulled up in any way. Before you use this method to introduce new things, the horse must be used to being tied up in this way and have totally accepted that, because it cannot get loose, there is no point in fighting. I learnt this method when working in other countries and have used it for many years. It gives a small person very good control over a big, strong horse and the horse soon learns to accept that it cannot get away. Never abuse this system by frightening the horse through progressing too quickly; be just as careful and thoughtful as if the horse were being held.

This is a much safer method for you to use when introducing new aspects of the horse's education but, unfortunately, very few people start early enough, or spend long enough on teaching a young horse that when it is tied up it cannot get away.

Safety Measures

Never tie any horse up with the rope so long that should the horse lower its head and paw with a foreleg it could get the leg over the rope. This could lead to a really nasty accident and the horse might even come down.

Never tie a horse up, especially a youngster, just inside or outside an open doorway. If the horse tries to go through this, the sudden pull on the head collar can bring it down in the doorway and it could prove very difficult for it to get up again with its head twisted round. It would also be very difficult for you to help.

Inside the stable, tie your youngster up well back from the door so that it cannot try to shoot out as you enter.

Outside the stable, shut and bolt the door and make sure there are no protruding fixtures for the head collar to catch on.

Never tie a young horse up anywhere and leave it unattended. If it loses its footing and goes down, it could hurt itself badly. Always remain within earshot in case of trouble.

LOOSE-SCHOOLING

If you are not experienced at lungeing, you will find loose-schooling easier, providing you use a secure working area.

You will need:
- A safe, enclosed area 20–30 m (22–33 yd) in diameter.
- Protective boots all round, plus overreach boots if the horse is shod or the going is deep.
- A short whip (to be held in your front hand).
- A long whip (to be held in your rear hand).
- A hard hat (to protect your head if the horse should rear and strike out or kick at you).
- Patience, sympathy and understanding.
- The ability to concentrate, observe and anticipate.
- The ability to co-ordinate your movements.
- Several days' practice with an older horse under expert tuition.

Reasons for Loose-schooling

We loose-school in order to work the horse in a way that will teach it to balance and carry itself and move in an even, rhythmical stride. There is no artificial, outside influence to put strain on the horse. (When lunged, a young horse will often pull against a lunge rein, swinging its hindquarters out and knocking its hind fetlock joints. The act of pulling away will unbalance the horse and put extra strain on its muscles and joints and also on the horse's back which will twist against the pull.)

A horse that has learnt to go in rhythm and balance through loose-schooling will be far easier to lunge later on. Even a yearling can do ten minutes of loose-schooling a day.

Loose-schooling is a comparatively safe method of teaching an inexperienced person how to control a young horse. The knowledge this person will gain of how much their own body position can influence the horse will be of great advantage when they come to lunge the horse. There is nothing for either horse or trainer to get tangled up in! The inexperienced trainer will learn how to observe and understand the horse's mental and physical reactions and should also be able to see how the horse's carriage, balance and rhythm change and improve during this work. This knowledge will be of tremendous help when the trainer not only lunges, but also long-reins or rides the horse at a later stage.

The Working Area

The area to be used must be strongly and safely enclosed so that there is no possibility of the horse attempting to jump out. Loose-schooling is easiest in a round area of 20–30 m (22–33 yd) in diameter. If the area is square, poles can be put across the corners.

A wild or excitable horse is most likely to try to get out through the gate it came in by, so make sure this is not the lowest point in the wall round your circle and, if necessary, put a piece of thick rope or a pole above the gate. A big horse may attempt a jump of up to 1.5 m (5 ft) so make sure the wall of your enclosure is high enough. Many horses have been hurt attempting to jump out over fixed post and rails or over the gates of a school.

An indoor school can be made smaller by using poles and jump stands but these must be securely lashed together and, if necessary, supported from the outside of the circle. Poles lying on the ground at the foot of the jump stands (but where the horse cannot step on them) making a complete circle, will help to guide the horse. Construct your circle at the end of the school nearest the door as your young horse will keep trying to come down to this end anyway.

By watching your horse's ears and eyes, you will learn to 'read' its thoughts and to anticipate its next move. By observing its stride and balance, you will see how the young horse is frequently off-balance at first and keeps changing its rhythm and length of stride. You will learn to notice the relationship between the action of the forelegs and the hind legs and to observe whether the hind legs are tracking up (the toe of the hind foot coming right up to the heel of the front footprint, or, with a fitter, more experienced horse, even onto the print left by the front foot).

This action shows that the horse is pushing itself forward correctly from behind and that it is well balanced. Many young horses are 'on their forehands' – their centre of gravity is too far forward. In this type of horse, the hind foot will come down several inches behind the front footprint.

Because you have no lunge rein to worry about, you are free to observe all these things. You will quickly learn that if you get the very slightest bit in front of the horse, it will stop and may even whip round and go off in the other direction. You must always feel that you are driving the horse forward. Your body position has a tremendous influence on the horse and moving even a foot in the wrong direction can make the difference between success and failure when loose-schooling (or lungeing).

Be very aware that there is a certain danger in loose-schooling in that the horse can turn its hindquarters towards you and deliberately kick out at you or simply kick you accidentally while giving a cheerful buck. Your most vulnerable moment is when you step back after releasing the horse in order to start working it. Think ahead of your horse and anticipate what it might be about to do.

Method

The horse should preferably have been worked in hand already and been taught your words of command. It can be loose-schooled in just a head collar or in a saddle and bridle with the reins and stirrups removed or made safe. If used, side reins can be attached to the side Ds of a cavesson or head collar, but they should not be necessary at this stage in a young horse's training, other than to prevent it from eating grass.

Boots should be worn all round for the horse's protection and overreach boots should be worn if the going is deep or the horse is liable to overreach for any reason; they should always be worn if the horse is shod. (See page 37.)

With a lead rope on the head collar, lead the horse from the near side. Carry both whips in your left hand, pointing them downwards and to the rear. Take the horse to the outside of the circle, facing left (most horses prefer the left rein, so always begin in this direction). Halt the horse and remove the lead rope. Step backwards towards the centre of the circle, keeping your eye on the horse the whole time because, as stated, at this moment you are very vulnerable and can easily get kicked.

Move into a position where your body is in line with, or just behind the line of, the horse's flank. Use the vocal command 'And walk on!' in a high, encouraging tone of voice if the horse has remained at halt where you left it. If it shot forward the moment you released it and is now tearing round and round the circle, stand still, however long it may take, until it becomes calmer and slows itself down. As the horse is either excited or worried or both, it is not going to listen to the vocal commands you have taught it when leading in hand, while shouting will only make matters worse. Remember to keep the whips still at this point unless the horse actually comes in too close to you and you think it is going to try to kick you.

The horse does not yet understand the new aids, given by your own body position and the whip, which you are about to teach it, so anything you do, other than using a quiet, calming voice, is likely to prolong the time the horse will take to settle down.

When the horse finally slows down or stops, try to take control by using the vocal command it is familiar with − a long, drawn-out 'Aaaand whoooa'. To slow the horse down, move a little sideways until your body is in line with its shoulder. If it ignores you, move further over until you are almost in line with its head (moving further than this point may cause the horse to whip round, so watch for signs of this and be ready to stop).

If necessary, lift the front whip slowly until your hand is level with your head. (This whip should be in your left hand when the horse is going round on the left rein). The back whip should be pointing downwards and to the rear when you are asking for a decrease of pace. Watch the horse and, as it begins to slow down, gradually lower the whip in your left hand if you wish

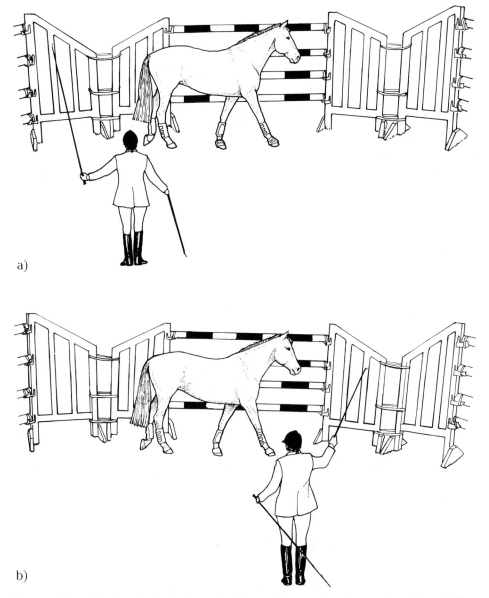

a)

b)

Figure 3.1 *The handler's body and whip positions when loose schooling. a) The 'driving' position just behind the line of the horse's flank. b) The slowing, or stopping, position in line with the horse's shoulder.*

the horse to continue going forward at the slower pace. If you want it to halt, keep the left-hand whip up and still until the horse obeys, then lower it and, with both whips in one hand and pointing downwards behind you, go slowly up to the horse, stopping if it seems the slightest bit frightened of your approach. Talk to it, stroke it and praise it.

To change direction, turn the horse round, change your whips over, so that the short whip is now in your front (right) hand and the long whip is in your back (left) hand. With both whips pointing back and down, step towards the centre of your circle again, once more keeping a close eye on the horse in case it kicks.

Move to the left so that you feel you are driving the horse forward slightly with your body position, and use your vocal command 'And walk on', only moving the long whip if the horse does not respond.

You should have the feeling that you are working your horse between the two whips; the short, front whip emphasising your vocal and body commands to slow down, the long, back whip emphasising your vocal and body commands to go forward if necessary. If you wish, you can use just the one, back, whip, making your front hand − either lowered or raised − the slowing down signal; an open palm towards the horse's head (like a policeman directing traffic) being the halt signal.

As in riding, you should always begin with the slightest possible aids, only increasing them if you receive no response. The horse should then become more responsive and almost seem to answer to your thoughts. If you start with strong aids, you will always have to use them.

To slow down, use a slow, long-drawn-out, deep-voiced command. Ask for the gait required with that one word only, but always precede it with a deep, slow 'Aaaand'. This will act as a warning signal to the horse and draw its attention to the fact that you are about to ask for something different. For example, use 'Aaaand walk' to come from trot to walk. If the horse ignores you, move over until your body is more in line with your horse's head. If it still ignores you, raise the short whip held in your front hand.

To increase the pace or change gait through an upward transition, use a short, brisk, higher tone of 'And' and ask for the gait required in the same way − 'And trot!'.

Always use the same one or two words of command in the same way and in the same tone of voice. Use only the familiar tones of one or two words of praise. Do not chatter on to the horse because you will only confuse it.

At first, work the horse once (or better still twice) a day for ten minutes. You will be surprised how quickly the horse begins to go in a regular, rhythmic stride and how soon its balance will improve. An intelligent horse will watch your every move. It will never take its eye off you and will almost begin to anticipate your thoughts.

When the three-year-old horse is going calmly and is well balanced in trot, with a rhythmic stride, you can ask for canter. (Work only in walk and trot with most two-year-olds. An exceptionally well-balanced one may canter voluntarily and thus show that it can do so effortlessly. *In this case only*, a little cantering will do no harm.)

To get an upward transition to another gait, use your warning word 'And' in a higher, quicker voice, followed by your word of command for that gait in a higher, brighter and quicker tone, using your voice to convey a sense of urgency to a lethargic animal. The second syllable of 'can-ter' can be on a much lighter note so that the horse will be aware of the difference. Do not canter if the horse finds it difficult and becomes unbalanced.

As your control, observation and knowledge of the horse's balance and gaits improve, you can concentrate on these. Try never to let the horse drop heavily into a downward transition. It must always appear to go forwards and on into downwards transitions, carrying itself lightly. You should not hear heavier footfalls as the horse decreases pace or changes gait. Think 'trot' and 'trot on' or 'walk' and 'walk on'. Do not think of a decrease of pace as a 'stopping' transition.

The sound of the horse's footfalls will tell you a lot about its mental state. A tense, worried horse hits the ground hard as it moves and the difference in sound can be heard even in sand or shavings. Notice that as the horse relaxes, its footfalls will become softer and quieter. This should also be apparent as the downwards transitions improve.

There is a tremendous amount to be learned about a horse when you work it loose and this knowledge and understanding of your horse's mental and physical make up could be invaluable to you during future training.

Length of Loose-schooling Sessions

Yearling − 10 minutes a day − mainly in walk with a little trotting.
Two-year-old − 20 minutes (or better still two 10-minute sessions) − mainly in walk and trot, with a little cantering only if the horse volunteers this and finds it easy.
Three-year-old − 30 minutes (preferably in two 15-minute sessions). If all in one session, give a several minutes' interval in walk. Canter if the horse does not become badly unbalanced; if it does, you must be patient and work in trot for several more days before trying again. All horses are different, some will cope with canter after one week's daily loose-schooling, others will need three weeks.
Four-year-old − start with two 10-minute sessions and gradually build up to two half-hour sessions. Do not work the horse for longer than half an hour or it may become tired and bored.

Loose-schooling is an excellent way of reschooling horses that are really naughty on the lunge. There is nothing for them to fight and I have found that I can quite quickly make such horses obedient and much happier in their work by this method.

If you have already begun backing your youngster (see pages 49 and 56), continue to sit on it after each loose-schooling session, getting a leg up from an assistant who can then lead you about the box or work area.

Constant repetition of this will help your horse to learn to accept being ridden without problems.

LUNGEING

Lungeing places a great strain on a horse, especially a young one, and very little should be done with a two-year-old. Only begin this part of the horse's training if you are sure it is well developed and strong enough to make a start. Ten minutes' lungeing once a day, with only a little trotting, is sufficient at this stage. Work only on large circles of about 20 m (22 yd). A small circle will put extra strain on the horse. You must work equally on each rein.

Early Lungeing

You will need:
- An enclosed area, 20–30 m (22–32 yd) in diameter.
- Lungeing cavesson.
- Lungeing whip.
- Protective boots all round, plus overreach boots if the horse is shod or liable to overreach or the going is deep.
- A hard hat for your own protection, and gloves to protect your hands against rope burns.
- A lot of experience in lungeing several different, and some difficult, older horses before you attempt to lunge a youngster.
- A good knowledge of your horse's character, gained through working it loose.
- Patience, sympathy and understanding.
- The ability to concentrate, observe and anticipate.
- The ability to co-ordinate your movements, and the possession of 'good hands' (created by having supple shoulders, elbows and wrists) that will enable you to follow and control the movement of the horse smoothly.

Reasons for Lungeing

A young horse is lunged to teach it to obey your vocal commands and to accustom it to going forward on its own without being led. Lungeing also teaches the horse to be controlled by a contact on its head and to go in a rhythmical, balanced manner in walk, trot and, eventually, canter.

Later, lungeing can be used to improve an animal's way of going but only a very experienced trainer would be capable of doing this. It is also used to exercise a horse that cannot wear a saddle because of a temporary injury to its back, or to settle a very fresh horse before riding it.

Lungeing Equipment

Fitting Boots

The horse should wear *well-padded* boots all round to avoid injury. Some horses are terrified of boots, so introduce these carefully in the stable. Tie the horse up securely, as it may kick and panic at the feel of something attached to its leg. On this first occasion, do the middle straps up quickly so that the boot is secured at the centre and will not flap about so much if the horse panics. A boot attached by only the top strap will flap. Try to do the straps up fairly quickly so that the boot is secure, then step well back out of range in case the horse kicks. Put the front boots on first and introduce just one boot at a time.

If you use boots with Velcro fastenings, remember that some horses take a little while to get used to the noise made by this material, so fasten and unfasten them a few times while standing near to the horse's head before you attempt to put one on a leg, otherwise you may never get it off again without the horse kicking.

The fastenings or straps of the boots should do up towards the rear. Once the horse is used to the boots, do up the top fastenings first, then slide the boot down until the inside of the lower part of the fetlock joint (where the horse is likely to brush) is covered, before doing up the lower fastenings.

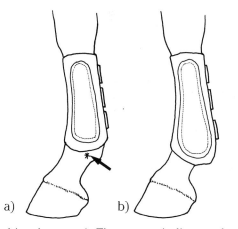

Figure 3.2 *Brushing boots. a) The arrow indicates the vulnerable part of the fetlock the boots are designed to protect. This boot is too high. b) A brushing boot in the correct position over the whole fetlock joint.*

Make sure the front boots are thick enough and strong enough to protect the tendons from a blow from the hind shoes if the horse is shod.

If the ground is deep or the horse is unbalanced or very lively, put overreach boots on the front feet as well. Always put these on if the horse is shod. The solid circular kind should be turned inside out to put them on, so that the widest part is ready to take the foot. It is sometimes quite difficult to

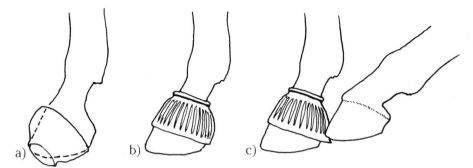

Figure 3.3 *Overreach boots. a) Fitting a solid, circular overreach boot by turning it inside out so that the widest part takes the foot. b) An overreach boot in position. c) A boot protecting the foreleg from a blow from the hind leg.*

pull these on when new and soaking them in hot water first often helps. Once they are on, turn them over so that the widest part is at the bottom, covering the hoof. If your horse has very wide feet and you find these boots too difficult to get on and off, try the Velcro-fastening type or the 'petal' type.

If overreach boots are too long, so that they trail on the ground behind the horse's heels, the hind feet may tread on them and whip them off or even cause the horse to trip or fall.

Fitting a Lungeing Cavesson

The most common type of lungeing cavesson fits at the same level as an ordinary cavesson noseband, but has two extra straps; one is a throatlash to be done up loosely; the other is fitted a little lower down and must be done up more firmly because its purpose is to keep the cheek straps of the cavesson away from the horse's eyes. The noseband should be done up tight enough to prevent it from slipping round.

A Wels cavesson gives a little more control because it is fitted lower, like a drop noseband, and so can be very useful for controlling a strong, stroppy youngster when leading it in hand before it has become used to a bridle. It must rest on the bony part of the nose, well above the nostrils.

For the first few sessions, a young horse can be lunged in a lungeing cavesson only. Attach the lunge line to the front D as this will give you more control. Some horses are frightened by the sight of a lunge rein on their noses so be prepared to attach it to the side D at first if necessary.

Get the horse used to all the lungeing equipment in the stable first. Tie the horse up and then pull the lunge line along the ground near to it but not close enough to frighten it. Next, lie the lunge line over the horse's back and neck and eventually pull the rein along the ground near the horse's hind legs. All of this may take several days before the horse accepts it but you must do this thoroughly before attempting to lunge or the horse may panic if it gets a leg over the lunge line or if you get into a muddle and drop the line. This careful preparation will prevent accidents later on.

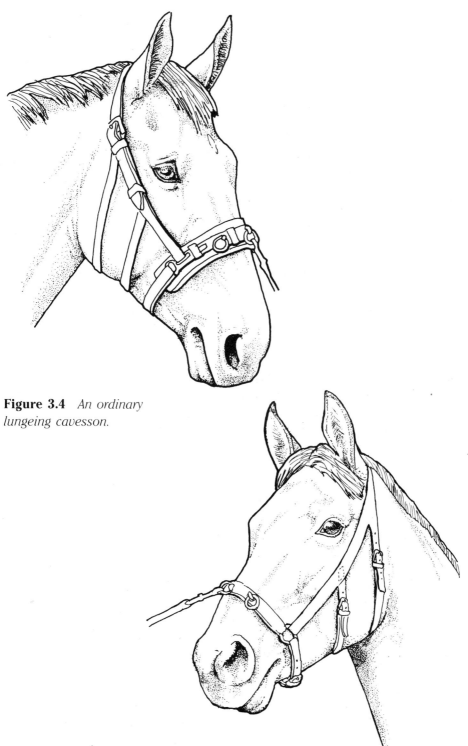

Figure 3.4 *An ordinary lungeing cavesson.*

Figure 3.5 *A Wels lungeing cavesson.*

Figure 3.6 *Wels cavesson (left) and ordinary cavesson (right), both worn over bridles.*

The horse can be 'lunged' in its loose box when it is calm and confident about the sight and feel of the lunge rein. (The loose box must be at least 4.3 m × 4.3 m [14 ft × 14 ft] for safety.) This will help it to understand what you want it to do when you lunge it outside.

Learning to Lunge

Do not attempt to lunge a young horse until you are capable of controlling an older horse when it misbehaves on the lunge. You must be really competent before you try to lunge a young horse or it will quickly learn to take advantage of you and a dangerous situation is bound to develop. If you have never lunged a horse before, you must take lessons in lungeing from a competent teacher. When learning to lunge, I also suggest that you 'lunge' another person and then change places so that you become the 'horse', letting them lunge you. The person who is the 'horse' has the lunge line in their hand; the lunger then works them as if they are a horse. The 'horse' is made aware of how much the body position and personality of the lunger affect a horse. As the 'horse' stops, cuts in or tries to whip round, the lunger learns to react quickly and find out where to move to have positive control. Then practise on an older horse that behaves perfectly, followed by practise on an older horse that is liable to play up.

When teaching a young horse to lunge, some people use an assistant to lead the horse on the circle until it understands that it must stay out on the circle, but two people both trying to control a horse and give it commands is very confusing for the horse. Whether leading from the inside or the outside of the circle, the person leading the horse is also placed in a very vulnerable position if the horse panics or misbehaves. In this situation, it is the responsibility of the person lungeing to make sure that they have control of the horse and know exactly what they are doing.

Lungeing a Youngster

Fold the lunge rein in large loops, about 46 cm (18 in) in diameter, over your left hand, starting from the end so that the loops will drop off your hand in smooth sequence. Carry the lunge whip in your left hand, with the whip end pointing behind you and low to the ground. Lead the horse with your right hand, knuckles uppermost.

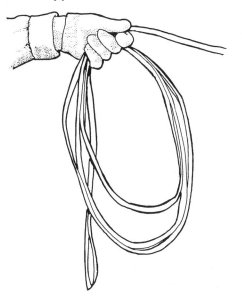

Figure 3.7 *Holding the lunge rein correctly with the excess rein in loops over the hand, and the index finger between the rein and the loops.*

For lungeing a young horse, use an indoor school, outdoor fenced manège or the corner of a small paddock, working in the area nearest to home, where the horse wishes to be. If you go to the far end of the field, your horse will be pulling and thinking towards home all the time.

If the horse is strong or wayward and you have no suitable enclosure, make a circle, just over 20 m (22 yd) in diameter, out of poles resting on straw bales, jump stands or large oil drums, high enough so that the horse will not try to jump out.

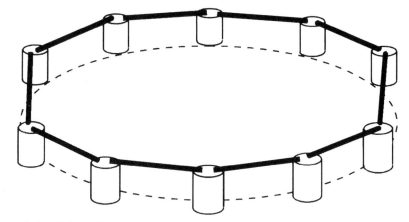

Figure 3.8 *A lungeing circle.*

Figure 3.9 *A homemade lungeing circle built in the corner of a field.*

If you are working in a field or outdoor school, shut the gate in case the horse gets loose.

(Never, ever work, lead or ride a young horse if there are other horses or ponies loose in the same field. This is asking for trouble.)

Check that the lunge rein loops are still neatly in sequence on your left hand and that the swivel where the lunge rein is attached to the cavesson is turned towards you. Begin parallel to a fence, or facing a corner, with your whip pointing behind you and held low in your right hand. Start on the left rein because most horses prefer going in that direction. Step back a little and towards the horse's quarters, asking it to 'Walk on' in the tone of voice it is used to from your work when leading. Be ready to take enough contact on the lunge rein to prevent the horse turning its quarters in and kicking at you if it is very lively. From your lessons in hand, however, it should know your words of command and respond to your voice.

Keep a straight line from your left elbow, through your hand and along the lunge rein to the front of the cavesson. The lunge rein is attached to the front D because this gives you more control and also encourages the horse to look a little to the inside and bend on the circle as you will want it to do when ridden.

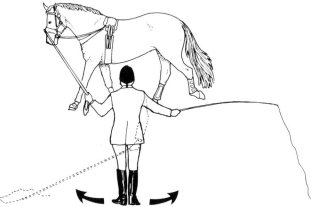

Figure 3.10 *Correct whip positions for lungeing: for slowing a horse (dotted-line whip), and for driving it on (solid-line whip).*

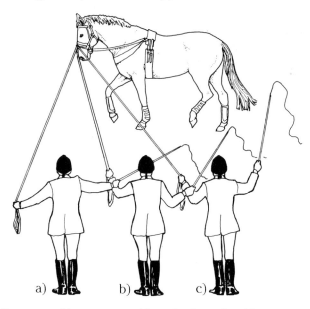

Figure 3.11 *Correct and incorrect positions for lungeing. There must be a straight line from the elbow through the hand to the cavesson. a) Incorrect, the lunger is too far in front of the horse. b) Correct position. c) Incorrect, the lunger is too far behind the horse.*

Always be in such a position when lungeing that you feel you are driving the horse forward, not *leading* it. Watch its eye; this tells you what the horse is thinking and prepares you for its next move. To encourage the horse forward, step a little towards its quarters and, if necessary, move your whip *gently*. To slow the horse down, step a little towards its head and lower your whip behind you.

When lungeing any horse, it is most important to be consistent in your commands, always using the same words and tone of voice. Most horses learn quickly to answer to a slower, deeper tone for a decrease of pace, and a quicker, higher tone for an increase. Do not talk, other than to say your words of command, except for the odd word to calm or praise, otherwise the horse will cease to concentrate.

At first you will probably need to walk in a circle yourself to keep the horse going. When it is more experienced, you can stand still.

If you are lungeing in some form of enclosure, you will have far more control, because the wall or fence will keep the horse on the circle and it will not lean against you or pull outwards. If it does lean at all, do not hold on tight and pull against it. Just feel, feel, feel it in a little − *ask* it in; don't have a tight hand for it to lean against.

To change the rein, ask the horse to halt out on the track, always pointing your whip down and behind you for any decrease of pace at this stage. To keep the horse out, it may be necessary to 'snake' the lunge rein slightly, putting a ripple in it to work along towards the horse's nose. Do not allow the horse to come in to you, or it will continually be edging in hopefully.

When the horse has halted, walk up to it, looping the lunge rein over your right hand as you do so, so that it will be ready for working on the right rein. Keep your lunge whip behind you and pointing low down as you approach the horse. Notice its expression. Is it calm and confident as you approach or is it tense and ready to shoot away from you?

A caress and gentle word are reward enough for good behaviour. Horses that are always searching your pockets and nudging for titbits are a nuisance. They are also inclined to nip when they find out that for once you do not have anything for them.

Turn your horse round facing right, and, again, begin in a corner. Check that your loops will fall off your right hand in sequence. Make sure that the swivel near the nose is towards you. Put the whip in your left hand, pointing low and behind you, step back and towards the horse's quarters and ask it to walk on, if necessary moving the whip a little to encourage it forward and away from you. Move yourself into the centre of the 20 m (22 yd) circle.

If the horse keeps turning in to face you, it may be necessary to advance towards it and even to wave your whip at its head. This should persuade it to step back and you can then quickly try to drive it forward onto the circle again by stepping towards its quarters and pointing your whip at its shoulder.

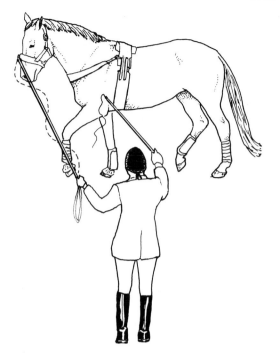

Figure 3.12 *Snaking the lunge line and pointing the whip at the horse's shoulder to stop it falling in towards the centre of the circle.*

Watch your horse's eye. If it even begins to think of whipping round, step towards its quarters and drive it forward with your whip. Horses soon learn to spin round if the person lungeing is standing too far forward, nearly level with their shoulder.

Never wrap the lunge rein round your hand, or allow the rein to slide through your hand, forming small, tight loops round it. People have been dragged and had their hands and fingers broken in this way.

Keep a light contact on the lunge line so that it is in a straight line from your hand to the cavesson. It should never be allowed to slacken or touch the ground. If this happens, the horse could get its legs tangled in the lunge line.

When the horse understands lungeing at walk, work in trot for a few minutes. Work equally on both reins and always begin each session in walk so that the horse will remain calm. Always work on a large circle so that the horse can balance itself.

If, when you first begin to lunge it, the youngster trots or canters off round and round and will not respond to your commands to slow down, walk forward until you are level with its neck. As it comes to the highest part of the wall of the enclosure (if there is a fence or hedge surrounding you on two sides), continue to walk forward so that you can stop the horse against the fence that is facing it. Only do this, however, if the fence is too high for it to jump or it may pop over. Go up to the horse, talk to it and lead it round on the circle once or twice then gradually move away towards the centre and see if the horse will now go more quietly.

Control When Lungeing

You may not have sufficient control of a strong or stroppy horse with the lunge rein attached to the front of the cavesson, so lungeing from the bit may be necessary. (You must accustom your horse to wearing a bridle first before you do this.)

Put on a strong head collar, the noseband of which must fit snugly. Over this put a snaffle bridle, minus the leather noseband, and tie the rings of the bit securely to the side Ds of the head collar. This will prevent the bit from being pulled through the horse's mouth when you lunge. The rein will be less severe if it is attached to both the bit ring and the head collar D, so try this method before using only the bit ring attachment.

One method sometimes used is to pass the lunge rein through the nearside bit ring, over the top of the horse's head, and attach it to the offside bit ring. I find that the disadvantages of this method are that changing the rein over takes time and that the upwards leverage (gag action) raises the horse's head, rather than bringing it in towards you so that you can have control. (When charging off, a horse straightens and stiffens its neck and goes out of the circle. To maintain control, you must be able to turn the horse's head inwards.)

The next method is *very* severe and should *only* be used if the horse has learnt to get away from you in a cavesson and you know it will succeed in doing it again. This frequently happens to inexperienced people. Regaining control of the horse and re-establishing its respect for you are absolute essentials if you are to continue to educate this horse successfully. You should ask a more experienced person to help you in the use of this method.

In such extreme cases, you can gain control by passing the lunge rein from your hand through the bit ring and attaching it to the girth or roller on the inside of the horse. The bit rings must both be securely tied to the head collar or cavesson so that the bit will not pull through the mouth. If a horse has learnt to get away from you, this method will make it respect you again. It is a very useful technique when reschooling animals that have learnt to take advantage. With this type of horse it is a good idea to have a second rein or rope to attach to the bit while changing your lunge rein to the other side.

If, when being lunged, the horse turns to face you and then rears, keep your lunge-rein hand high to try to prevent a foreleg from getting over the rein. When the horse comes down, try to drive it forward with whip and

Figure 3.13 *Lungeing from the bit and head collar. A snaffle bridle over a head collar (minus the bridle noseband), with the bit rings attached to the side Ds of the head collar.*

Figure 3.14 *Lungeing from the bit. The lunge rein is passed through the nearside bit ring, over the top of the horse's head, and attached to the offside bit ring.*

Figure 3.15 *Lungeing from the bit. The lunge rein is passed from the lunger's hand through the bit ring and attached to the girth or roller on the inside. This is a severe method of control and should only be used on a problem horse.*

voice. This will not be possible in an open field; you need to have some sort of fence or barrier behind the horse.

A horse may buck on the lunge from high spirits or it may buck because of the feel of the girth, humping its back. In either case, concentrate on keeping the horse going forward with voice and whip.

If the horse kicks out at you, take a good pull on the lunge rein to bring its head towards you, then use your whip once. Repeat this if necessary. When lungeing a horse that is inclined to kick at you, be careful never to let the rein fall slack. Always be ready to bring its head in towards you the minute it attempts to kick.

When both leading and lungeing, you should always wear gloves to protect your hands against rope burns if the lunge line should be pulled through them. You should wear a hard hat to protect your head if the horse should stand up and strike out at you. Also wear boots with a good heel so that you will not slip.

Length of Lungeing Sessions

Yearling − 10 minutes at walk with a little trotting.
Two-year-old − 10 minutes (or two 10-minute sessions) at walk and trot.
Three-year-old − 15 to 20 minutes (or two 15-minute sessions)
Four-year-old − 20 minutes (or two 15-minute sessions).

BACKING BAREBACK

If your two-year-old is physically strong and well developed and is quiet, calm and confident and has totally accepted the 'police horse' type of training with plastic bags on and above its back, neck and hindquarters (see page 24), there is no reason why a *lightweight* person should not lie across its back even if it has not been loose-schooled or lunged for several weeks first.

If the horse has been carefully and thoughtfully prepared for this new experience and has complete confidence in its handlers and all they do, being backed bareback will very rarely cause problems. I have used this method all my life and am convinced that it is the best way to back a horse and that it can safely be done early in its education.

By the time that you get on with a saddle, the horse will be well used to the feel of a rider on its back. It will then only have to get used to the feel of a saddle and girth (the latter often causing the most trouble of all) which is one of my reasons for preferring to get on bareback at first.

Method

Work the horse first, in whatever method you are currently using (loose-schooling or lungeing), to get rid of any freshness and then lead it to the place chosen for the rider to lie across its back for the first time. This must be a place to which the horse is accustomed and in which it feels thoroughly at home. It should be a confined space, perhaps a small yard that has been well bedded down. In this secure area the horse will be easier to control and less likely to misbehave.

Remember that this should only be attempted in a box with a roof that is high enough to stay well clear of the rider's head whatever happens.

If your horse totally accepts being tied up (see page 29) use this method for introducing lying across, but always have an assistant with you. I have learnt to use this tying method when introducing new things to young horses and have found it highly successful and very safe. Once the horse has learnt to accept being securely tied and knows it is under control, it tends to accept new things (as long as it is carefully prepared for them) without protest. This method enables you to control a big, strong horse and when you stand beside horses that accept being tied up in this way, I am convinced that many of them think it is your strength that is holding them and thus have more respect for you.

When lying across a horse that is tied up, only one assistant is needed. Otherwise it is safest with two assistants, one to hold the horse and the other to leg you up.

Begin by repeating the work with the plastic bags until you are sure the horse is quite happy.

Do some preparatory jumps up and down on both sides of the horse, behaving as if you were about to vault on from either side. Continue this until the horse remains relaxed and completely unafraid, with a low head carriage, no white of eye showing and its ears moving slowly backwards and forwards. Both ears should often be pricked forward, proving that the horse is unconcerned by what you are doing and can happily think of other things.

Do not attempt to lie across until the horse is as confident as this, which may take several days or even weeks, so be patient. A horse that is frightened by the first feel of a rider on its back will remember this for months.

After your usual preparatory jumps up and down on both sides, get your assistant to take your weight as if they were going to give you a leg up. Your left hand should be holding the mane for stability and your body should lie across the horse's back so that most of your weight is on the same side as your assistant. In this way you can easily slide down onto your feet again. Never lie across so that most of your weight is over the far side of the horse's back because if the horse moves suddenly you could fall straight off onto your head. If the horse is completely unafraid, unconcerned and relaxed, with both ears moving slowly backwards and forwards, with a low head carriage and calm eyes, you can begin to wiggle about a little and gently stroke its back and off side with your right hand, while keeping a good hold on the mane with your left hand. Repeat this several times from both sides of the horse.

Once you are absolutely certain that the horse is completely unworried about you lying across it, you can lie a little further across the back and then very gently put your leg across the back, taking care not to touch the hindquarters. Keep your head down low so that you are lying along the neck at first, because the sudden sight of something tall above it can be very alarming for a horse. Sit up very slowly. Do not grip with your legs as this can also terrify a horse. Sit quietly and hold the mane. Gradually begin to swing your arms and legs and move your seat, only proceeding if the horse remains quite unafraid and is not looking back at you with raised head, worried eyes and increasing tension in its body, which you will feel through your seat and legs.

Continue with this work two or three times daily for a few minutes until the horse does not mind what you do on its back and is completely relaxed and confident. The next move is to get your assistant to lead the horse forward for a few steps while you are on it and turn it quietly in both directions.

All through the rest of its training, continue to get on the horse in this way two or three times a week. The horse's reactions may vary; it may not always be completely quiet, so be prepared to go back to some of the early preparatory work if necessary. Learn to recognise the horse's mood each day. Strange horses or people in the yard, odd noises, a change of place or in the weather can all produce a different and sometimes unexpected reaction.

Warning

When you back a two-year-old in this way, you may feel its back sag a little under your weight or your assistant may see that this is happening. In this case do not get on the horse again until it is three years old as it is not yet physically mature enough to carry you. When the horse is ready to be backed it should carry your weight without any sagging of the back.

LUNGEING WITH SADDLE AND BRIDLE

This is done in the same way as early lungeing in every respect, except that you must introduce the horse to the saddle and bridle in the stable until it becomes accustomed to wearing them. Only then can you think of lungeing the horse in saddle and bridle. Lungeing in a saddle will get the horse used to the feel of a tightish girth while on the move. Some horses buck at the feel of the girth, others never do. Lungeing should get rid of the bucks caused by the girth before you begin to ride the horse.

Lungeing in a Saddle

When lungeing the horse in a saddle, use a numnah for comfort and put on a breast girth (or use a tail bandage as a substitute) to prevent the saddle from slipping back. If the horse runs up light (the lower line of its tummy slopes upwards behind the girth), the girth cannot be held naturally in the correct place and will slip back, causing the saddle to slip back too, and possibly upsetting the horse and making it buck.

First remove the irons and leathers so that they will not bang and flap, or else fix them safely by running the stirrups up in the normal way, then passing the looped leathers horizontally through the irons towards the rear, putting the end of the leathers through the loops and then through the keepers on the saddle.

Fasten a surcingle over the saddle to hold the flaps down. If they suddenly blow up in the wind they can terrify a young horse. Each time the wind gets under the flaps on the lungeing circle, up they go and off goes the horse! Tie the surcingle to the girth just behind the forelegs so that it cannot slip back.

Remember that any fright can cause a long setback in training, so think ahead and plan to avoid these things happening.

Even if you think your horse is now perfectly used to the girth, continue to turn it in a circle to each side inside the box after saddling up and still take this precaution even when you start to ride the youngster. The day usually comes when your young horse will quite unexpectedly buck at the feeling of the girth.

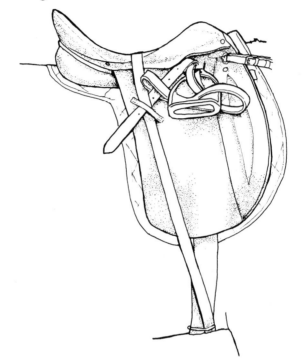

Figure 3.16 *When lungeing the horse in a saddle the stirrup irons must be removed or secured to ensure that they do not flap about. The saddle flaps should also be secured.*

Lungeing in a Bridle

The bridle is put on before the lungeing cavesson (minus the bridle noseband which would get in the way). The headpiece of the lungeing cavesson is put on over the headpiece of the bridle but the close-fitting lungeing cavesson noseband passes inside the cheekpieces of the bridle before being done up snugly so that it will not slip.

The noseband of a Wels cavesson is done up below the bit in the same way as a drop noseband. The noseband must be fitted high enough to rest on the bony part of the nose.

The reins should be removed from the bridle or made safe by twisting them many times one over the other, then passing the throatlash through one loop of one rein only and doing it up.

Figure 3.17 *Lungeing in a bridle. The lungeing cavesson is fitted with the headpiece over the bridle's headpiece, but with the lungeing cavesson noseband inside the cheekpieces of the bridle. The reins should be removed or secured by twisting and held by the throatlash.*

Figure 3.18 *Lungeing in a bridle. The noseband of a Wels cavesson is done up below the bit like a drop noseband, and must rest on the bony part of the nose.*

If necessary, the lunge line may have to be used on the bit (or bit and cavesson or head collar D) to control the horse when lungeing outside in an open field. Remember that you must fix the bit securely to the side Ds of the cavesson or to the side rings of a head collar before a' ching the lunge rein to it. Otherwise the bit will be pulled through the   orse's mouth.

When lungeing from the bit you must realise that you can bruise, hurt or even finally deaden the horse's mouth if you are severe or heavy-handed on the rein or if the horse fights you. It is essential, however, that the horse does not get away from you so this method might only be needed early on with a stroppy horse, until it accepts your control. Only attempt to control a horse outside in an open field if you are already able to control it easily in an enclosed area and it has proved calm, sensible and amenable. Even then, work in the corner of the field nearest to home because the fence or hedge on two sides will help to control the horse.

Two short lungeing sessions are better than one long one, during which the horse may become bored, and both mentally and physically tired.

SIDE REINS

Side reins can be used on a young horse but you must realise that if they are adjusted even a fraction too tight, they will shorten a horse's stride. The pressure of the bit on the mouth from overtight side reins may deaden the mouth. Pressure on the tongue from overtight side reins may cause the horse to bring its tongue over the bit to avoid this. (Once learnt, this habit is extremely difficult to break.) The horse may also learn to go 'overbent' (with head too low and tucked in towards the chest, with the front of the face at an angle behind the perpendicular).

All of these problems may also occur if the side reins are attached too low down on the saddle or roller. If you are going to use side reins, do not do so without getting expert advice initially and then have constant monitoring, as the reins may well need adjusting to a slightly different length or position each day, or even during one session, depending on how the horse is going in them.

Irreparable harm can be done by using side reins incorrectly. It really does take a very experienced person to improve a horse's way of going in side reins. The trainer must know how to adjust them and how and when to readjust them on different horses. The trainer must be capable of driving the horse forward so that it works through from behind and goes forward and down onto the bit. Very few people have this knowledge and feel. If you have any doubts about your own ability, do not use side reins as, incorrectly used, they will do far more harm than good.

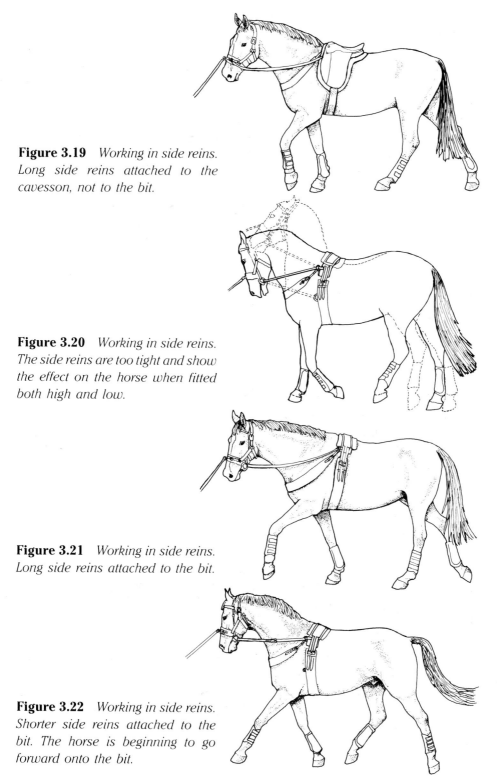

Figure 3.19 *Working in side reins. Long side reins attached to the cavesson, not to the bit.*

Figure 3.20 *Working in side reins. The side reins are too tight and show the effect on the horse when fitted both high and low.*

Figure 3.21 *Working in side reins. Long side reins attached to the bit.*

Figure 3.22 *Working in side reins. Shorter side reins attached to the bit. The horse is beginning to go forward onto the bit.*

ANTI-GRAZING REINS

If you have difficulty in controlling the horse, or if it keeps trying to eat grass when you are lungeing in the field, you can use side reins in a different way to prevent this. Attach them to the side Ds on the roller, about 20 cm (8 in) below the withers on each side, and to the side Ds on the cavesson. If you are using a saddle, attach the side reins to the second girth strap. (If you put them on the first strap, the saddle may be pulled forward.)

If crossed over just in front of the withers and tied together where they cross, the side reins can be fitted quite loosely yet still prevent the horse from getting its head down to graze or really buck. Have them loose enough so that they will not come into contact unless the horse dives its head down, but tight enough to prevent the horse's head going below knee level. Fitted in this way the side reins will not shorten the horse's stride.

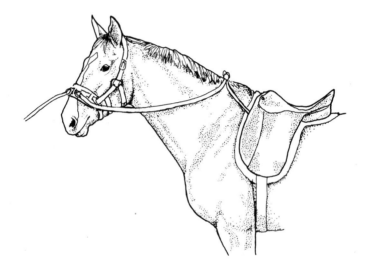

Figure 3.23 *Anti-grazing reins prevent the horse from trying to eat when it is being lunged in a field. These reins are attached to the side Ds of the cavesson, crossed over and tied on the crest of the neck, and attached to the second girth strap of the saddle.*

BACKING USING A SADDLE

When backing a horse with a saddle on, remove the irons and leathers for reasons of safety. (If something went wrong your foot might get caught in a stirrup.)

Use the same method as described for backing bareback (see page 49). Always lunge the horse in the saddle first, however, so that the saddle will be warm against its back and it will have felt the girth tighten against its sides. Always do a little canter on the lunge on both reins before you back a

Figure 3.24 *Backing with a saddle. The rider is legged up by the handler to lie across the saddle initially.*

horse in a saddle. I have known very many horses which appeared to accept the girth totally in trot work but absolutely exploded when first cantered in a girth. If this is going to happen (and it may do so quite unexpectedly one day), it is better discovered and worked out before you get on the horse.

If the horse is not completely used to the feeling of the girth under all circumstances before you back it with a saddle on, it may tense up and hold its breath when it feels you on its back. This sudden tensing on the horse's part tightens the girth even more and it may buck in panic, not at you but at the girth. A horse bucking because of the girth does not kick up its heels behind it; it lowers its head, rounds and arches its back and leaps like a broncho, with all four feet off the ground.

Do not attempt to get on with a saddle if the horse still frequently and unexpectedly bucks at the girth on the lunge. Some young horses are never worried by the feel of a girth; others strongly object to it and some will do so all their lives, putting on a broncho act every time the girth is first done up after only a few weeks off work.

If your young horse is even slightly worried by the girth, always turn the horse in a circle in both directions if you have had to pull the girth up a hole after lungeing the horse and before getting on it. Tightening the girth by even one hole can give it a very different feel and restart the bucking. Always tighten the girth very gradually and do not have it tighter than necessary to keep the saddle in place if the horse does buck. Use a wide, soft girth as this is usually more comfortable for the horse.

If the bucking at the girth persists, make sure that no part of the tack is uncomfortable and that there is no pinching from the numnah, saddle or girth on the horse's back, sides or belly. To overcome this problem it n y be necessary to leave a well-padded roller on this type of horse for sev l hours every day. If the horse continues to buck try a girth with an ela c insert; the slight 'give' eliminates the feeling of imprisonment.

Work the horse loose or on the lunge in its saddle several times a day until it accepts the feeling of the girth. This problem can really slow up your progress and be very depressing for the trainer, but it is a fairly common one. Be patient and do not be tempted to get on and try to sit the bucks as a horse that has learned that it can buck you off will be even more of a problem!

It is well worth spending a lot of time on this as it will really pay off when you ride the horse out and find it is calm and confident, not tensing up and looking back at you, both of you wondering fearfully what is going to happen next.

Depending on the horse's temperament, it may take a few days or as long as two weeks of sitting on the horse every day with a saddle on before it is calm, relaxed and confident. Continue to sit on its back with the saddle on two or three times a week after the lungeing or loose-schooling sessions so that when you do begin to ride the horse it will be well used to the feel of the saddle, girth and rider.

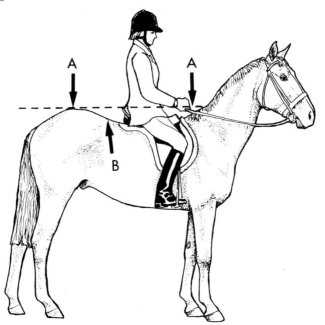

Figure 3.25 *An immature two-year-old not strong enough to be backed. The horse is higher behind than in front (shown by dotted line A), and there is a marked dip to the back (B).*

Figure 3.26 *A mature two-year-old whose back is taking the weight well.*

Remember that, while some two-year-olds are mature enough to be backed, others are not, and you must assess each youngster individually.

A mature two-year-old may feel big and strong, but do not be tempted to work it longer or do more advanced work with it; its bones are still soft, its limbs are not used to carrying weight, and it has no muscle.

4 THE THREE-YEAR-OLD

Like children, horses mature at different rates, both mentally and physically. You may find that your youngster takes to it all like a duck to water and learns without much effort or stress. On the other hand, it may be easily confused or tired, suffer from amnesia or simply fall over its own feet the whole time. With either type of horse it is important that you do not rush the training, while, especially with the second type, it is *vital* that you take things slowly and allow the horse to learn at its own pace.

Just as you may have found that your two-year-old could only cope with the early stages of the work described in the section on two-year-olds, so your three-year-old may proceed very slowly through the work described in this section and you may wish to spread this out over the third and fourth year. Use your own judgement or ask for experienced advice but *do not* rush things. It is far better to turn out a well-schooled, sensible five-year-old than try to reschool a confused four-year-old that has learned a little about many things but does none of them properly. If the work goes wrong at this stage, you will still be paying for it at nine and ten, so take your time and get it right.

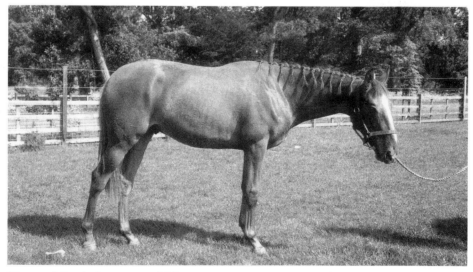

Figure 4.1 *A three-year-old horse.*

60

If you have not lunged your horse as a two-year-old, now is the time to do all the work on lungeing and/or loose-schooling described in the previous chapters.

LUNGEING IN SIDE REINS

Some people never use side reins attached to the bit because they believe this can alter a horse's natural way of going and encourage a stiff, set head carriage. If they are used with care and thought, side reins can do a great deal of good, but badly used, too tight or too low, they can shorten a horse's stride, prevent the horse from using its shoulders freely and stop it bringing its hind legs well forward underneath it so that it does not work through from behind properly.

Side reins should not be attached to the bit when leading a horse to or from the work area, in case the horse is upset by the sudden contact if it happens to leap or buck. Make the side reins safe by clipping them onto the Ds on the front of the saddle or roller. Always begin each session by lungeing without the side reins to allow the horse to stretch, relax and settle.

Start with the side reins so loose that there is no contact on the mouth. Fix them high enough to the saddle or roller so that there will never be any backward tension. As work progresses, gradually tighten them a little at a time, making sure the horse is always going freely forward and working down onto the side reins. With your voice and whip, you must encourage the horse to work from behind and really use itself. Try to get it going in an even, rhythmic trot at a steady, active pace, using its hocks, pushing itself forward from behind and looking as if it is really going somewhere. Watch the inside hind leg and see if the horse is stepping forward and under with it, tracking up to the hoofprints of the forelegs. At this stage the horse's natural head carriage should be low and its loins should be rounded slightly, not hollowed.

Some horses work better with the inside side rein one or two holes shorter than the outside one; others go better with both reins at equal length. Some people swear by one method and condemn the other. You must find out which method encourages your horse to go forward freely with a slight bend to the inside.

Remember that side reins at the right length for trot may shorten a horse's stride in walk, because there is a natural difference in head carriage between the two gaits. Work as little as possible in walk if the reins are adjusted for trot and let them out a little for longer periods of walk. Lengthen them still more, or undo them, for periods of rest at walk, when the horse must be encouraged to go forward and stretch its neck out and down.

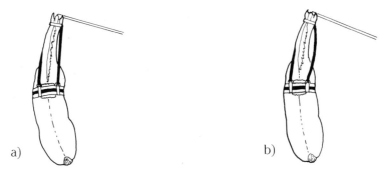

Figure 4.2   *Horse being lunged with a) the inside side rein slightly shorter than the outside rein, and b) the side reins of equal length.*

If you are using a shorter side rein on the inside, remember to alter the length of this each time you change the rein and make sure that the horse is not carrying its hind legs to the outside instead of making them follow in the same track as the forelegs. If this does happen, adjust both side reins to the same length and ask for an inward bend with the lunge line by feel, feel, feeling gently on the lunge line.

When changing the rein, lead the horse forward and turn it away from you, very gradually, on a big circle so that the horse does not receive a conflicting pull on the outside side rein as it turns.

Remember that as you progressively shorten the side reins, you will have to work harder to keep the horse really going forward onto the bit. Do get expert help and advice when using side reins. If in doubt keep them loosely adjusted.

The three-year-old horse is very young and must not be allowed to become tired or bored by this work, so twenty minutes of real work a day is sufficient, interspaced with rest periods at walk. Keep your youngster on a large circle, say, 20 m (22 yd). Small circles can cause muscle tension, loss of balance and strain on limbs.

CANTERING ON THE LUNGE

Do not canter until the horse carries itself in trot in a good rhythm and with a correct bend to the inside through its neck and body. At first, canter with very loose side reins, or preferably none at all, so that the horse can find its own balance. When it is cantering smoothly and evenly, you can very gradually start to tighten the side reins, but the horse must never be pulled back by them. You must always make it work forward and down onto them. From the beginning, check that the horse starts canter on the correct leg. If it is wrong, immediately ask for trot again, establish a good trot, don't hurry, then ask for canter once more. Nearly all horses have a preference for leading on a certain leg and it may take time and patience to get your horse going equally happily on both leads. It is sometimes easier to get canter on the correct lead if you work on a circle in the corner of a field where there is a solid-looking fence, hedge or wall, and ask for canter just as the horse comes into the corner. This is the easiest place for the horse to pick up canter in an indoor school or manège.

EARLY LONG-REINING

Long-reining is not essential in your training programme, but it is very interesting and most worthwhile. Your two- or three-year-old should be ready to long-rein when it is lungeing at walk and trot on both reins and responding well to your commands.

Long-reining requires speedy, rhythmic movements of your hands and body and great co-ordination. Do not attempt it on a young horse until you are very capable when working with an older horse. If you have never long-reined before, get some lessons from an experienced teacher.

You will need:

- A lungeing cavesson.
- A pair of long reins.
- Boots all round plus overreach boots if the horse is shod or liable to overreach or the going is deep.
- An enclosed area or very small paddock in which the horse is used to being lunged.
- A horse that is already lungeing calmly and sensibly.
- The ability and experience gained from long-reining many older horses, including some difficult ones.
- Patience, sympathy and understanding.
- Good hands which can keep the reins in a straight line and maintain a gentle contact even through changes of direction.
- Anticipation, co-ordination and quickness of hand and eye.
- Gloves.

The horse should have been made accustomed to the feel of two reins along its back and round its quarters and sides while in the stable or in a small enclosure. It should also be unworried by the sight of a long rein lying still or moving on the ground beside its feet. It should be willing to stand quite still when asked so that you can adjust the tack safely.

If you have *any* doubts about your ability to long-rein a horse, don't do it.

Reasons for Long-reining

Through long-reining, you can train a horse to be supple and very responsive without putting a saddle on its back, so that even a very young or not very strong animal can be worked in this way.

You have very accurate control of the whole horse and can influence its forehand or hindquarters.

If the horse showed a tendency to turn in on you when it was being lunged, you can keep it out with the second rein.

If the horse tends to cut in on part of the circle, again, you can keep it out with the second rein.

Small ponies can be worked and schooled to a high standard by this method.

Working on a circle with two reins improves a horse's rhythm and balance. With two reins it is easier to encourage the horse to really work through from behind and to track up.

When driving the horse, always walk over to one side or the other so that if the horse suddenly tries to take off you are in a better position to turn it onto a circle to regain control. It is quite impossible to control a horse which is trying to rush forward if you are directly behind it because it will just tow you along. By driving the horse you can make the horse walk on in front of you past frightening objects. You can teach it to go towards and away from home alone. You can supple it by driving it in and out of trees, cones, etc. changing the side on which you are walking as you do so.

The feel of the second rein on its side gets the horse used to the feel of your legs before you ride it. It can learn the beginnings of lateral work (moving away sideways and forward from your leg). When it is eventually ridden, lateral work will come more easily to it if it has done this work in long reins.

Even a two-year-old can do this work at walk for 20 minutes a day because it puts no strain on the horse when done by a knowledgeable person. A horse that has been long-reined is far easier to control and guide when first ridden.

Method

Many horses panic completely when they first feel the back rein (i.e. the rein on the outside of the horse) round their hindquarters so you must get them used to this in their own stable first. Do not attempt to work like this outside until the horse is calm and confident when the rein is round its hindquarters and hind legs (to where the reins may easily fall if you get in a muddle). The process of getting the horse used to two reins on the ground, round its hindquarters, round its hind legs and being pulled gently along the ground around its hind legs may take several days. You must make quite sure that your horse will not panic when you do this sort of thing outside. (Many dangerous situations can be avoided throughout the horse's life if it will stand quite still when told to. Teach this lesson well; be consistent with the wording of your command and the tone of voice, and practise this exercise with the horse several times a day in the stable, field or school.)

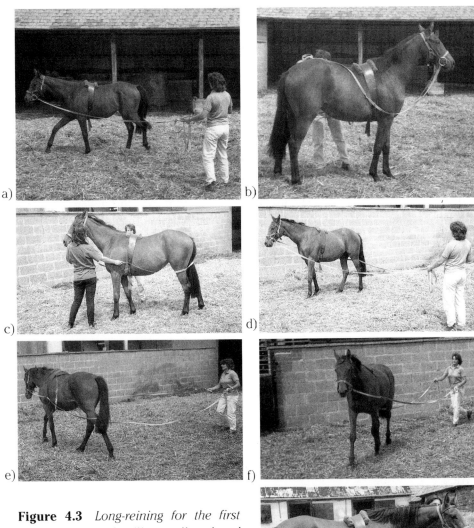

Figure 4.3 *Long-reining for the first time in a safe, familiar, well-enclosed yard. a) Lungeing on a straw surface in a roller. b) Introducing the second rein ready for long-reining; the horse is a little worried and has its attention directed back towards the trainer. c) The second rein is now round the horse's hindquarters; the horse is still concerned and has both ears cocked back and its head raised. d) Starting to work on a circle using the two reins; the horse is more relaxed, but the head is still raised. e) The horse is more relaxed with a lowered head carriage. f) Driving the horse in long-reins for the first time. The trainer walks behind the horse, but a little to the inside. The horse is relaxed and happy. g) The lesson has finished, and the horse is relaxed, confident and unafraid of the reins touching its leg or trailing along the ground.*

Begin in a small enclosure, such as a large loose box (4.3 m × 4.3 m [14 ft × 14 ft]) or an indoor school. You will need a pair of reins 9 m (30 ft) long. The horse should wear the same equipment that you use for lungeing. Attach one long-rein to the nearside D of the cavesson and hang the loops over your left hand, ready to unwind in sequence. Attach the other rein to the offside D of the cavesson, passing the rein over the neck just in front of the withers, and arranging the loops in sequence over your right hand.

Long-reining is easier without a whip. At first, walk the horse round the box so that it gets used to the sight and feel of the two reins. Let it become accustomed to the sight of a rein being pulled along on the ground beside it.

Halt the horse and walk towards it, looping the reins onto alternate hands as you go. Do not allow the horse to turn in towards you.

At halt, gently 'stroke' the right rein along the horse's back and allow it to fall down to rest just above the hocks. (Some people flip the rein along the back and down over the hocks but this is an unnecessarily frightening method to use.)

At first the horse may shoot forward, but don't pull on the back rein; just maintain sufficient contact to keep it above the hocks. To change sides, drop the back rein, go to the off side and turn the horse a little to the right so that its hind legs are well clear of the back rein on the ground, then

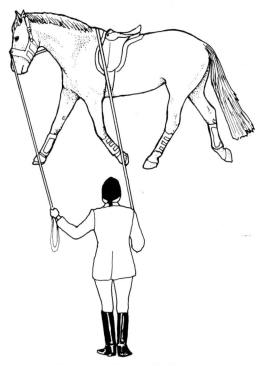

Figure 4.4   *The first stage of long-reining with the outside rein coming over the neck just in front of the withers.*

gradually reel the rein in. Put the new back rein over the withers and gently work it down over the quarters. Work in the same way on both reins, not taking the horse out of the loose box or enclosure until it is relaxed and happy with the back rein lying above its hocks.

The next step is to take the horse out to the usual lunge area and work it on a circle on both reins, again starting with what will be the back rein coming over near the withers. Halt the horse and walk towards it, looping up the reins onto your left and right hands as you go. Now 'stroke' the rein that was over the withers back along the quarters as before and allow it to fall gently to rest just above the hocks. At this point, the horse may jump forward. Use your front rein (i.e. the rein on the inside of the horse) to keep it on the circle. Whatever happens, *do not* pull on the back rein, just maintain enough contact to keep it above the hocks and talk to the horse to calm it.

You must have supple shoulders and elbows to allow your hands to follow the horse's movements and thus keep an even contact on both reins. If your horse bucks, it may get an outside hind leg over the back rein. If this happens, drop the back rein, halt the horse or bring it in to you and then halt. Quietly move round the front of the horse to the other side, take up the outside rein and start again from the beginning. If the back rein drops below the hock, you may be able to get it above the hock again by raising the hand holding the back rein as high as possible.

If, in bucking, the horse gets the back rein under its tail, it will clamp the tail down very tightly onto the rein and probably rush forward. Keep the horse on the circle and do not feel the back rein; keep it very loose and hope the horse will relax, in which case the rein will slide down into place

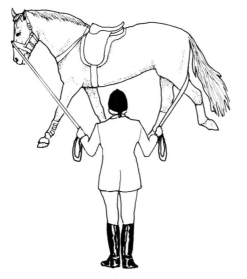

Figure 4.5 *The second stage of long-reining with the outside rein resting just above the hocks.*

again, above the hocks. If this does not happen, drop the back rein and go to the horse's head at which point it may relax. If you have to take hold of the tail to release the rein, be careful that the horse does not kick in fright.

When you change the rein, halt, drop the back rein, loop up the front rein, go in front to the other side of the horse and slowly reel in the back rein. Do not stand still in front of the horse in case it rushes forward when the rein touches its hind legs.

Once the horse accepts the sight and feel of a rein in all possible positions, then, if you do get in a muddle, it will not panic.

Work on both reins equally. If the horse is lazy, you can encourage it forward with a flip of the back rein above its hocks. You can ask it to halt or decrease pace by using your voice and a slight feel on both reins, remembering not to use too much back rein or you will pull the quarters inwards and confuse the horse. If your horse has been turning in on the lunge, or cutting in on part of the circle, the back rein can now be used to keep it out on the track, not by holding the rein tightly but by a gentle feel; feel the rein *just before* you come to the part of the circle where the horse starts to cut in.

Close your hands on the reins with your fingernails turned slightly upwards, so that you have a soft elbow and shoulder and there is a straight line from your elbow through your hand and along the rein.

When the horse is happily accepting the back rein in both directions, you can turn and change the rein without going up to it. If the horse is walking round on the right rein, step forward towards it and, at the same time, bring your right hand across to take up a loop of the left rein and place it on your left hand, feeling it a little. This feel on the left side of the cavesson and the slight pressure on the near side of the quarters will turn the horse to the left. As the horse turns, be ready to let a loop of rein out quickly from your right hand, as this will now be the longer rein, passing round the quarters. Start your turn towards an open part of the field so that the horse will have room to turn, or, if you are in an enclosure, bring the horse in a little towards the centre before starting your turn, so that it has room to turn outwards. You must walk forward quickly for three or four steps as the horse turns outwards away from you because it will make a sweeping outward curve to turn rather than swivel round on the spot.

Remember, as the horse feels the new back rein come against its quarters, it may jump forward; do not pull back, just follow the movement with your hands. Adjust the length and tension of both reins as necessary after the turn.

When you are both expert at turns in walk in each direction, you can try them in trot. For this, your change of rein aids has to be very quick and precise and you have to step further forward and more quickly to allow the horse to make the larger arc necessary when turning outwards at trot.

If the horse becomes tense or worried, this is a sign that you are doing

a)

b)

c)

d)

e)

Figure 4.6 *Driving the horse out and about on long-reins. a) Long-reining in a roller with the reins attached to the bit and threaded through the Ds on the roller. b) Long-reining the horse round a farmyard to get the animal used to strange and 'spooky' objects. c) Long-reining round a yard in a saddle with the reins threaded through the stirrups; the stirrups are tied together underneath and secured to the girth. d) Long-reining round the lanes to meet traffic. e) Long-reining past other horses.*

too much too soon, or that you are not yet experienced enough for the horse to understand what you want.

Your movements do have to be very co-ordinated but once you have the feel for it you will really enjoy this work. Because the reins are attached to the cavesson, not the bit, you cannot hurt the horse's mouth as the pressure of your reins is only on the nose. Unless you are very experienced, it is better not to attach the reins to the bit as it is very easy to upset a horse this way, and/or spoil its mouth.

When the horse is turning happily in both directions at walk and trot and will keep an even rhythm in trot during and after the turns, you can begin to drive it about the field and in and out of barrels and trees.

While you are changing direction on a circle, having the reins threaded through the stirrup irons would be a nuisance, because you would have to keep unthreading the inside rein. Working with the inside rein through a stirrup when on a circle would give a backward feel, discourage the horse from going forward freely and could shorten the stride because the stirrup would act as a lever.

When you are driving the horse about the field, however, you may find it easier to thread the reins through the stirrups because you will be using shallow loops and straight lines, frequently moving from the horse's near side to the off side as you change direction. Have the leathers very short, so that there is no downward pull, and tie your stirrup irons together by passing a string underneath the belly on top of the girth, securing the tie to the girth so that the stirrups will not lift up or slide back. Never walk directly behind the horse, because, at this stage, you will have no control from this position if the horse takes off; it would simply tow you along, using the strength of its neck.

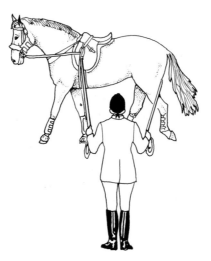

Figure 4.7 *If the inside rein is threaded through the stirrup when long-reining on a circle, the rein will give the horse a 'backward' feel and shorten the stride.*

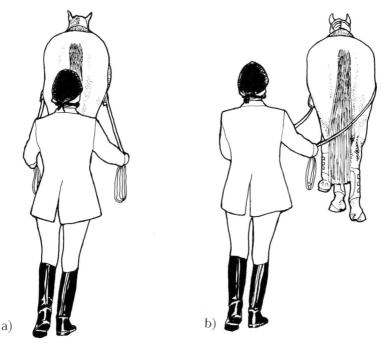

a)   b)

Figure 4.8 *Incorrect and correct positions of the trainer when driving a horse on long-reins. a) Incorrect, the trainer is standing directly behind the horse. b) Correct, the trainer is standing a little to one side of the horse.*

As stated before, always walk fairly close to the horse but out to one side a little, so that the back rein comes slightly round the quarters. From this position you can, when in trouble, get on to a circle again by using one rein. In real trouble, you could then drop the back rein and use both hands on the front rein. Here, the lever of the stirrup iron would help you to regain control by bringing the horse round and inwards onto a circle.

When driving, work equally from both sides so that you are sometimes walking a little way out to the horse's left, and sometimes out to its right.

When turning left, walk a little way out to the horse's left. Your left rein asks for the turn and your right rein round the quarters controls them and encourages the horse to go freely forward through the turn. When turning right, walk a little way out to the horse's right side and reverse the rein aids.

Prepare the horse for changes of direction by half-halts, thinking 'Whoa' and slightly checking the forehand while encouraging the hind legs to step further under the body. Co-ordinate your aids so that your reins are always in a straight line and the horse has a feel from both your hands through the reins on to both sides of its nose. A sudden turn by the horse is usually caused by loss of contact on the outside rein. Learn to co-ordinate your aids so that the horse turns smoothly, is correctly bent through the body and is always looking in the direction it is turning.

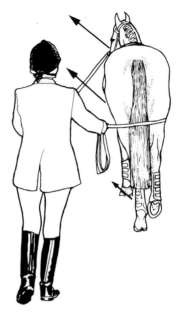

Figure 4.9 *Starting lateral work in long-reins. The horse is moving forwards and sideways (the arrows show the direction of movement).*

Once you can do this, you can teach the horse to move sideways. This is a useful preliminary to teaching the horse to move away from your leg when ridden. Use a small half-halt before any change of pace or direction. To move forward and sideways to the left, walk a little behind the horse and over to the left, with your right rein going round the quarters. Watch the off hind leg. When riding or long-reining, you can only influence a horse sideways to the left when its off hind is *not* on the ground. Take a little more contact with your left rein, asking the horse to look slightly to the left, and, as the off hind *begins* to come off the ground, feel on the right rein so that it is pressing against the off hind leg and asking the horse to step across, forward and over. Ease the right rein as the horse takes a step across. Work in a rhythm − feel and ease − then drive the horse straight forward again.

You must not *stop* the forward movement but simply change it to forward and sideways movement. When driven on long-reins or ridden, the horse must step under its body with its hind legs and actively push itself forward to work correctly. Never hold the horse back with too much rein, causing a shortening of stride and loss of forward movement.

To move sideways to the right, walk a little over to the right of the horse. With your right rein, ask for a slight bend to the right. Feel with the left rein round the quarters as the near hind *begins* to come off the ground and ease the rein a little as the horse takes a step, again, working in a rhythm. Do not ask too much at first − two or three steps are enough − then straight forward again.

As you drive in and out of trees or barrels or in serpentines, you must change your position so that you are always a little way out on the side towards which the horse is turning.

Do not get cross if the horse does not understand immediately. Check that your aids are co-ordinated and in rhythm. Have patience and you will both succeed.

Remember that 15 minutes of serious work is sufficient. A young horse cannot be expected to concentrate for long. Two short sessions per day are better than one long one, during which the horse may well get tired, cross and bolshy. Instead of trying to make the horse do something it is finding difficult, ask for something easier and when it does this correctly, stop. Learn to stop on a good note. Avoid battles and have patience.

Watch for signs of weariness, clicking or forging (striking the toe of the hind shoe on the toe of the front shoe), brushing or dragging the hind toes, and be ready to give the horse two or three weeks rest in the field before continuing its education.

As soon as you are sufficiently capable and co-ordinated you can long-rein from the bit. A big, strong young horse may need to be controlled by the bit when driven in long reins.

LOOSE-SCHOOLING OVER POLES AND SMALL JUMPS

If you set this exercise up carefully and thoughtfully, it is an excellent way of teaching a horse to jump because the horse wears no equipment to interfere with its performance or distract it in any way.

Jumping a horse loose is safer and easier for an inexperienced horse and trainer than jumping on the lunge but, even so, you should not attempt it until you have practised this method of jumping using an older horse and are competent to cope with any problems that may arise.

The horse can wear just a head collar or a saddle and bridle. In the latter case the reins must be made safe by twisting them one over the other many times and then passing the throat lash through one rein before doing it up. The reins must not be passed behind the stirrups to keep them out of the way as they will pull on the mouth and restrict the horse's head and neck when it jumps. For the same reason, side reins should never be worn when jumping.

It is best to remove the stirrups, but if you leave them on, secure them firmly, as shown on page 52, and put a surcingle round the saddle to stop it from flapping. Some people prefer to loose-jump a young horse without a saddle as they feel this frees the back so that the horse will round its back (bascule) properly as it jumps and will not be distracted by the saddle moving and flapping.

For safety, the horse should wear boots all round, and if shod, it should also wear overreach boots.

You must use an area with a solid, high fence or other barrier that the horse can neither jump nor try to barge through. The horse should have been worked on the flat in this place several times so that it is quite at home there. The going should be level and not too deep or too hard.

The area can be oblong, oval or circular. The length of the short side, or the diameter of the circle, must not be less than 20 m (22 yd). The area must be small enough for you to be able to control the horse accurately and, with the help of wings or poles, guide the horse into the fence. You should carry two whips as you did when loose-schooling on the flat (see page 33).

Erect the wings or guide poles and, with nothing on the ground between them, work the horse through the empty gap in both directions. The gaps must be at least 3 m (10 ft) wide. When the horse is trotting rhythmically and calmly through the gaps, place one pole on the ground between one set of wings and walk, then trot, the horse over that. (Use only rounded poles as square-sided ones can injure heels and fetlocks).

Now place a second pole 2.7 m (9 ft) away from the first and between a second set of wings. Work the horse in trot over the two poles in both directions before inserting a third pole in the gap between the first two so that the three poles are now 1.3 m (4½ ft) apart. Work the horse over these poles in trot on both reins and check that the hind foot is stepping exactly in the centre of the gap between the poles. If necessary, move the poles by about 15 cm (6 in).

If the hind foot falls in the centre of the gap between the first two poles but beyond the centre of the gap between the second two, the distance may be too short for your horse, so move the first and last poles 15 cm (6 in) further away from the centre pole.

If the hind foot falls in the centre of the gap between the first two poles but before the centre of the gap between the second two, then the distance may be too long for your horse. In this case, move the first and last poles 15 cm (6 in) closer to the centre pole.

Only alter the distances between the poles if you are certain the problem is not caused by the horse hurrying along with a long stride, or being lazy and just bumbling in on a short stride.

Next, set up a single crossed-poles fence to encourage the horse to come in straight and to the centre of the fence. The horse must want to jump — never chase it over the fence. Ask the horse to jump only four or five times at most in each session and not more than twice a week. Keep your fence small and solid-looking and change its appearance frequently by using different fillers.

Stick to a single fence until you are sure the horse will meet it right and then, if you are working in an oval or oblong area, try a second fence. This must be at least 5.5 m (6 yd) away from the first fence (for a horse) and be on the long, straight side of an oblong or on the longer, curved side of an oval. This distance will give a horse one non-jumping stride. (A second jump on a 20 m (22 yd) circle would be too tight for a young horse.)

Introduce your second fence as a pole on the ground on the approach to your original fence. You will need to set up more wings and poles to guide the horse in, and a barrier between the jumps so that the horse cannot run out.

Gradually raise the fences but do not go over 61 cm (2 ft) with any fence at this stage. The horse must enjoy its work and jump calmly and confidently. If the horse stops, runs out or rushes into the fences, you are doing too much too soon, your actions are uncoordinated or the jumps are not correctly set up. If things go even slightly wrong, go back to something the horse will do happily and then stop on that good note. Ask for expert advice and help before asking the horse to jump again.

RIDING YOUR THREE-YEAR-OLD FOR THE FIRST TIME

Read the sections on backing bareback (page 49) and backing with a saddle (page 56) before you attempt to ride your horse.

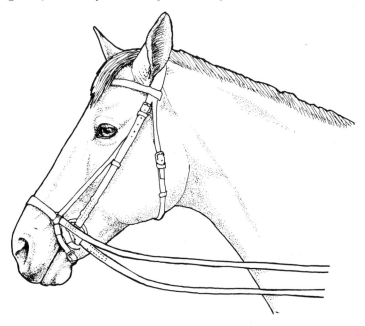

Figure 4.10 *A young horse is used to the feel of instructions via the nose from a lungeing cavesson. When it is ridden for the first time it helps the horse if you maintain that feel by using two sets of reins. One set is attached to the rings of a drop noseband and held like the bradoon reins of a double bridle. The other set is attached to a snaffle and held like the curb reins of the double bridle.*

REIN CONTACT

So far, all your rein aids have been on the horse's nose, via the cavesson. To me it is logical to continue with this when you first ride the horse, as it understands the feeling. Put a drop noseband on the bridle, using one that has biggish rings where the noseband and cheekpieces meet. Now, when you ride the horse after each lungeing or long-reining session, use the snaffle-bit rein and a second rein attached to the drop-noseband rings. Hold the reins as if the drop-noseband reins were the bradoon (controlling and guiding rein) of a double bridle and the snaffle-bit reins were the curb reins of the double bridle.

Check that the drop noseband and its headpiece are not too loose or the cheek part of the headpiece may be pulled across into the horse's eye as you feel on the rein on the opposite side. (If you have never ridden with two pairs of reins, practise this arrangement on an older horse but with both reins on a snaffle bit. This is also a good way of improving your own 'feel' and co-ordination.)

Make sure you have the drop noseband rein fractionally shorter so that it comes into contact before the bit rein. The horse will understand the feel on the drop noseband because it will be the same as the feel on the lungeing cavesson.

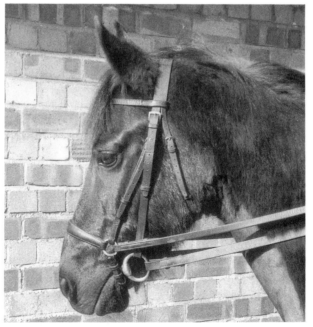

Figure 4.11 *A young pony wearing the 'double bridle' arrangement of one set of reins to a drop noseband, and one set to a snaffle bit. Note the large rings on the drop noseband which make it easy to attach the reins.*

Rein Contact with Young Ponies

Ponies need to be ridden by a lightweight, experienced person at first. A lightweight adult or an older child who is not nervous is ideal. A child might find two reins difficult to hold and use accurately, so pelham couplings or Ds can be used, one end attached to the bit ring, the other to the drop-noseband ring. The pony then has 50 per cent of the guiding and controlling pressure on its nose and 50 per cent on its mouth. The rider only has one rein to cope with and cannot be severe on the pony's mouth.

When the pony is going happily, the bit rein alone can be used, but it is a good idea to revert to the pelham coupling for the first Pony Club rally or 'interesting' outing. Too much bit rein on an overexcited pony causes far more trouble than too little. Nose pressure seems to be much more readily accepted in stressful conditions and the pony is then less likely to start going backwards or rearing.

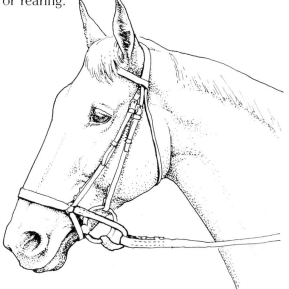

Figure 4.12 *Young ponies are often ridden by experienced children, but a child may have trouble using two reins when worn as in Figs. 4.10 and 4.11. It is, therefore, easier to use one rein attached to a pelham rounding. The rounding is attached to the drop noseband rings and the snaffle bit.*

RIDING IN AN ENCLOSED AREA

Put on the saddle and a bridle with two sets of reins. Have a neck strap in case you need something to hold on to. Make sure the stirrup irons are big enough for your feet to slip out easily. Get a leg up onto the horse in the box or enclosed area it is used to. Only if it is calm and relaxed should you proceed to riding in a larger, enclosed area.

Figure 4.13 *The single rein, pelham rounding arrangement in action on a child's pony. Fifty per cent of the pressure is on the pony's nose, and fifty per cent on its mouth.*

If this is the first time your horse will have been ridden outside the box, get an assistant to leg you up in the usual work area and to lead you about to begin with. Just lie across the horse's back at first and repeat all the stroking and wriggling of your first backing session. Do not be surprised if the horse is worried. That which is accepted in the box can receive a very different reaction outside. Watch the height of the horse's head − a raised head, ears held back towards you and eyes looking back at you indicate a worried horse. Do not go any further until the horse relaxes, lowers its head a little and its ears move slowly backwards and forwards, occasionally both going forward, proving the horse has the confidence to think of other things. When you swing a leg across and sit up, do so very slowly, re-membering that the sudden sight of you so tall on its back can be alarming to a horse.

Get your assistant to place your feet in the stirrups in case you accidently nudge the horse's side with your toes in searching for them.

At first, get an experienced person to lead you on a lunge rein so that they can help to control the horse if necessary.

When you first guide the horse while riding it, use an opening rein − i.e. the hand (with fingers upwards) is held out a little to simulate the feel and angle of the lunge − and gently use your inside leg on the girth to keep the horse going forward and encourage it to move its ribs and shoulders. Keep your outside leg quietly on its side, behind the girth, to control the quarters. Feel the horse round with your inside rein, and make the turns very gradual curves. It is safer at this stage to have a good hold of the mane in your outside hand, so that you will not touch the mouth and are more likely to keep your balance if the horse does leap about.

To halt, use your voice aid, sit tall, think halt and ride the horse forward into a slightly raised hand that applies a little gentle pressure on the noseband. Do not close your hand and take a hold on the mouth, or the horse will quickly learn to lean on your hands in downwards transitions and to slow down on its forehand, or to hollow its back and raise its head to evade your hand. Continue to use your voice aids so that the horse will learn to associate the new, ridden aids with the familiar voice aids.

Halt

From the beginning, both when in hand and ridden, try to teach your horse to halt square, with its weight evenly distributed on all four legs. Correct the horse by making it step forwards, not backwards. Even in hand, check the horse a little with a half-halt before saying, 'And Whoa!'.

When riding a halt, use a half-halt to get the horse's centre of gravity further back and bring its hind legs further under it; this will make it easier for the horse to perform a correct square halt. At first, use your voice as well as the other aids. Bring your weight smoothly back a little, lift your hands a fraction and ride the horse forward into a very slightly holding hand. Correct the horse by asking for just one step forward until it is standing square. The horse must always step forward, it must not learn to step back from halt.

If the horse's position is very bad, walk on and begin again with the preparatory half-halt. Only practise for a very short time and do not upset or worry the horse if at first it does not understand exactly what you wish it to do.

Half-halts

A half-halt is used to steady and rebalance the horse by moving its centre of gravity further back and so lightening its forehand in preparation for a change of gait or direction or shortening of the stride.

The rider closes the lower leg to ride the horse forward into a slightly checking hand, thus asking the horse to step further underneath the body with its hind legs. The rider must think 'Whoa!' without actually halting, giving a tiny, momentary check that is so slight as to be hardly visible to an onlooker.

Half-halts should be used all the time when riding, not only as a preparation for changes of gait or direction, but also during the changes of direction and again, after changes of gait or direction. They make the difference between a smooth, co-ordinated performance by horse and rider and a rough, jerky performance lacking in rhythm, thought and preparation.

Leaping and Bucking

If the horse leaps and bucks, your assistant should be ready to pull it in towards him or her, thus bringing it off balance and making it a little more difficult for it to misbehave. When leaping and bucking, as in jumping, a horse needs to push off equally with both hind legs. Turning its head sideways puts more weight on one hind leg and makes this movement awkward for it.

If the horse misbehaves, try not to grip with your legs. The new feeling of a rider's legs clamping on to its sides can make a youngster explode into broncho-type bucks in an attempt to get rid of the frightening feeling. It is very important that you do not fall off at this stage because then the horse will learn that it can get rid of you and this is not something you wish it to find out (see page 132).

RIDING OFF THE LUNGE

If the horse seems relaxed and happy, your assistant can take off the lunge rein and you can try turns, circles and halts by yourself, still using your usual vocal aids in conjunction with the rein and leg aids. (It may be a few days before the horse is ready for this, so be patient and do not push things.)

Work only in walk for the first two or three days, then, if the horse is completely calm and relaxed, ask for a few steps of trot using your usual vocal aid for trot, together with gentle leg aids. Sit lightly on the horse's back with your weight slightly forward in the saddle so that if the horse does shoot forward you will be in balance and go with the movement. Gradually include trot in your practice of turns, circles and transitions.

For safety, continue to lunge or loose-school your horse for a few minutes in an enclosed area before getting on its back. You must go through all of these preparations for several days before you get on your young horse in the field. You will then be able to 'read' your horse's mood each day and know at once if it is in a tense or nervous state, in which case you should go back a step and stay in the enclosed area.

Be very aware of the horse's mood each day. If it is unusually jumpy, don't do anything new and perhaps only sit on its back in the box for a little while. If your horse is a mare and you think she is in season, be prepared for a change in temperament and avoid upsetting her. Wind and rain can make a horse jumpy even if you are riding in an indoor school, so be aware of possible problems before they arise. Every day is different. Be sensitive to your horse's mood and act accordingly.

MOUNTING WITH THE STIRRUP

Get the horse used to being mounted in the usual way, by putting your foot in the stirrup, but try to get on from a mounting block or step to avoid undue pressure on the off side of the back and withers as you mount. Be very careful to keep the toes of your left foot down as you mount, so that you do not prod the horse's side, and come down very, very gently into the saddle, without touching the hindquarters with your right leg as it goes over.

The mounting block must be introduced with care; you should practise leading the horse up level with the block and make it stand close to it and remain still for a minute or so before being led on. Do not let your horse get into the habit of swinging away from the block as you mount or of walking off the minute you are on. Both of these habits can lead to an accident. The horse should stand still until you have checked your girth and adjusted your stirrups etc. and even then it should only move off when it is asked to do so. If you insist on good manners from the start, you will have a lot less trouble in times of crisis.

Initially, when mounting, ask an assistant to hold the noseband – not the bit rein. Later, try to get the horse used to standing still without being held.

EARLY SCHOOLING

To remain in balance with your horse, your own centre of gravity must be directly above the horse's centre of gravity. On the horse you are the equivalent of a heavy rucksack on a person's back. If the rucksack is in balance with the person, above their centre of gravity, it makes the load easier to carry. If the rucksack is behind the person's centre of gravity, they will find it difficult to go forward and the weight will make them stiffen their back. The rucksack is then behind the movement. In the same way, when a rider's weight is behind the movement it makes carrying them uncomfortable for the horse and extra hard work.

If the rucksack is in front of the person's centre of gravity it will push them forwards and put extra weight onto their toes. The person may now stumble quite easily. In the same way, if the rider is in front of the movement it puts more weight over the horse's forehand, unbalancing it.

You must sit centrally on a horse. If you sit over to one side you will unbalance the horse. Think how many times a walker will hitch a rucksack into the centre of their back because it has unbalanced them by slipping over to one side.

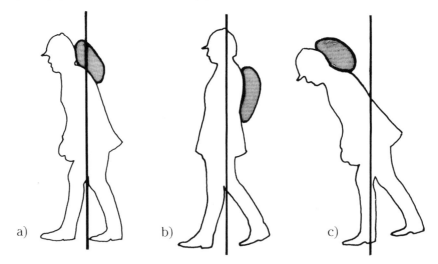

Figure 4.14   *The centre of gravity for a man with a rucksack: a) Weight directly over the centre of gravity is easier to carry. b) Weight behind the centre of gravity causes tension in the back and loss of balance with more weight on the heels. c) Weight in front of the centre of gravity causes loss of balance with more weight on the toes, and a tendency to trip.*

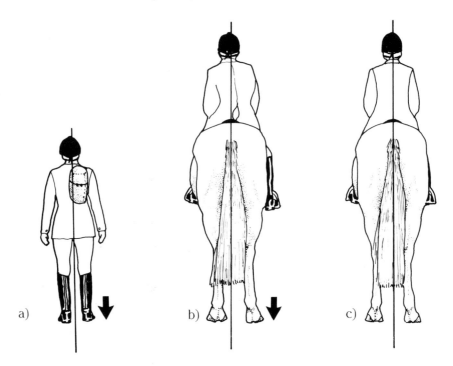

Figure 4.15   *Weight placement: a) The rucksack on one side unbalances the man with the weight pulling down on the right side. b) Similarly, the rider sitting to one side unbalances the horse. c) The rider has the weight correctly centrally balanced.*

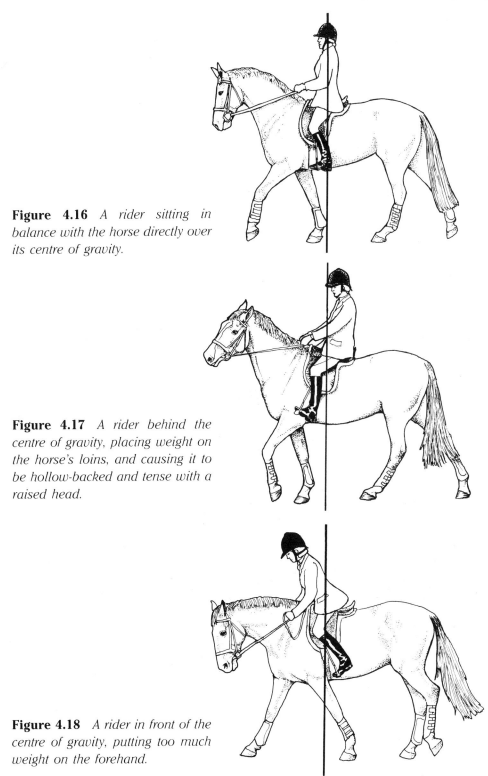

Figure 4.16 *A rider sitting in balance with the horse directly over its centre of gravity.*

Figure 4.17 *A rider behind the centre of gravity, placing weight on the horse's loins, and causing it to be hollow-backed and tense with a raised head.*

Figure 4.18 *A rider in front of the centre of gravity, putting too much weight on the forehand.*

Any alteration of your weight, as you change gait or direction, must be done very smoothly and gradually so that the horse can make adjustments along with you and remain balanced. If you are riding in balance you should be in a position whereby if the horse was magically whipped out from underneath you, you would land in balance on your feet.

A horse that is consistently ridden behind the movement may become stiff, tense and worried as soon as the rider mounts. A different rider, who can sit quietly in balance, on a loose rein, gently stroking the horse's neck in an even rhythm and having no weight on the back of the saddle, will quickly make a truly astounding difference to the horse. The new rider must never, even for a second, go behind the movement, however, or the horse will lose its new-found confidence in this rider as well.

Your Hands

Do not worry about the height of the horse's head carriage at this stage. Make sure that your reins are in a straight line, with a light contact on the horse's mouth. Many people think 'good hands' means allowing both reins to hang in loops. This is not true, because then the horse receives no messages from the reins, does not know where it is supposed to go and wanders about.

If you ride with your reins in loops or have an intermittent contact, you will not be able to teach your horse to go in straight lines or to follow an accurate circle. You must have a good contact on both reins so that

Figure 4.19 *There should be a straight line through the elbow, wrist, hand and rein to the bit, with the correct contact and the palms turned up slightly.*

messages can go from your hands to both sides of the horse's mouth. You will find it easier to maintain an even, sympathetic contact with the mouth if you turn your hands over a little, palms slightly upwards, so that you can just see your fingernails. This action frees your elbow and shoulder joints and thus allows your hands to follow the movement of the horse's head.

If your horse has a naturally high head carriage, your hands should be held higher than if it has a low head carriage. Never think of keeping your hands down; think instead of your horse's natural head carriage and keeping a straight line from the elbow through the wrist and reins to the bit. Do not think of keeping your hands still because this creates stiffness.

Remember to keep your hands one on each side of the horse's neck. If, in turning left, you carry both hands over to the left, the horse will feel a stronger contact on the right side of its mouth, which will confuse it. To help to correct this very common riding fault, think of pushing the outside hand forward a little, while still maintaining a light contact on the horse's mouth. Remember that while you are slightly shortening the inside curve of the horse's neck as you turn or circle, you are also lengthening the outside curve and your outside hand must allow this to happen.

The outside hand controls the amount of bend in the neck and this should not be greater than the bend through the rest of the body as the horse turns.

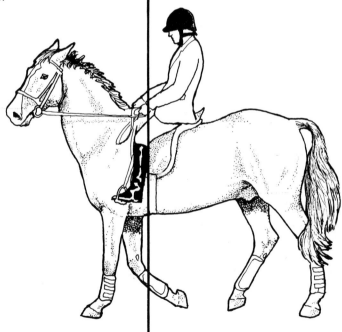

Figure 4.20 *Common positional faults: the hands, elbows, shoulders, knees and ankles are stiff, the feet braced against the stirrups, and the hands are trying to 'ask' the horse's head down.*

The commonest hand faults when riding are:

1. Pushing down with the hands, with stiff elbows and shoulders, in downward transitions (often accompanied by a stiffening of the knees and a bracing of the feet against the stirrups). These faults will cause the horse to raise its head and stiffen and hollow its back.
2. Pulling on the reins in downwards transitions, causing the horse to raise its head and stiffen and hollow its back.
3. Lowering the inside hand on turns and circles, which stiffens the elbows and shoulders and gives you a resisting hand. All of this will shorten the horse's stride and prevent it from stepping underneath the body with its inside hind leg as it should.
4. Thinking you can bring a horse's head down with your hands by lowering and stiffening them. This is sometimes referred to as 'asking your horse's head down' and either the fingers are wriggled about busily or the hands are used alternately — left, right, left, right — producing a constant left, right swing of the horse's head.

Your Legs

Your legs must always be in contact with the horse's sides, holding the horse gently in the track that you want it to follow. You should be able to feel the warmth of the horse's body through your boots at all times. Learn to use each leg independently. It is often necessary to use one leg actively while the other one remains passive against the horse's side. One leg is often used further back than the other, as in turns and circles.

When asking the horse to go forward, squeeze inwards with the inside of your lower leg, gently at first, then, if necessary, give quicker, stronger nudges with the inside of your lower leg, not your heels. If you still get no response, it may be necessary to give the horse a tap with a schooling whip. Never, never kick. Any horse, no matter how common, fat or lazy, can be taught to answer to light aids. If you start off with a kick or a wallop with a whip, you will always have to use strong aids, so begin with the lightest aids and only increase them if you do not get a response.

The commonest leg faults when riding are:

1. Bracing against the stirrups and stiffening the knees in downwards transitions (instead of letting your weight remain on your seat bones and riding the horse forward into your hands).
2. Kicking with the heels (instead of squeezing with the insides of the lower legs).
3. Gripping with the calves and toes turned out (instead of allowing the inside of the lower leg to rest against the horse's sides and keeping the feet parallel with the horse).
4. Pointing the toes downwards and riding with the lower leg, and stirrup leathers, too far back (thus making the rider tip forward; a problem that

is sometimes caused by the stirrup leathers being too long) instead of the heels being a little lower than the toes, and the stirrup leathers hanging perpendicularly.

5. Stiff ankles, making the rider appear to be standing on their toes on the stirrup irons and making the heels come up (instead of supple ankles, allowing them to absorb the movement of the horse, for example when landing after a fence).

USE OF THE WHIP OR SPURS

You want your young horse to be responsive to the lightest aids, so always begin your training by *using* the lightest of aids; a slight change of weight, gentle pressure of your leg inwards on the horse's side, a feel on the reins as a signal to the lips. If necessary, gradually increase the aid until the horse responds.

If you start off with a strong aid, you will always have to use one. If you start off with a light aid, the horse may eventually respond to your very thoughts, which will have produced an unconscious tightening of your muscles.

The Whip

If a horse is lazy and unresponsive to quick, active leg aids, follow them immediately with one very sharp smack with a whip just behind your leg to emphasise and strengthen that aid. By doing this you will give the horse a quick, short, sharp shock to make it more alert. If it goes forward speedily on being hit, allow it to do so. Then once more ask for an increase of pace with gentle aids. You may not need to hit the horse a second time, but do so if necessary until it wakes up and learns to respond to the request made by the first, light aid. I feel that this is a much better method than continually prodding at a young horse with spurs, often completely deadening its sides for ever.

Be very careful how you first use a whip. If you carry a short stick or whip, you must remember to put both reins into one hand and use your whip in the free hand to avoid jerking the horse's mouth. It is easier to use a long schooling whip on a young horse so that you do not need to take a hand off the reins. If you want the horse to go forward, a whip used on the shoulder is not a good idea because it can make the horse back away from it, instead, use the whip behind your leg to emphasise the leg aid.

Get your horse used to you carrying a whip in a small, enclosed area. A horse can quite unexpectedly panic at the sight of a whip being carried. If the horse leaps forward or bucks, or bends its neck towards your whip hand when trying to evade your aids, you can, unintentionally, touch the horse's

Figure 4.21 *Touching the horse unintentionally with the whip may frighten it. The rider may be unaware this is happening, but should try to avoid the circumstances when this may happen. Ensure that the horse is used to seeing the whip being moved over its back from the ground before carrying a whip when riding it.*

side with the whip and frighten it. The act of changing the whip from one side to the other can frighten the horse and make it run off. Should your horse suddenly look back at the whip, tense up and try to shoot forward in fright, drop the whip.

In an earlier training session you waved your arms about while mounted to get the horse used to your movements, now do the same with the whip, moving it slowly, gently and silently at first. Move the whip up and down from both sides and then stroke the horse with it. If the horse is of an even slightly nervous temperament, do all of this from the ground in the stable before you attempt to do it while mounted.

A horse that accepts a short whip happily, may be very upset at the introduction of a long schooling whip, so carefully repeat the preliminary work of getting the horse used to this also.

To change a short whip from one hand to the other, put both reins and the whip in one hand. With your free hand turned over, fingernails upwards and thumb nearest to the knob of the whip, take hold of the whip and draw it up through the other hand. Take the reins back into the normal position again.

It is important to carry a whip with a large knob on the top as this will prevent the whip from sliding through your hand. You can then hold the whip softly so that the horse receives the same feel on its mouth from both of your hands. A whip that does not have a knob on the top can slip through your hand and has to be clutched more firmly, often causing tension in the whip hand and wrist and on down the rein to the horse's mouth.

To change over a long whip, put both reins and the whip into one hand. Turn the free hand – with fingernails away from you, knuckles upwards and towards you, and your elbow towards the horse's ear – and take hold of the whip with your thumb nearest the knob. Swing it slowly upright over the withers and down onto the other side. Take the reins back as normal again.

This action of swinging a long whip up and over the withers may frighten a horse so practise this first on foot in the stable and then mounted and at halt in an enclosed area.

Spurs

Spurs do have their place but not when worn by an inexperienced rider or when riding a young horse. The possible exception is a horse that jibs (see page 128), when the totally unexpected and quite new feeling of spurs, applied at the exact moment when the horse comes to a dead stop, may surprise it into going forward.

Spurs should only be used by experienced riders who can apply them in exactly the right place and at exactly the right moment and will never use them by mistake or through habit. Spurs can be used by expert riders to help to correct a problem of stiffness, encouraging the horse to bend, or to give a refined and delicate aid by just brushing the hair on the side of a horse schooled to an advanced standard.

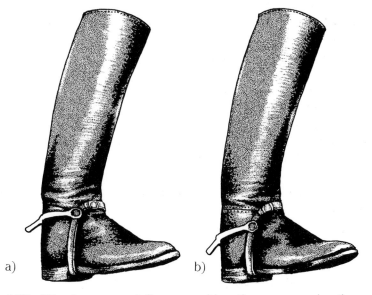

a)   b)

Figure 4.22 *Wearing spurs: a) Correct position, the spur covering the seam of the boot. b) Incorrect position, the spur is lying too low.*

It is a sign of bad training if a horse needs to be ridden or jumped in spurs in order to just make it go.

Spurs should be worn high enough so that the spur covers the ankle seam on your boot.

LENGTH OF STIRRUP LEATHERS ON A YOUNG HORSE

Do not try to ride long and deep on a young horse. Your position will be more stable with the leathers slightly shorter than usual. At even one hole too long you will be totally ineffective; sitting on your fork and inclined to tip forward in the saddle.

YOUR WEIGHT

Your weight is the first early warning signal to your horse that you are about to do something different. It is your most important aid and a horse that is trained from the start to answer to a fractional movement of your weight, looks and feels as if it is responding to your very thoughts. In fact, it often is because when you think of a movement that you want from the horse, you will unconsciously alter your muscles and weight.

A young horse needs more time than an experienced horse to notice, think about and respond to a weight aid. Begin with a tiny transfer of weight and only increase it a little if the horse does not react. In this way the horse will become more attentive to you and will soon answer to a very slight aid. Sometimes a horse, that is normally ridden by an experienced rider who has trained it to respond to tiny weight aids, is very puzzled and uncertain when ridden by someone who does not realise how their varying weight and position can affect the horse.

A rider sitting in balance with a horse, so that their centre of gravity coincides with that of the horse, is far easier to carry.

Riding Uphill

To maintain this balance when going uphill, get your seat out of the saddle, bring your shoulders forward to help the horse and sit still, as you would at take off when jumping. If you tried to walk carrying an unstable pack on your back you would find it unbalancing and tiring for you. If you were walking up a hill, you would hitch your backpack further forward, nearer to your neck and shoulders, because you know that this will make it easier to carry. You are, in fact, moving the pack so that its centre of gravity will coincide with yours. You are the pack on your horse's back, so ride with thought and consideration.

Figure 4.23 *Correct position when riding uphill.*

Riding Downhill

When riding your youngster downhill, sit forward, in balance with your horse, in the position you would be in when landing from a jump. Ride straight down a hill; do not let the horse drift sideways. A horse can cope with a steep gradient as long as its hind legs are directly behind its forelegs. The horse will slip and may fall, if asked, or allowed, to come down a steep slope or even a small bank at an angle. When you are sitting forward going downhill, your legs and hands are free to keep the horse straight.

Figure 4.24 *Correct position when riding downhill.*

When approaching a deep, muddy patch of ground on a descent, move your weight back by bringing your upper body back thus putting your weight further back on your seat bones. Ride your horse forward into a checking hand (think 'Whoa!') and you will move your horse's centre of gravity further back, thus lightening its forehand so that it will not stumble or overreach.

Riding on the Flat

Horses that go crooked (hind legs not following in the track of the forelegs) often do so because the rider is sitting off-centre and has slipped to the outside. It is very easy to be totally unaware of such faults in your riding, so ask someone experienced to check your position in the saddle from time to time while schooling your horse.

A horse naturally follows the movement of your weight, so be very conscious of your weight aids in training. If your weight goes slightly forward, the horse will go forward; if your weight goes back slightly, the horse will slow down or stop. If you put your weight into your left seat bone (think 'Left knee forward' to advance your left seat bone slightly), the horse will turn left. If you put your weight into your right seat bone (think 'Right knee forward' to advance your right seat bone slightly), the horse will turn right. Thinking 'Right knee forward' rather than 'Right seat bone forward' makes the rider softer and less inclined to stiffen the back, pelvis and hips when transferring the weight.

It sounds incredibly simple, and is simple when ridden thoughtfully and carefully. Many young horses will answer to these simple aids at walk within a week of first being ridden.

USING YOUR BACK

Allow your back to follow the movement of the horse. At walk, the small of your back must absorb the movement and should move from upright to forward. Many riders slouch in walk, so that the small of their back moves from a slight backward curve to a greater one. Don't think of sitting up straight, which makes your back stiff and rigid. Think of filling your lungs with air to lift your upper body softly. Breathe in and imagine shouting to someone over the top of a high roof; this will lift your back and head softly.

Sit on a four-legged stool in the riding position and practise tilting the stool on to its two front legs while keeping your shoulders upright. Adjust the position of your seat, feet and shoulders until you can accurately and gently control the forward tilting onto two legs and the soft return to all four legs of the stool.

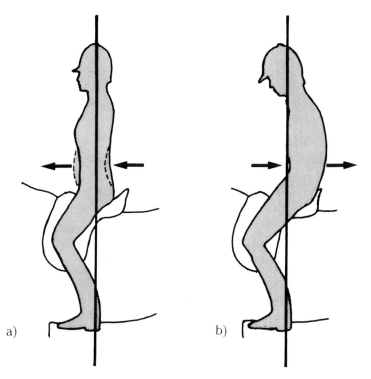

a)   b)

Figure 4.25 *Using the back: a) Correct movement of rider's back in walk and sitting trot (the arrows show the direction of movement). b) Incorrect movement of the rider's back in walk and sitting trot; the back is collapsed (the arrows show the direction of movement).*

When you use your weight aids, you are also using your back, so think about and feel this. You can use your back to 'push' an obstinate horse forward: your pelvis tilts backwards slightly and your seat bones press down into the saddle. Combined with your legs, this is a strong aid and should be used gently on young or sensitive horses. Strong use of the seat bones can make a horse hollow its back and 'leave its hind legs behind', so be conscious of this and notice what effect your riding is having on the horse.

A capable rider, who is able to use the seat and back effectively, will be able to ride a horse more accurately and is more likely to get an awkward or lazy horse to respect their wishes. Watching such a rider, you should feel that their seat and back are pushing the horse forward in the direction in which they wish it to go. When doing this, the rider's shoulders must be above, or slightly behind, the perpendicular.

A rider who is unable to use their seat and back will sit with their shoulders in front of the perpendicular and very little weight on their seat bones. They will look as if they are tipping forwards and an unwilling or argumentative horse will refuse to move or will whip round or go backwards with them as they are totally ineffective in this position.

As stated the seat and back should be used gently on a young horse, but if it is being awkward and obstinate, they may have to be used more strongly to make the horse obey.

TURNS AND CIRCLES

Before starting a turn put a little more weight on your inside seat bone, use your inside leg to ask your horse to move its inside shoulder and ribs outwards a little. Then, with your inside rein, ask the horse to bend its neck and head in the direction in which you wish to go. The outside rein controls the amount of bend in the neck and also the pace at which you want to go. Remember that, as you turn, you are slightly shortening the inside of the horse's neck by bending it but that at the same time you are also lengthening the outside of the neck, so your outside hand must move forwards a little to allow for this while still maintaining contact on the horse's mouth. Only when the horse is bent evenly throughout its neck and body should you begin your turn.

Control the amount of bend in the neck, and the speed, with the outside rein. There must not be more bend in the neck than there is in the rest of the body. Use your inside leg to ask the ribs and shoulder to move over and do not *start* to turn until you have felt this movement and the horse is looking in the direction that you want to go. Your outside leg on the horse's side behind the girth controls its quarters and keeps them following in the same track as the forelegs; your inside leg keeps the horse going forward in

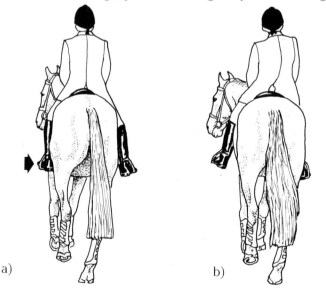

a)   b)

Figure 4.26 *Turning to the left showing a) correct, and b) incorrect, position of the rider's back and placement of weight.*

an even rhythm. Plan changes of direction in good time, remembering that a young horse needs twice as long as an older horse to prepare for and carry out an order smoothly. Think well ahead and co-ordinate your aids, remembering to put your weight onto your inside seat bone as a preparation for turning and when riding a circle.

Prevention is better than cure, so if you never allow your horse to turn until it is looking in the required direction, and has moved its ribs and shoulder, it will not learn to anticipate turns, or fall in and lead with its inside shoulder with its head looking to the outside. Keep the same rhythm. Ask the horse to step under with its hind legs and for a little more self-carriage; lightening its forehand and moving its centre of gravity further back by using half-halts before and after every change of direction. Allow sufficient time to straighten the horse. Change your weight and the horse's bend before turning in the new direction.

SUPPLING

To supple the horse place large oil drums in a line to ride in and out of, or round, or put them in a pattern of four, six or eight about 15 m (16 yd) apart to ride through and round. The height of these drums encourages a horse to move its ribs and shoulders, so it is less likely to cut in and lead with its inside shoulder than with smaller markers.

After a turn in one direction, remember to straighten your horse for a few strides, then ask for movement in the ribs and shoulder and the new bend in the neck and body before changing direction. Move your weight smoothly onto the inside seat bone. Sit upright. Do not lean to the inside or allow your seat to slip to the outside. Keep your weight equally on both seat bones when your horse is straight, then change it smoothly to the new inside seat bone. Your inside leg is active, asking the horse to bend round it and to keep going forward at the same pace. Your outside leg stays quietly in position behind the girth to control the hindquarters. As you ride serpentines and changes of direction, watch your horse's ears; if they stay pricked and the horse changes direction smoothly, you are telling it clearly what you want, but if its ears flick backwards and forwards, or if you feel it lean a little way to the left and then to the right, it is telling you that it is confused and does not know which way you want it to go. This shows that your aids are insufficient and uncoordinated and have not been given soon enough for the horse to respond smoothly.

If you have bought a young horse that falls in on turns and circles, carry a long whip and let this hang down the inside shoulder, near to the horse's elbow. Use your inside leg and, at the same time, tap, tap, tap with your long whip on the elbow or just in front of the girth. You will find out which place works best for your horse when you feel the movement of the

Figure 4.27 *Use of the whip on the horse's stiff side. With a horse that falls in on turns and circles, application of the whip at the elbow or just in front of the girth helps the horse to learn to answer to the inside leg.*

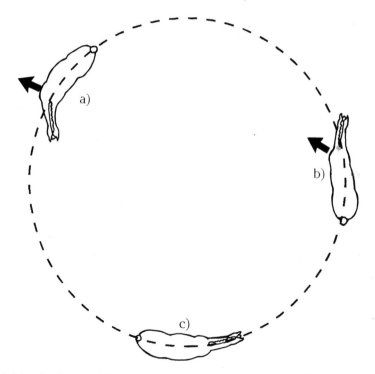

Figure 4.28 *Correct and incorrect bend in a horse on a circle. a) Incorrect, too much bend in the neck. b) Incorrect, the left shoulder is bulging inwards and the horse is looking to the outside. c) Correct, the horse is bent evenly throughout the neck and body.*

shoulder and ribs away from the whip. Again, do not ask for the bend or allow the horse to turn until you have felt this movement and do not attempt trot until the horse will bend equally on both reins at walk without the use of the whip. Be tactful — do not upset the horse.

If you get too much bend in the neck, perhaps on the part of the circle nearest 'home', the outside shoulder will escape and the horse will continue in the direction it wants to go, with its outside shoulder leading and its head bent to the inside. More inside rein (the reaction of most riders) only makes matters worse. Before coming to this part of the circle, ride forward onto much more contact with the outside rein to control the outside shoulder and the amount of bend in the neck. To prevent the horse bulging too much to the outside, use your outside leg and sit well down in the saddle to really ride the horse forward, using your seat and back. If you were riding in rising trot when the horse began to argue, sit now, as you will gain more control by being in closer contact with the horse. (Unless your horse is strong and mature, do not use much sitting trot when schooling at this age. It may be needed at times, as in this case, if the horse is disobedient.)

WORK IN TROT

Trot is a two-time gait, with the legs moving in diagonal pairs.

Rising Trot

In rising trot on a circle, you should ride on the outside diagonal, i.e. on the left rein, your seat should be going down into the saddle when the right diagonal (outside foreleg and inside hind leg) is on the ground, and you should be rising as the left diagonal is on the ground. Sit in balance with the horse so that its action pushes you easily up into the rise. If it is an effort to rise, you are behind the movement with your seat too far back and legs too far forward.

To change diagonal, sit for two beats instead of one, then rise again. Remember to change diagonals in rising trot, both when schooling and out on exercise, to ensure that the horse works evenly.

Sitting Trot

To accustom your young horse gradually to sitting trot, and to help prevent a hollowing or stiffening of its back, use rhythm rising. Providing you always sit for an odd number of beats you will remain on the same diagonal when rising. Try three beats first, i.e. sit, sit, sit, rise once, sit, sit, sit, rise once, etc. Then try sitting for five and seven beats each time with just one rise. It will also improve both your feel and sense of rhythm.

Figure 4.29 *The correct diagonal at the rising trot on the left rein.*

Do not do too much sitting trot on a young horse and remember to sit lightly. If the horse begins to hollow and poke its nose in the air, revert to rising trot because you are sitting too heavily to allow the horse to carry you properly.

In sitting trot you must sit upright and towards the back of your two seat bones. Do not grip with your legs. Allow the small of your back to absorb the movement by going from upright to forward. Do not stiffen and allow yourself to bounce. Take deep, even breaths and feel your stomach going forward, forward, forward with the rhythm of the trot.

UPWARD TRANSITIONS ON A YOUNG HORSE

For upward transitions, half-halt (think 'Halt'), ride forward into a slightly checking hand to rebalance the horse, moving its centre of gravity a little further back, and then ride forward again, squeezing inwards with both legs and allowing a little with your hands.

If the horse tends not to respond immediately, carry a long whip or a long, thin switch from the hedge. Squeeze, and if the horse does not go forward immediately, tap it behind the saddle with the whip. If you carry a short stick, you must remember to put both reins in one hand and use it with the free hand to avoid jerking the horse's mouth. It is easier to use a longer whip on a young horse because then you will not need to take a hand off the reins.

Remember, a whip used on the shoulder is useless for making a young horse go straight forward; the whip should be used behind your leg.

To go from halt to walk, close your lower legs with an inward squeeze just behind the girth, allow a little with your hands and incline your body forward very slightly.

When going from walk to trot, shorten the reins a little because horses have a higher head carriage in trot than in walk. Be careful, however, that your young horse does not learn to think that the action of shortening your reins is the actual aid to trot, so that it begins to anticipate the change of gait. To prevent this, stay in walk for a few strides with the shorter reins, then use a half-halt to rebalance the horse before asking for trot.

The half-halt and rebalancing are necessary with a forward- and free-going young horse, to keep it balanced and to prevent it from going onto its forehand. On a slightly idle horse, however, you will need to concentrate on getting it going forward freely and willingly, so a half-halt would not be needed.

Keep the rhythm of the gait you are in, using half-halts to check a keen horse. A very forward-going horse that is always wanting to go faster is best worked on a large circle where the continual bend of the circle and the need to step underneath itself with its inside hind leg will help to keep the horse balanced and under control. You must avoid the feeling of always having to hold the horse back or it will learn to lean on your hands and will get more and more on its forehand.

DOWNWARD TRANSITIONS ON A YOUNG HORSE

For downward transitions, never pull back. Instead, ride your horse forward into a slightly 'checking' hand. Sit tall and aim to decrease the pace smoothly and change gait without upsetting the horse's balance or head carriage and without the horse stiffening its neck and back or resisting your hands.

Do not stiffen your knees and brace your feet against the stirrups, pushing yourself up out of the saddle. This will only make the horse stiffen and hollow its back and set itself against your hands.

Relax your knees and thighs, allow your weight to remain quietly on your seat bones and, without any extra pressure on your stirrups, ride the horse forward with your legs into a slightly holding hand. Think forward and onward into a downward transition and use half-halts to rebalance the horse as a preparation for the change of gait. The horse's hocks will then be brought further underneath it and it will find it easier to slow itself down as its centre of gravity will be further back.

Riding should be approximately 90 per cent legs and body and only 10 per cent hands. Try to think of this when riding downward transitions. You and the horse will find it much easier if you practise on a circle, turning inward onto a slightly smaller circle as you ask for the decrease in gait, because, when turning in, the horse steps under itself more with its inside hind leg and carries its own centre of gravity further back.

Do not aim to change gait exactly at a marker at this stage or you are likely to use too much hand. Aim, instead, to change gait without any resistance in your horse's mouth and without any stiffening or hollowing of its back.

Listen to the horse's footfalls in downward transitions. If they become louder and heavier, the horse is stiffening and resisting. If the horse is correctly prepared and ridden the footfalls should remain soft and light.

WORK IN CANTER

Cantering in a School

Do not ask for ridden canter in an indoor school or manège until the horse has cantered loose or on the lunge and will answer to your spoken canter aid. The horse must be able to carry itself in a rhythmic, balanced trot before it is asked to canter. The surface must not be deep or heavy or the horse will find canter too difficult.

Work in walk and trot until the horse is quiet, but not tired, then trot a circle and, as the horse comes towards the wall of the school, lean forward and slightly inward (thus freeing the outside hind leg to take the first step of canter), squeeze the horse with your legs and use your spoken canter aid. Repeat the canter aids at every stride to keep the horse in canter and follow the rhythm of the canter with your body, still sitting forward, with your seat just out of the saddle, and a very light contact on the reins.

Figure 4.30 *Sitting in balance at canter with the seat just out of the saddle and a light contact on the reins.*

The canter aids are:

1. The inside rein asks for a slight inward bend.
2. The outside rein steadies the speed of the trot.
3. Your inside leg, used on the girth, encourages the horse forward.
4. Your outside leg, used behind the girth, asks for canter.

At first, the horse may find a 20 m (22 yd) circle in canter too difficult, so be content with a few strides of canter on either rein, asking for canter as you go into a corner. If the horse strikes off on the wrong leg, trot and start again. Make very sure your outside rein is not tight as you ask for canter, thus preventing the outside hind leg from taking the first step of canter.

Canter is a three-time gait. The canter sequence is:

1. Outside hind;
2. Outside fore and inside hind together;
3. Inside fore (leading leg).

Try not to let the horse 'run' into canter, trotting faster and faster before finally falling into canter. Keep the even rhythm of the trot, use two or three half-halts and ask for canter with a little inside rein to get the bend, place your inside leg on the girth to keep the horse going forward and your outside leg behind the girth asking the horse's outside hind leg to take the first step of canter. Put your weight onto the inside seat bone to free the horse's outside hind leg to start canter. Any tightening or lowering of your hands will prevent the horse from cantering, or, if it does canter will make it break into trot again. Let your hands follow the movement of the head and 'allow' the horse to canter.

If a horse will not lead on a certain leg in canter, and is a calm, unworried character, you can try using your whip in your outside hand, behind the saddle, as you ask for canter. Apply it as you go into a corner exactly as the outside foreleg and inside hind leg are about to come to the ground in trot. You are using the whip to encourage the outside hind leg (which is free at exactly that moment) to take the first step of canter.

With an older horse that is difficult to get onto the correct leg on one rein, or with a young horse that has begun to learn to jump and always takes one lead in preference to the other, you can use a sloping jump pole to get the correct lead. Put the pole across the outside track going into a corner, with the outer end on the ground up against a jump stand or cone. Raise the inside end to approximately 76 cm (2½ ft). Come into the pole in trot and apply the correct canter aids at the take-off point, with more weight on your inside stirrup iron. You should land in canter; if you are on the correct lead, keep the canter.

A horse that always leads on its favourite leg and will not use the other one will wish to *start* canter with its *inside* hind leg when you work it on its less-favoured rein – thus putting it on the wrong lead. By raising the pole on the inside, you make the horse aware that it is likely to bang its *inside*

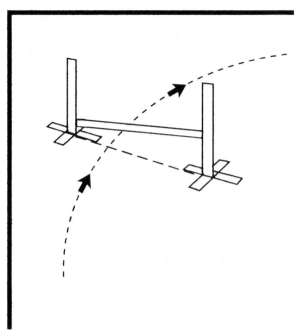

Figure 4.31 *Pole and jump stands positioned to aid the correct strike-off in canter; the pole is positioned for an off fore lead.*

hind leg if it uses this first. Because the lowest part of the pole is on the outside this encourages the horse to start canter correctly, with its outside hind leg. This method does not usually worry or upset a horse, but you must be able to ride accurately enough to ensure that the horse takes off from trot, lands in canter and keeps cantering. Progress to starting canter with the pole lying flat on the ground, then into canter at the same place but without a pole there.

TEACHING THE HORSE TO MOVE AWAY FROM YOUR LEG

Moving sideways comes naturally to the horse. When shying at a frightening object it moves sideways away from it while still looking towards it. (It is looking away from the direction of the movement.)

You need to teach your horse to move away from your leg to avoid rabbit holes, wire, another horse about to kick, to get onto the grass verge, to avoid approaching traffic and to open and shut gates.

When your horse is responding to your aids calmly and rhythmically and is fairly supple on turns and circles you can begin to ask it to move away from your leg. Remember that in any lateral work you are not stopping the forward movement, you are just changing it to forward and sideways. The rhythm of the gait should stay the same.

Start by riding on an inside track and asking the horse to move forward and sideways onto the outside track. (Horses seem to find it easier to work towards the wall than away from it to start with.) If you are on the right rein ask for a slight bend in the horse's neck with your right hand and leg and ride forward into a slightly checking left (outside) hand for a half-halt. Keep your hands up. Do not drop them or you will stop the horse. As the horse begins to pick up its off hind use your right leg to ask the horse to move sideways. (You cannot influence a horse sideways with your right leg when all its weight is firmly planted on its off hind so you must be aware of when each leg is moving.)

Your left leg controls the hindquarters and the amount of sideways movement, and also helps to keep the horse going forward. A little more weight should be in your left seat bone (the one the horse is moving towards). Think, 'Forward, half-halt and sideways' in a very gentle, soft rhythm. Be tactful and be pleased with a very little response. If you feel you are beginning to use strength to get a result things are going wrong. Your horse may not be ready for this yet or you may need an experienced person to watch and help you at first.

Start at a walk and try on both reins. Most horses respond better on one rein than on the other so concentrate on the good rein at first, because the horse will learn more easily. When it understands and responds, praise it with your voice and a stroke on the neck. Then try the more difficult rein. Again, be pleased with even a little response. Do not be tempted to think, 'I will go on until we get it right'. A few minutes and finishing on a good note are all you can ask of any horse if it is to enjoy its work.

To see someone hanging on to their horse's head to stop it going forward and kicking like mad with one leg to try to get it to go sideways, rocking their bodies from side to side in their efforts, is a horrible sight!

RIDING OUT IN COMPANY

A young horse soon gets bored with just schooling, so start to ride out for a short time accompanied by a sensible horse as a schoolmaster. Do not ride out with a horse that shies or is bad in traffic because young horses, like children, are great copycats.

If the horse seems a little skittish, lunge it for a few minutes before you ride in order to help it to settle.

If you have to ride out without the company of another horse right from the beginning, lead or long-rein the horse along the chosen route first so that it will be familiar with it. Choose somewhere as safe and unalarming as possible, and ask someone to go with you on foot to help you if necessary. *Never* ride out entirely alone on a young horse at this stage of training.

If your horse is frightened of passing something, your helper can walk on in front to give the horse confidence. As a last resort, they can lead it past the spooky object.

Carry a longish twig out of the hedge, which you can use if need be to keep the horse going, but which you can drop if the horse is afraid of it.

Do not ride a young horse out on the roads until you have introduced it to traffic in hand and you are sure it is used to the idea of cars whizzing past. Lead your youngster out to stand near a road, taking a couple of traffic-proof horses along for company. Once your youngster seems happy about the sight and sound of traffic, lead it along wide verges, keeping your own body between it and the traffic. Again, have a quiet horse with you for company and to give yours a lead if necessary.

When leading or riding a young horse out on the road, it is a good idea to wear a tabard that says 'Young Horse' or something similar. Very large L-signs will do just as well and can often give drivers a far better idea of what you are trying to tell them. Most drivers have no idea what behaviour to expect from a young horse, but do know all about learner drivers! Do not forget to introduce your horse to the tabard or L-plates and do not make them out of anything crackly.

When riding across fields, along bridle paths or through gaps, be aware of your horse's probable reactions to things. Many young horses are afraid of the noise made by their legs going through leaves or straw stubble. They may shoot forward and then, as the noise becomes louder, may panic. Turn the horse in a tight circle and, if necessary, dismount and lead the horse away from the scary situation.

Be careful if riding in fields where there is hay in big round bales or straw in long rows waiting to be baled. Some young horses imagine that there are dragons hiding in these and will leap up in the air or try to whip round and go home.

Old tree trunks and logs lying on the ground can be very alarming. Creeping cautiously up level with them and then rushing past is normal behaviour at first. Sit upright and ride forward with your seat and legs as you approach and, as you draw level, incline your body forward to go with the horse should it shoot forward. Failing to do this will result in your being left behind and the horse will receive a jolt on its back and a jerk in its mouth, both of which are very disconcerting and add to the horse's anxiety.

A young horse is also likely to be frightened of branches brushing against its side or against your leg or coat as you ride through woods or bushes, especially if the branches are prickly, like gorse. Again, sit in balance with the horse, ready to go with it if it shoots forward or sideways or leaps upward and forward. A sudden jolting on the horse's back can make it more frightened and cause it to buck. If this happens often, the horse may begin to buck in anticipation of the rider being left behind.

When approaching a narrow gap in a hedge, try to work out what your horse is thinking. Is it looking at and through the gap into the area beyond, i.e. thinking forwards? If it is, you can sit forward during the approach, ready to go with it if it rushes through or jumps the long grass or thistles that may be growing in the gap.

If, in the approach, the horse is looking to left or right for an alternative route or is even trying to run backwards or out to the side, you must sit upright and use your seat and legs to push it forward, your reins to keep its head pointing towards the gap and your voice to encourage it forward with the words and tone it has already learnt to obey on the lunge. Only incline your body forward when the horse begins to look and think through and beyond the gap and you feel it intends to go through.

Just as the open countryside has many scary things to frighten a horse, so also do towns, villages and farmyards. People cutting hedges or lawns, slamming their garage doors or standing on ladders can all make a young horse jump. Look ahead and watch out for possible problems, especially when you are on a new route or on one where unpredictable things happen. Ride forward and do not communicate tension or apprehension to your horse by gripping with your legs or overtightening the rein.

Your reins should be at a length at which you have control in all situations. Do not slop along with loose reins that can be whipped out of your grip, but also ensure that they are not so tight that you invite the horse to rear if it does stop or nap. If it begins to lift its front feet off the ground and you think it is likely to rear, give with your hands and drive the horse forward with your legs, using the switch, if necessary, behind your leg. If the horse does rear, go forward with it and throw your arms around its neck. Do not pull on the reins because this could make the horse fall over backwards.

Sitting in balance with your young horse is desperately important to its calmness and peace of mind and to give it confidence in the rider. Some young horses tend to trip, stumble and fall about on every bit of uneven ground. This can be very depressing for the rider, but most horses will grow out of it. Like young children, some young horses are better balanced, more athletic, better co-ordinated and more alert than others.

After riding out in company for the first couple of times, try to get your young horse to go in front unless you come to something really frightening. It can then be given a lead by an older horse. If it is always given a lead it will not learn to think for itself or gain enough confidence to be ridden out alone.

First, get your horse used to being ridden level with its companion, and then go in front. Make your youngster follow one route to the right of a clump of trees, while the other horse goes left. Do not ask too much at first. Trot on in front, while the other horse walks. Ask your horse to halt until the other horse catches up. However, do not expect it to walk or halt while the other horse trots on away from it. That is asking too much at this stage because your youngster may think it is being left behind for good and panic. Similarly, ask your horse to go on alone towards home while the other horse turns and goes away from home, but not vice versa.

Young horses are easily bored working in the same schooling area, so use any suitable places out on exercise to practise serpentines and circles. Practise moving your horse sideways away from your leg in rhythm with its stride. When moving to the right use your left leg as the near hind leg begins to come off the ground so that you are asking the horse to step under and over to the right. Keep the impulsion; do not stop the forward movement, just change it to forward *and* sideways using half-halts to balance the horse. A young horse will find this movement easier if its head is bent slightly away from the direction of movement (in this case towards the left). This comes naturally to the horse; it is the position adopted when shying.

Gradually work up to half an hour's ride twice a day and, as soon as possible, omit the short lungeing or long-reining session before your second ride of the day.

Always put a numnah on under the saddle to soften the unaccustomed pressure and allow it time to warm up before you mount or tighten up the girth. In very cold weather it is a good idea to warm the bit in your hands before putting it in the horse's mouth.

Continue to turn your horse in both directions before you mount. Remember to check your girth before mounting and again after you have ridden for 10 minutes or so. Do not overtighten the girth, but ensure that it is not loose enough for the saddle to slip if the horse suddenly moves sideways.

If you are unable to ride your horse for some days, go back several stages when you next ride it. Lunge the horse before you ride it and watch its eyes and ears, they are good indications of the horse's mood. If it is calm and relaxed, its head will be low with the ears and eyes moving quietly. The horse's mood may vary from day to day and close observation will help you to decide what work to do that day.

MARTINGALES

If your young horse is apt to throw its head up when scared or napping, a running martingale can help to keep the head in a more controllable position and also gives you a neckstrap to hold on to if needed. When fitted correctly, the martingale should be long enough for the rings to reach up into the horse's throat when the other end is attached to the girth. It should not come into action unless the horse puts its head up beyond the normal level.

Sometimes it is suggested that a running martingale can be correctly fitted by taking the rings back to the withers when the martingale is attached to

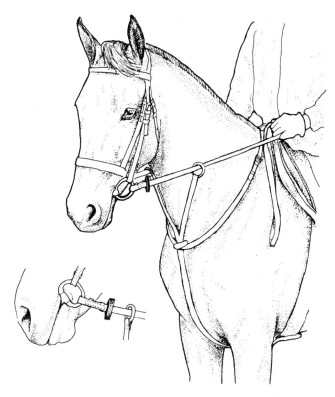

Figure 4.32 *Correctly fitted running martingale. Inset: martingale stop.*

Figure 4.33 *Incorrectly fitted running martingale; the straps are too tight and are pulling the reins down.*

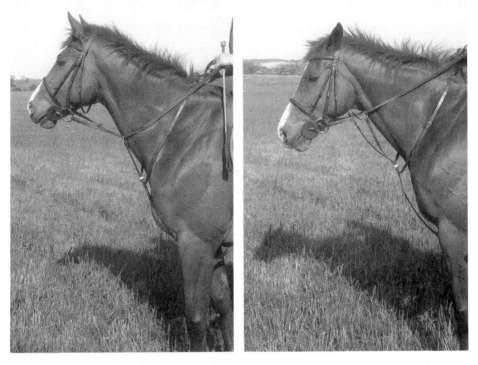

Figure 4.34   *The running martingale: (left) The martingale is too tight, pulling the rein down, and giving the rider indirect contact on the horse's mouth. A tight martingale can also shorten the horse's stride. (right) These martingale straps are the correct length; the martingale rings will reach up to the throat. Note: the throatlash is too loose and the bit too wide for the horse's mouth.*

the girth. This method does not work because you are measuring only the shoulder, not the length of the neck.

Martingale stops must be put on the reins between the rings and the bit to prevent the rings catching on the buckles or stud billets.

If the horse learns to lean against the martingale it will develop a bulge of muscle on the underside of its neck with a consequent hollowing of the top line of its neck and an angling of its head back towards you. If this does happen, a Market Harborough may help to lengthen the top line of the neck. This must be fitted by an experienced person and used at first only under their supervision. The rein should come into action just before the Market Harborough.

A standing martingale is attached to the girth and a cavesson noseband. It should not be attached to a drop noseband. This martingale is not a good idea on a young horse because most horses learn to lean against it and then, as with the running martingale, they develop a large bulge of muscle under their necks which prevents the development of a good head carriage.

Figure 4.35 *The Market Harborough.*

Figure 4.36 *(left) A Market Harborough adjusted too tight; the Market Harborough rein is coming into action before the guiding rein which can be seen hanging slackly. (right) This Market Harborough is correctly adjusted; the guiding rein comes into action first. The Market Harborough rein is slack where it is attached near the chest.*

Figure 4.37 *Standing martingale correctly fitted to a cavesson noseband. It should not be attached to a drop noseband.*

No horse, especially a young one, likes to feel that its head is restricted. If it feels trapped in this way, the horse may become restive and fussy in its head, constantly tossing it and trying to free it. Try to allow the horse some freedom by using a giving hand.

If you have to rely on excessive use of artificial aids for control, perhaps you are not yet experienced enough to work with youngsters.

If you are not using a martingale, put a neckstrap on the horse in case you need something to hold on to if the horse plays up.

IMPROVING RHYTHM AND BALANCE

To improve your horse's rhythm and balance as it learns to change its centre of gravity, work in walk and trot up and down slopes and over undulating ground. You must learn to change your position in the saddle smoothly so that your centre of gravity always coincides with that of the horse.

Walk through water and over small ditches and logs. Concentrate on keeping the horse going forward happily and confidently. Do not ask too much. Remember to sit forward when walking through water as the horse may take an enormous leap over it. Also sit forward at a ditch, where the horse may drop its head to look and sniff, bend its knees and think about jumping, then suddenly jump very high and wide over it. If you sit forward you are safe whether the horse walks or jumps. Small ditches can be approached in walk and jumped from a standstill. Do not allow the horse to turn away. Keep it facing the ditch and quietly encourage it to look, think and go.

CANTERING OUT ON A RIDE

Cantering for the first time out on a ride is easiest and most safely done when going uphill. Get your schoolmaster to trot up a slight hill in front of you and establish a steady rhythm in rising trot. Let the schoolmaster break into canter first. Bring your weight a little forward out of the saddle and squeeze the horse into canter, using your vocal aid for canter as you do so. Sit quietly in balance, with your seat just out of the saddle and, should it be necessary, try to steady the horse to maintain an even canter rhythm.

When cantering uphill the horse is less likely to increase pace, cannot get onto its forehand and will most probably come back to trot again voluntarily, having become tired and puffed after a few yards. When cantering on the flat, a young horse can get onto its forehand very easily. Once unbalanced, it can find it difficult to stop itself. For this reason, never trot or canter a youngster down even the slightest slope. Even when on an older horse you should avoid trotting or cantering down sloping ground as this puts extra stress on the joints. (Obviously, these things happen occasionally, when out hunting or at cross-country competitions for example.)

Only canter for short distances at first and use the uphill direction to accustom the horse to cantering slowly. Never get into the habit of always cantering in the same place or the horse will begin to anticipate the canter gait and may become excited and try to take off. Never ask for canter until the horse is going calmly and in an even rhythm in trot.

As you progress, remember always to establish a good steady rhythm in trot, with the horse perfectly calm, before asking for canter. Only canter for a short distance and keep an even rhythm. Gently check, check, check with your hands in the rhythm of each stride to ensure that every stride is the same length as the stride before it. If you allow the strides to get longer and longer, the horse will soon be out of control. The action of pull and let go, pull and let go, so often seen, is an impossible way to steady a horse.

A Dangerous Place to Canter

It is extremely dangerous to canter any horse, no matter how quiet, along a roadside verge. If there is any traffic on the road and the horse shies out into the road it could get hit or cause a vehicle to brake suddenly and/or swerve. This is extremely frightening for the rider, the horse and the motorist and is one of the things that give horses a bad name among drivers, insurance companies and the police. Accidents can happen all too easily on our busy roads without irresponsible riders increasing the risks. Even if the road is empty, a horse shying out onto tarmac could slip and come down.

Many serious or fatal accidents have been caused by cantering on a roadside verge with small drainage ditches set at intervals in the verge. A horse can stumble at the first and fall into the second, giving the rider a horrible fall. I know several people who have been killed or paralysed in this way.

MEETING OTHER HORSES

When you first meet other horses when riding out alone, your youngster may either totally ignore them or with a wildly beating heart give massive bucks out of excitement. There is no way to predict this before it happens. If the other horses are walking along quietly, however, your horse is more likely to remain calm. No well-mannered rider would ever trot or canter past another horse going in the opposite direction along a road, lane or track.

If you are riding in the open country, however, and you suddenly see two or three horses cantering wildly across a field, perhaps accompanied by several dogs, that is another story! If you are riding with a group of horses, put your horse in the middle of the group and all the riders should then turn their horses heads away from the source of excitement. Keep walking and try not to tense up or hang on to the reins too tightly. Talk to your horse and you may be lucky enough to feel its heartbeat return to normal as it relaxes.

Bridging Your Reins

If your horse does begin to leap and buck in this situation, you may feel more secure if you put your reins in a 'bridge'. This means that your left rein goes across through both your hands, entering your right hand near your index finger and leaving it near your little finger, while your right rein also

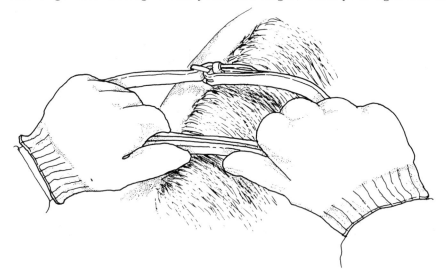

Figure 4.38 *Bridged reins.*

goes across through both hands, entering your left hand near your index finger and leaving it near your little finger. There should be a gap of 5–10 cm (2–4 in) between your hands. This keeps your hands together. Now, if the horse bucks, the bridge of rein between your hands will come onto the horse's neck and prevent your hands from being pulled down on each side of the neck. This will help you stay on board in a crisis. The bridge can also prevent the horse from plunging its head down and pulling you forward out of the saddle.

A neckstrap or a good handful of mane will also help you to stay on. It is far better to hold on to something and stay on the horse than to let it know it can get you off. Unfortunately, having successfully dislodged you once, many young horses will try again, so be prepared to do almost anything to avoid being put down by a young horse.

SAFETY FIRST

If you are riding a young horse in the country, never go out alone until you know how your horse will behave when it meets others galloping about.

If you see another rider approaching you, always walk in case either of you has a problem. If you wish to overtake another rider, ask the rider if their horse will mind if you go on and leave it behind you. Even if their horse will not mind at all, it is polite to warn the other rider what you are about to do. You must rely on other riders to treat you with the same consideration. If you feel someone is about to trot or canter past you, a polite 'Young horse, walk please' may do the trick.

Remember that a frightened or loose horse will usually go to another horse for security, which is a good reason for always riding out with a companion.

Riding in the country has hazards of its own such as rabbit holes, loose barbed wire, pigeon-scarer guns, loose hedge clippings and streams to cross, so think, look and listen all the time and be aware of what is going on around you. Plan ahead how you will cope with potential problems. Your horse needs to have learnt to move away from your leg obediently in order to avoid holes or wire.

Remember that a horse will leap sideways and upwards away from a suddenly moving object such as a pheasant flying up or a flapping paper bag, but it will stop dead and perhaps try to whip round when confronted with a stationary object that it finds frightening.

Loose hedge clippings or long trails of undergrowth can get caught in a horse's tail and cause total panic. The 'horror' seems to be chasing the horse so it tries to run away because this is its natural reaction to danger. If your horse is terrified by something caught in its tail, turn it to the left in a small circle, take your feet out of the stirrups and get off quickly. (It is easier to get off on the near side.) If you have a companion, ask them to dismount too and hold the horse for you. They must keep the horse turned to the left and put one cupped hand behind its left eye like a blinker so that it cannot see what is stuck in its tail. You must attempt to remove the object while standing on the near side (not behind the horse where you could get kicked). Untangle the object carefully − do not just catch hold of it and tug!

If you are alone, you must attempt to remove the branch from the tail while holding the horse yourself. This can be a bit tricky but is made easier if the horse is beside a fence or hedge. Talk calmly to it and try to reassure it before attempting to remove the obstruction.

Do not remount immediately after any form of mishap in which the horse has received a bad fright. Lead the horse until it is calm and relaxed. Even if you no longer usually ask someone to hold it when you mount, do so on these occasions in case it is still a bit panicky.

OPENING AND SHUTTING GATES

Introduce your horse to this exercise by leading it. Teach it to stand close, and parallel, to a gate, with its tail towards the hinges. Open the gate wide and lead the horse through, being very careful not to let any part of the gate touch the horse and not to let go of the gate if the horse shoots forward because the gate may then bang against its heels. Close the gate, bringing the horse round to stand parallel to the gate, again with its tail towards the hinges. Repeat this exercise every day until the horse knows exactly what you want and is quite calm about it.

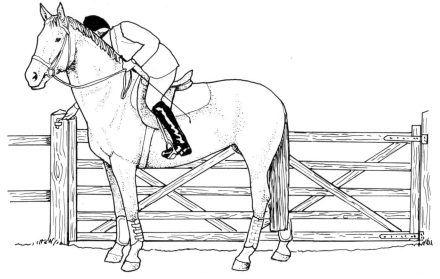

Figure 4.39 *The correct positioning of the horse when opening or closing a gate: the horse stands parallel to the gate with its tail towards the hinges.*

Figure 4.40 *Opening a gate: the pony is standing calmly in the correct position, the rider's reins and whip are in her right hand, the hand furthest from the gate, while her left hand opens the gate.*

Figure 4.41 *Closing a gate: The rider shuts the gate with her right hand having changed her reins and whip over to her left hand, and the pony is in the correct position parallel to the gate with its tail towards the hinges.*

Only attempt to open a gate when mounted if your horse is calm and sensible and will stand quite still. Choose a gate that will open easily and does not require lifting. The gate must open away from you. Gates that open towards you should only be opened from an experienced horse because they can trap you and the horse. If the horse tries to push through the gate, it will close on the horse and may make it panic. The more the horse pushes, the tighter the gate will press against it and against your leg. If your leg gets caught on the gate and the horse goes on pushing, you could be pulled off the horse. Many accidents have occurred in this way.

Be quiet and patient when you try to open a gate. Again, stand the horse parallel to the gate with its tail towards the hinges. Put both reins and your whip into the hand further from the gate. The reins must be kept short enough to give you control and the rein further from the gate must be fractionally shorter than the other rein in order to keep the horse's hind-quarters parallel to the gate. Open the catch with the hand nearer to the gate and push the gate open wide enough for the horse to pass through easily. Keep a contact on the reins to prevent the horse from rushing through. Once through, turn the horse so that its tail is again towards the hinges, change your whip and reins into the hand that is now further from the gate and shut the gate. Make the horse stand still for a few seconds more so that it will not develop the habit of moving off the moment it hears the latch click shut.

Remember that as you bend down to open or shut a gate it is very easy to let your rein hand slide unconsciously down the horse's neck on the side nearer the gate. This will cause a pull on the side of the horse's mouth that is further away from the gate and will make the horse turn away from the gate. Before you get cross with your horse for moving away, make sure this is not happening without you realising it.

Use your legs to ask the horse to move sideways towards or away from the gate, for example using your right leg to ask the horse to move to the left, while keeping your left leg absolutely still against the horse's side, ready to stop the sideways movement.

When going through a gate that opens towards you, never try to pull the gate shut behind you as you go through because it is then liable to catch on your horse's heels and this will make the horse rush through the next time to avoid being hit.

Make sure you open the gate wide enough and watch out for hooks or knobs that stick out and could catch in your stirrup or strike your horse's side. If your horse wears a martingale, make sure that neither this nor the reins can catch on any part of the gate as you bend down to reach the hook or bolt.

If someone holds open a gate for you to pass through, always put both reins and your whip into the hand that is further from the gate so that you are ready to catch the gate if it is accidently let go and swings towards you.

Be very careful that a young horse receives no frights connected with gates. Your horse will never forget having a gate dropped on it or having its heels rapped by a gate as it goes through. This will cause it to panic next time you open a gate and it will then either try to rush through or swing away as you bend down to lift or drop the catch.

Be calm, patient and gentle when training a young horse to open and shut gates. Only do easy gates at first. Once the horse behaves perfectly at these you can progress to the more awkward ones. It does take time to teach a horse to stand quietly when you sometimes need both hands to open or shut a gate. An intelligent horse soon understands what you are doing and will sometimes even try to help!

If you have to ride through a gate that opens towards you, make sure that it is open really wide so that there is plenty of room for your horse and your legs to pass through easily.

If you are mounted on an excitable horse, never attempt to open a gate that opens towards you because the horse may try to dive through before the gate is properly open. In this case either dismount or, preferably, get someone else to open the gate. Even on a calm, sensible horse, have your reins short enough to give you very accurate control, because gates that open towards you are potentially dangerous to any horse.

Some gates are better opened on foot. These include the heavy type that will not stay open and begin to swing shut as you go through. For safety's sake, dismount and run up your stirrups or cross them over the saddle. Open the gate and walk the horse through, keeping your body between the horse and the gate. Close the gate and insist that the horse stands quietly while you mount again. Be aware that if the ground is wet or muddy, the soles of your boots may now be slippery against the stirrup irons.

RIDING ON THE VERGE

You will often wish to ride at walk on the grass verge to save the horse's shoes or to avoid slippery or icy tarmac. (As mentioned in a previous section, trotting or cantering on verges can be very dangerous.)

Many people find it difficult to keep their horse on the verge because, when they wish to ride on the left-hand verge, for example, they use only the left rein and right leg. The horse then bends its head to the left but bulges its right shoulder out to the right and moves away from the grass.

To ask your horse to move left onto the verge, ride a half-halt to steady the horse, use your right rein to keep the right side of the horse's neck straight and to prevent its right shoulder going out, use your right leg to push the horse sideways to the left and your left rein just a little to lead the horse onto the verge. As in lateral work, you must change the forward movement to forwards and sideways.

When the horse is on the verge, continue to use your right rein to prevent its neck from bending left and its right shoulder from bulging out to the right and continue to keep your right leg on its side to keep it on the verge. Think of leg yielding (see page 201).

CONTROL

If you think the horse will refuse to go over or through something, do not ask, it is too soon. You must try to avoid any argument or battle that you cannot win. Also, by hitting the horse and trying to force it to do something it is truly frightened of, you may teach it to rear, nap, whip round, kick and buck or try to get you off. Once learnt, these evasions will be made use of, so avoid this situation. If you do have an argument, be calm and firm, and if trying to pass something frightening accept a wide loop round it, rather than fighting to achieve a direct route past it. Quietly, but firmly, apply the aids and talk to the horse to give it confidence. If the horse is prepared to stand facing the direction you want, sit still and give it time to assess the situation; perhaps it is not as frightening as the horse first thought − it may then walk on. If you make no progress, try using your whip once or twice. If still unsuccessful, dismount and lead the horse past, but do not do this often or it can become a habit. If the horse refuses to pass an object or go beyond a certain point on a ride, get an assistant with a long whip to hide nearby. Then, as soon as the horse *begins* to slow down they can drive it forward.

Train your horse to turn, circle, change gait and direction calmly, smoothly and with a good rhythm. Put it into the gait and rhythm you want, and teach it to maintain this, even when heading towards home on a hack. If the horse quickens pace or leans on you, check it gently and when it lightens and returns to the rhythm you want, soften your hand. Be very quick to feel when the rhythm first starts to change and immediately correct the horse. If you teach it to work in a slow but active trot it will learn to carry itself. Many people trot a young horse too fast so that it learns to run and go on its forehand.

Frightening Situations

A young horse may be frightened by:
- Flapping clothing worn by the rider. (Never, ever take off or put on a coat or jacket when mounted.)
- Something rattling in the rider's pockets.
- Something rubbing or tapping on the saddle.
- A violent sneeze or cough from the rider.
- A waving handkerchief or loud blowing of the nose.

- The rider flapping a piece of paper, such as a map or newspaper.
- A sudden movement of the whip.
- A sudden change of balance in the rider (never, ever carry anything — knapsack, haynet, macintosh, etc. — when riding a young horse).

Other potentially frightening things include cows, sheep, goats, donkeys, dogs and particularly pigs; many horses are terrified of the smell of pigs and often refuse to go past a pig farm even when the pigs are out of sight.

A pony pulling a cart can also cause panic, as can bicycles and prams.

When riding through a field of cows or bullocks for the first time, always go in the company of an experienced horse and keep very close to the fence or hedge so that the cattle cannot surround you. Have the young horse against the hedge, with the experienced horse between the youngster and the cattle. Be aware that young cattle will often tear towards you all together, bucking and kicking. They are only being inquisitive and playful but a young horse may think they are going to attack and decide to run away from them.

If a dog chases you, try to stand still. The dog will often cease to attack if the horse's legs stop moving. Speak sharply to the dog (it's quite an advantage if you know the dog's name) but do not yell as this may upset your horse.

Small animals and birds can be frightening. Hares may get up almost under the horse's feet, as will pheasants. Pigeons will fly noisily out of the hedge; ducks may get up from a pond or ditch with much quacking and flapping. Some horses find even small deer very frightening and dislike their smell.

Flapping plastic sheeting, piles of plastic bags, dustbins, straw bales, bonfires, any kind of smoke, small pieces of paper or branches blowing about can all cause a problem. Add to these strange noises like bells, sirens, the cry of hounds, dogs barking, guns, music, people shouting or a farmer calling his sheep or cattle and you have more than enough to scare a young horse.

If you need to check your girth while out, remember to do so slowly and gradually. If you want to blow your nose, do not bring your handkerchief out, shake it about and give a trumpeting blow or you may part company. Coughing and sneezing can also make a horse jump or shoot forward until it gets used to such things.

Do not go out wearing a kagoule or plastic mac that will flap in the wind. This noise can really panic a horse. Make sure your horse is quite used to seeing you in a riding mac before you try to mount in one. Never try to take off a jacket or jumper while seated on a young horse. If the horse spooks at the sight of you flapping and struggling out of the sleeves, you could have a bad fall.

When riding along bridle paths and quiet tracks, practise swinging your legs and arms slowly, banging the saddle and making a variety of noises and movements until the horse is quite unbothered by them.

Traffic

Do not attempt to ride your young horse in traffic until you have held it (in a bridle for safety) nearer and nearer to a road to accustom it gradually to the sights and sounds of vehicles. It may be possible to turn it out in a field beside a busy road to get it used to the constant flow of traffic.

Only when it is calm and unworried by traffic and obedient to your aids should you attempt to ride on the road and even then you must take another calm, sensible horse with you.

Most horses will accept small cars passing them but some are frightened of a stationary car. Tall vehicles can be a danger, particularly in a narrow lane, where the horse feels trapped between the vehicle and the hedge or fence, and may try to whip round. If the horse does whip round it may get hit by the fence or the vehicle and be terrified for ever more.

Try to get large vehicles, or vehicles pulling trailers, to stop if you meet them in a narrow lane. Get your horse into a gateway if you can, where it will have more room. Position its hindquarters towards the gate and let it see what is coming. Remember that if there are several big vehicles coming, your horse may get more and more frightened as each one approaches. Airbrakes can terrify a horse, so make sure you ask lorry or tanker drivers to stop or slow down in good time, not as they draw level with you.

If there is something spooky on your side of the road, stop and wait to pass it when there is no traffic coming in either direction. Otherwise, your horse may be hit by a vehicle if it shies out into the road.

Remember to ride on the left of the road (unless in a country where the traffic drives on the right) and keep well in to your own side of the road on blind corners. If you feel your horse is going to shy at something (raised head, pricked ears, tension, a change of rhythm in the stride), ride forward and use your right leg and right rein more strongly than your left rein and leg to keep the horse going forward and prevent it from shying out into the road where it may get hit by an approaching vehicle.

Remember to give clear hand signals without waving your whip about (practise these in a field so that they will not alarm the horse). Above all, you must thank drivers. Even if they have not slowed down, thank them and smile. If you cannot take a hand off the reins, bow your head, smile and say 'Thank you'. They might remember and slow down next time. When drivers *have* taken the trouble to slow down, they find it very annoying to be totally ignored.

When riding in company on any road, everyone must stay on the same side of the road. Even if the verges are very wide, do not separate. A young horse will often try to join another horse by going out into the road and trying to cross it. It is also very difficult for a car driver to look at both sides of the road at once and try to anticipate what each rider is going to do. (Drivers always assume that riders are in complete control of their horses!)

When crossing a road in company, always cross together. If left alone at a road crossing, even an older horse may try to take the rider across the road when there is traffic coming.

On a wet day the swish of car wheels through puddles and the splash of water onto the horse's legs as a car passes can be very frightening. If a horse has been badly splashed by a passing car, it may think that every car is going to 'throw water at it'.

Remember that any fright is a real setback with a young horse and that the horse may take months to forget about it. An extreme fright, such as seeing a motorbike skid and crash near the horse, is likely to be remembered all its life. As soon as it hears a motorbike engine, the horse will tense up, and may panic as the bike comes closer.

If a big lorry comes up behind you, make sure, by using your right rein and right leg, that your horse sees the lorry out of its right eye, then if it is frightened it will keep its right eye on the lorry and its quarters will not swing out into the road. This applies when riding all horses in traffic and could prevent many accidents; nearly all horses are hit in the hindquarters which swing out into the road because the rider has used the left rein.

Do not shorten your reins and 'prepare' for the horse to be frightened in traffic. If you do, the horse will receive the message via the reins that you are tense and worried and you may actually make the horse afraid when it was not before.

Most horses become quite used to cars, motorbikes and bicycles, provided they pass slowly and at a distance.

Get your horse used to the traffic on quiet roads before riding out on busy roads and, even then, only ever ride on the busier roads if it is really essential. If your horse is at all nervous in traffic, avoid these busy roads. Never ride out on a youngster in fog or if it is growing dark. In poor light things are seen indistinctly and become more alarming because of this. The horse may be frightened by vehicles' headlights and drivers will not see you clearly nor in good time.

Shying

If your young horse shies at something, do not force it to go up to the object and do not hit the horse. Remember that in the wild a horse will circle something it is frightened of, moving in ever-decreasing circles until it finally stretches its neck out and sniffs the object. If a horse shies at something to the left of the road and you use your left rein, the horse will think you want it to go up to the object. It will then shy even more and its

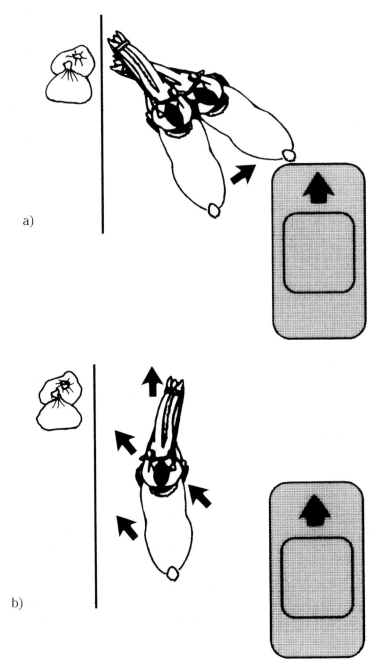

Figure 4.42 *Positioning the horse when in traffic, or when it shies at an object on the nearside of the road. a) Incorrect; the hindquarters are being allowed to swing out into the road because of the incorrect use of the left rein. b) Correct; the head is being bent towards the road by the right rein, and the right leg holds the horse's hindquarters straight.*

quarters will swing out into the road. If you use your right rein to control the right shoulder and right leg to control the quarters, the horse will immediately become less frightened because it is being asked to look and bend away from the object.

If the horse shies away from something on the left and there is a deep ditch or something similar on the right, do not pull its head round to the left. If you do, the horse will continue to charge over to the right with both eyes fixed on the frightening object on the left. It will not see the deep ditch and may well fall into it.

Try, instead, to get its head round to the right so that its sense of self-preservation will prevent it from going into the ditch. In some horses this sense is naturally well developed and it is a great relief when you find that your young horse will look after itself and you.

If your youngster shies frequently, try to find out why, if it is genuine fright the horse will look at the object with raised head and eyes popping; you may feel its heart thumping if you are riding it or see the quickened rhythm in its flanks if you are leading it.

The horse may look at the object then look forward to the path beyond the object, trying to decide whether it dare proceed past it. It may shy out away from the object, but you might feel that it is at least plucking up the courage to go past. You will usually know what a nervous horse is shying at, but a typically brave horse may, quite unpredictably, shy at something you cannot even see or at something it has never experienced before; a horse pulling a cart for example.

Try to keep the horse thinking forward. Give it time to assess the situation, then ride it firmly forward with your legs. Lift your hands and maintain just enough contact with the reins to guide the horse. Never, never let the horse feel that the reins are tight and that you are holding it back, or it will learn to whip round.

Do not expect the horse to pass close to the frightening object. Your aim must be to keep going forward, so accept a large curve round the object. If possible, repass the object several times going in both directions and allow the horse to go up and inspect it with eye and nose. If the horse was genuinely frightened and is given the chance to investigate the object thoroughly, it should then have the confidence to pass it next time.

Is the horse shying from sheer naughtiness? Do you feel that any excuse to whip round will do? Is a large leaf moving or a tuft of grass of a different colour sufficient reason? This sort of horse will whip round in a flash and give you absolutely no warning. It may also shoot off at a gallop, possibly dropping its shoulder as it does so and then giving a little buck to help you off! This is not pleasant but a great many horses do it and it is probably the commonest trick learnt by young horses. To cope with a horse like this you must be an experienced rider with a very firm seat and absolutely no fear of the horse. If your horse has put you off two or three times in this way and you both know that the horse can do it again whenever it likes, the situation can only get worse. Admit now that this horse is not for you before long-lasting mental damage is done to the horse.

A strong, capable rider who is unafraid of the animal could probably sort this out before the habit became too firmly ingrained in the horse's mind.

When a horse of this type comes to a frightening object, it will not even look at or think about the path beyond the object. All its thoughts will be back behind it and its one aim will be to whip round. It will either do this immediately and extremely quickly or, if it is a more ponderous type of animal, it will either stand rooted to the spot and turn its head to look back or it will run backwards away from the object in the direction from which it has come. It will at no time think or look in the direction in which you wish it to go.

If you set about the horse with a stick at this point you will only have a fight on your hands because until it is at least beginning to think and look forward, you cannot make it go forward. There is no point in starting a battle with a horse unless you think you can win.

An extremely strong, experienced, capable, determined rider might be able to get the horse past the object, using a lot of whip, but are you sure you fall into this category?

Your best bet is to work on getting the horse to stand still facing in the direction you wish to go and out a little to one side of the frightening object so that the horse can see that there is a clear passage for it to pass along. Each time the horse tries to turn or go backwards, quietly but firmly reposition it and wait for that magic moment when it begins to think and look forward. Given the chance, this moment will nearly always come, even if only because the horse has become bored with the situation. When you can feel that there is at least some forward thought, ride firmly on in your chosen direction, using your whip, hard, once or twice if the horse attempts to stop again.

Some horses will shoot sideways at a strange sound, for instance an unseen bird rustling in the hedge, but will pass without problem a 'spooky' object that they can see. Others ignore strange noises and are only frightened by what they can see. Some are afraid of moving objects but not stationary ones, others shy at parked cars. Notice what your horse reacts to because you will then be more aware of its probable behaviour. Be ready for a 'spook' but do not tense up or overshorten your reins quickly in anticipation of the horse shying because, as mentioned, you may in fact make it shy by communicating your fear to it via the tension on the reins.

On a cold, wet or windy day, most horses will shy to some degree but a really naughty horse can be an absolute devil in these weather conditions. Be aware of this and plan your work with a young horse accordingly rather than meet trouble head on. Bad habits learnt on a day like this are not forgotten, so it may be better to give the horse a day off.

If your horse shies and whips round often, try not to ride out alone. At first let the horse follow another past the 'spook', then ride side by side with your horse furthest away from the object. Finally ask your horse to go in front.

Rearing

A horse will sometimes rear when forced to do something of which it is frightened or which it obstinately does not wish to do. Ask yourself why the horse is rearing.

If it is through fear, can you make it easier for the horse to obey you by taking a route slightly further away from whatever it is afraid of? If necessary, lead the horse up to the object for a better look.

If the horse is just being obstinate, it could rear on being asked to leave the stable yard or turn away from home, if you meet another horse heading towards home when you are going away and your horse wishes to follow it back, or if you pass other horses in a field and your horse does not wish to leave them.

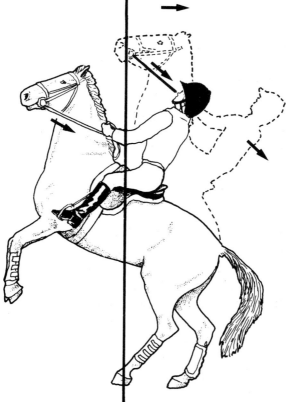

Figure 4.43 *The incorrect way to sit a rear; the rider overbalances the horse by hanging on to the reins, and pulls it over backwards.*

Figure 4.44 *The correct way to sit a rear; the rider leans forward, and, by wrapping her arms round the horse's neck, slackens the reins, thus avoiding pulling the horse over.*

If you are alone, it is often very difficult to succeed. Get off and lead the horse forward only as a last resort, but even this is better than giving up and allowing the horse to turn round. Having had its own way once, the horse will undoubtedly try this again in the same place, and unless you ride out in company, you will never succeed with this horse.

Someone on foot with a lunge whip is better than nothing but they must be very experienced with young horses to know how, when and where to use the whip to encourage the horse forward. In this situation an inexperienced person will do more harm than good.

How do you stay on when a horse rears? The first thing to remember is that a horse will hardly ever rear and come over backwards without a rider on it. When a ridden horse rears and falls over backwards it is usually because the rider has pulled it over by hanging on by the reins and overbalancing the horse. As soon as you feel the horse go up, you must lean forward quickly and put your arms round its neck, leaving the reins loose. Turn your head to one side so that your nose will not get banged and when the horse comes down onto its forelegs, try to keep it facing in the direction you wish to go.

If you are quick enough to feel the rear just before it happens, while both front feet are still on the ground, or if you think the horse is going to rear again, pull its head right round towards your knee and force the horse to go forward — it cannot rear while moving forward as it needs to get both hind legs right underneath it first.

Rearing to Avoid Pain

Rearing can sometimes be caused by the rider hanging on to the reins tightly and at the same time urging the horse forward. The reins are saying 'Stop'; the rider's legs are saying 'Go'. The worried horse does not know which way to go so it goes up and thus learns a new habit.

Slowing a young horse down very suddenly and with very heavy hands can make it rear to get away from the pain in its mouth. Very sore gums or sharp teeth can make a horse rear out of pain when ridden by someone with rough, jerky hands or who hangs on to the reins tightly. Inward pressure on each side of the withers, caused by a badly fitting saddle, can also make a horse rear, as can a severe bit.

Napping and Jibbing

Napping and jibbing are both results of the horse objecting to the rider's chosen route. The better-bred young horse is more likely to show its feelings by the more active resistance of napping, i.e. whipping round to face the direction in which it wishes to go. The commoner sort of horse is more likely to resort to the more passive resistance of jibbing, i.e. it may just stand there and refuse to move.

In both cases the reasons, similarly to rearing, are a dislike of leaving the stable yard, an objection to turning away from home, passing another horse going towards home when your horse is being asked to go away from home, going out with other horses and then being asked to continue on alone, not wanting to leave other horses in a field along the route, or not wanting to pass something frightening. The last reason can be caused by genuine fear and is acceptable at first in a youngster.

In every case, keep the horse facing in the direction you wish it to go. If it whips round, turn it to face the required direction and try not to let it whip round a second time. Use your legs and voice to encourage it forward and, most essential, lift your hands so that there is no backwards or downwards feel on the reins. The horse must feel that your hands are keeping it straight but are still allowing it to go forward freely.

If this does not succeed, hit the horse behind the saddle, very hard, once only. Be prepared for the nappy horse to whip round like lightning, perhaps bucking as it does so, and maybe shooting off in the direction in which it wants to go. Stop it, turn it round and use your voice and legs once more to encourage it forwards, plus, if necessary, one more hard smack with your whip.

It is often almost impossible to get a horse like this to go forward without mounted or dismounted help. The more often the napping occurs and is successful, the more it will stick in the horse's mind, so if you cannot make the horse obey you, even on only one occasion, do not go out alone again until you have sought knowledgeable help, either mounted or on foot.

Jibbing is passive resistance. The horse just stands rooted to the spot, wooden and immovable, totally ignoring you. When you hit it you may get a hump of the hindquarters and a swish of the tail in return or the horse may start to go backwards. Not very much happens. Sometimes, if you sit absolutely still and do nothing for five minutes, then very, very suddenly hit, kick and shout all at the same time, you can shock the horse into going forward. Sometimes, if you turn the horse round, you can get it to go backwards in the direction in which you wish to go. Every few yards, turn it round and ask it to go forwards again. If it refuses, go in reverse once more.

If it will not even go backwards, you can sometimes succeed by turning it round and round in tight circles several times before once more giving it the chance to go forward.

Some horses only jib more if they are hit and must be cajoled and persuaded to do as you ask. Others, which are hit when they are going forward slightly reluctantly in trot or canter, will stop dead and may even buck as well.

Jibbers often react better to spurs than to a whip, so *blunt* spurs, used only when the horse jibs, may be the answer. However, other horses buck every time the spurs touch their sides.

Bucking

Many horses will buck as you go into canter, especially out of doors. If this is the case with your young horse, try to maintain an even rhythm in trot and then ask for canter while still in rising trot with your weight forwards out of the saddle. Canter for just a few strides and then go forward to trot again and repeat the exercise. A horse lifts its back just behind the saddle as it prepares to strike off into canter and your youngster may resent your weight there at first.

A cheerful buck after a few strides of canter is acceptable but should not be encouraged.

In the early stages of training, broncho-type bucks — all four feet off the ground, back arched and head down — are usually caused by the feel of the tight girth. These bucks can happen suddenly when a horse shies, when it first strikes off into canter and when it first goes downhill. You will feel the horse take a quick intake of breath and stiffen under you. Try to get its head up and to keep it going forward. It should grow out of this habit quite soon.

Figure 4.45 *A cheerful buck.*

Figure 4.46 *A broncho-type buck is usually caused by the feel of the tight girth.*

When a horse bucks, your main object must be to keep it going forward, prevent it from getting its head down and regain the rhythm of its stride. If you feel a buck coming, ride forward into a holding, lifting hand.

Many young horses will hump their backs when going downhill for the first time. In this situation the horse is very conscious that your weight is altering its balance and may find this difficult to cope with, so that it will often try to go sideways. Horses must remain straight when going downhill to avoid the risk of a fall, so it is a good idea, at first, to dismount and lead your youngster down steep hills. Trying to carry your weight down is not only uncomfortable for the horse, it is also a strain on its legs and back.

Bucking and Discomfort from Saddlery

Why is the horse bucking? Does it buck as soon as you get on? This can be caused by an ill-fitting saddle, so get someone experienced to check the fit. If the horse begins to object as soon as you put your foot in the stirrup, the discomfort is more likely to be in the front of the saddle where you are causing pressure at that moment. (Make sure that your left toe does not stick into the horse's side as you mount.)

If the bucking is of the slowing down, humping of the back kind, it may be caused by the unaccustomed pressure of the saddle with your weight in it. The horse's back feels hot and itchy and it may attempt to roll. Be prepared to get off, loosen the girth and lead a young horse for a few minutes to rest its back.

Perhaps the movement of the saddle as the horse walks has slightly 'scalded' its back. The movement of the saddle creates heat through friction and the skin can become moist and sore. If, when you take the saddle off, you find wet, sticky patches on the horse's back, this is what has happened. Do not put the saddle on for a few days and bathe the back twice a day in salt water (one tablespoon of salt in 500 ml [1 pt] of water) to harden it off. Surgical spirit can also be used in the same way to harden the skin. Again, check the fit of the saddle and use a good numnah.

The soft skin behind the elbows can be rubbed by the girth, causing girth galls which will hurt and may also cause the horse to buck. Each day, when you remove the saddle, check the back and girth area for the slightest sign of soreness. If you see any, harden off the skin and, if necessary, put a sheepskin sleeve over the girth.

Obviously, it is essential that all tack is kept scrupulously clean and supple. Also remove all sweat from the horse, by sponging if the weather is warm enough or by leaving it to dry and brushing it off if the weather is cold.

If a horse that has previously stood still begins to fidget when you pick up the reins in preparation for mounting, suspect that there might be discomfort under the saddle and that the horse is anticipating the pain it will feel as you get on.

Likewise, if, as you lean forward to dismount, the horse throws its head up, perhaps laying its ears back, suspect that the saddle is giving it an inward pinch on each side of the withers. Leaning forward to dismount will accentuate this pressure.

Remove the saddle and look to see if the stuffing is hard or uneven. See if the horse shows discomfort when you press the area on each side of the withers, where the saddle sits, with your hands. If so, rest the horse's back for a few days and then use a different saddle after checking the fit carefully. If in doubt, get advice from someone more experienced, and possibly have the saddle restuffed.

Running Away

The start of this problem is nearly always a bad fright, usually caused by the rider or by something that the horse sees or hears. The horse may leap forward and then, if the rider gets left behind and bangs down on the rear of the saddle, at the same time jerking the horse in the mouth, it may take off in a panic. A loose anorak flapping in the wind, something jangling in your pocket, a scarf or your handkerchief waving about, a cough or sneeze can all be the cause of panic in a nervous young horse.

A bird flying out of the hedge, dogs suddenly appearing, prams, bicycles, low-flying aircraft, branches from a hedge touching its side or thistles touching its legs or belly, the noise the straw makes while riding over a stubble field, all these things can cause a young horse to run away.

At this stage the horse is trying to get away from something it is frightened of and will nearly always stop when the frightening thing is no longer happening.

If any parts of you or your clothing are causing the problem, make quick adjustments to stop the noise or flapping, then try to stop the horse in a normal way, also using a calming voice. If this fails, and if there is room to do so, turn the horse onto a large circle and then onto ever-decreasing circles.

If something about you, the rider, has frightened it, the horse may be very tense and shaking with fright when it eventually stops. It will be looking back at you in anticipation of more terrifying flaps and noises to come. In this situation, you must dismount the very second the horse stops as it is likely to take off again if there is the slightest recurrence of the sight or sound that scared it. Do make sure you have a firm hold on the rein, however, in case the horse now tries to pull away from you.

Calm the horse down, run the stirrups up and lead it for several minutes. Remove or readjust whatever was causing its fright before remounting. If, as you put your foot in the stirrup, the horse becomes tense and still appears terrified, *do not* get on again.

In this sort of blind panic, when running away from something on its back, a horse is almost impossible to control, so think carefully, especially on a windy day, and try to avoid the situation occurring in the first place.

A horse that has been frightened in this way may need a few days' reschooling, with flapping or noisy objects held over its back from the ground, before you mount, and gently repeat these movements while on its back in an enclosed area. Do not ride out again until the horse has calmed down and is no longer tensing up and looking back at you when you ride it.

Unfortunately, once a horse has run away over some distance, it may learn that it can take charge. It may then run away towards home just because it wants to get there quicker or after it has napped or had a fright. If you are in a straight, narrow lane this is very difficult to cope with because you cannot turn the horse onto a circle. The common practice of pull and let go, pull and let go, so often seen, will never stop a horse that is running away. The horse is probably already going very fast and so has the advantage. The reins may have slipped through the rider's hands as the horse whipped round and the rider has possibly been thrown out of balance.

Quickly take up the reins and make them very short. Taking a strong contact on the reins, put one hand on the horse's neck just in front of the withers and in such a position that it cannot be pulled forward by the horse. Stiffen that hand and arm against the horse's neck. Keep a strong contact on the rein in your other hand and, working with the rhythm of the horse's stride (this is most important), feel, feel (or even pull, pull) more and more strongly on this rein, only giving the slightest amount between pulls. A dead pull will not work — there must be some movement of the bit in the horse's mouth.

This can work and is probably the best thing to do in this situation. It is also the best method of keeping a strong, keen horse under control when cantering, where your aim is to keep each stride as short as the previous one. Your rein hand thus checks the horse, saying 'Steady, Steady, Steady'.

This type of horse does not get out of control immediately. It gradually gets into a longer and longer stride until it becomes unbalanced and cannot stop itself. This is particularly the case when going downhill, so bear this in mind when you are still in control and steady and rebalance the horse before even a slight downward slope and go more slowly. If in doubt, go in walk. it is not a good idea to trot a young horse down slopes as it may be having difficulty with balance anyway.

Falling Off

Obviously it is better for you and the young horse if you do not fall off, but it can happen. A sudden movement, the youngster bucking in protest at the girth, shying; all can dislodge a rider.

Figure 4.47 *The application of rein and arm to control a keen horse. One hand takes a strong contact on the rein and is placed on the horse's neck just in front of the withers; the other hand also takes a strong contact, and, in rhythm with the horse's stride, applies an even pull, pull, giving only the slightest amount between pulls.*

Initially the horse is probably not deliberately trying to get you off, but if it learns that it can do so, dropping the rider could become a habit and may develop into a problem that will require sorting out by an experienced rider.

When you fall do not hold on to the reins; a young horse may kick in fright or tread on you. Only remount a young horse if it is totally unconcerned by your fall; do not remount a horse that is obviously terrified. Lead it home and be prepared to go back several stages in the horse's education, repeating the preliminary backing lessons and the early riding lessons. If you do remount a frightened horse it may panic and shoot forward or sideways, and, if you come off again, you compound the problem.

Observe the youngster's reaction to this situation, think, progress slowly and carefully, and remember to go back several stages if you have to.

The Jogging Habit

This habit normally starts through nervous tension. The horse is not mentally relaxed and so will not walk. It keeps breaking into trot which then becomes an endless jog. Sometimes it starts with the excitement of turning in the direction of home when out on exercise alone. Sometimes it is caused by the frustration of being held back when in the middle, or at the back, of a group of other horses.

When riding in a group, let your tense, jogging horse take the lead. There is then no other horse in front of it which it feels it must pass and it may begin to 'think back' to the horses coming along behind and relax and slow down. If you are behind another horse and attempt to steady your jogging horse to a walk, it will get slightly left behind and become even more worried by the gap between it and the horse in front. Your only hope is to let your horse take the lead, then ask it to walk with gentle, tactful aids, using your walk command repeatedly in a calm, quiet voice.

Do not get annoyed or become strong with your aids or the horse will become even more tense and upset. The second it walks, give it a loose rein and keep your weight slightly forward to encourage it to relax its back and lower its head and neck to swing along in walk. A jogging horse has a high, tense head carriage and is tense through its back. It will not walk until it has relaxed its back and changed its head carriage so you must relieve the mental problem first. Only when you have solved that will the physical problem be overcome.

If this tense jogging goes on for more than five minutes, or if the horse begins to get even more worked up, dismount and lead it. Most horses will then relax almost immediately.

Many tense joggers will only do it on the way home and seem to know exactly when you have reached the halfway mark on a circular route, as that is where they will start to jog. When riding any young horse, avoid going out and back along the same route, so that you have to turn round (possibly at the same place each time) because the horse could become excited and could learn to nap if unexpectedly asked to continue away from home at this point.

Avoid trotting towards home on a tense horse and do not canter *any* young horse towards home as, even in a calm horse, this could cause excitement in the future.

If you are out alone on a jogging horse and cannot get it to walk, see if it will halt. The second it does so, relax the reins, keep your weight a little forward and hope that it will walk, even if only for a few steps. Repeat this if necessary but not if the horse becomes even more worked up. It is much better to get off and lead the horse rather than allowing it to get more and more worked up until it is perhaps dancing sideways or even fly bucking (taking big leaps into the air to carry it in the direction in which it wishes to go). Getting off and leading it is not a case of giving in to the horse. More harm will be done mentally and physically by staying on the back of an obstreperous horse than by leading the calmed horse home, even if you have to lead it home every day for several days.

Jogging can also be caused by taking your horse out with others that walk faster than it does. It will jog to catch up every time it gets left behind and then discover that if it goes on jogging it will not get left behind in the first place. It is better to ride out with horses whose paces are roughly the same as those of your horse (and also with riders who understand the importance of a young horse going in a steady rhythm in trot).

You can teach your horse to lengthen its stride and swing along in walk, really using its shoulders, by using your leg aids alternately. As the horse begins to pick up its near foreleg, you use your left leg and as the horse begins to pick up its off foreleg, you use your right leg. With an allowing hand, let the horse stretch its neck and use its shoulders freely to swing along in walk, while you pick up the rhythm of its stride with the left-right use of your legs.

Overshortening of the reins, causing shortening of the stride, will often make a horse jog. A nervous rider holding the reins too tightly will convey this nervousness to the horse and make it jog.

CONFUSION

Most horses will try to please. If the horse does not obey your aids, ask yourself why. Are you using too many aids too strongly? This is a very common fault. At first, use simple, basic aids, in the sequence of voice, weight, leg and rein, clearly and distinctly. Do not expect an instant response. The horse has to think about and understand your aids before it responds and some young horses take much longer than others to interpret your wishes.

If the horse does not respond, try again and at the same place in the schooling area. Do not get cross; a worried, tense horse will never relax enough to learn to feel your aids and think about what you are asking.

If you are absolutely certain that the horse does understand and simply does not want to obey — for instance, trying to stop every time you come to the door of the school — use your whip behind the saddle, hard, once. If the horse passes the door willingly next time round, finish the movement, reward the horse with a word of praise and a stroke or rub on its neck, and stop work on this good note.

Wanting to stop at the door could also be caused by boredom so do not go on and on to get something right (or go on and on polishing something that the horse is already getting right and that is taxing it mentally and physically). If something is not going right and the horse is becoming tired or bored, ask for something easier and when that is done quickly and correctly, stop. Always finish on a good note even if this means stopping a little sooner than you had planned.

PUNISHMENT

Punishment is of use only if the horse knows exactly why it is being punished. The punishment must follow the misdeed instantly and must take the form of a short, sharp shock. It must never be used to relieve your own feelings of frustration, fury or fear. If you give a horse a beating it will very rarely understand the reason why. Such action may be an outlet for your own tension but it will in no way help to educate your horse.

To punish from the ground, one hard hit with a whip (the stingy, pliable type, not a heavy stick), instantly applied on the area where the misdeed originated (in the case of kicking or biting) should be understood by the horse. Accompany this smack by a 'growly' vocal reprimand and this may be sufficient to prevent the misdeed from recurring.

If the horse will not stand still, punishment must still come from the front, so give a hard, downwards jerk on the head collar. This will give the horse a bump on its nose which should bring it up short. Immediately the horse stands still, slacken the lead rope. If the horse moves again, repeat the jerk on the lead rope.

If this is not working, give the horse a hard thump with your fist on the front of the point of the shoulder and at the same time feel on the front of the headcollar rope, always including your normal single word of command − 'Stand' or 'Whoa'.

If the horse will still not obey, try one sharp tap on the nose with a small stick and use your vocal command. Praise the horse and loosen the lead rope when it does stand.

Expect only a few seconds' obedience at first, then gradually lengthen the time for standing still. Do not shout at the horse, call it names, wave your arms about or slap it on the neck or belly as you will see other people do. It is precisely because these people behave in this way that their horses do not stand still for them.

Do not hit a horse that fidgets when you are grooming ticklish places, as this will only make it bad tempered. Remember that if you hit a horse in front of the girth area when it is tied up, it may run back, panic and perhaps break loose.

If your horse kicks or bites at another horse when you are leading it, reprimand it with your voice and a tap on the nose for biting. You are unlikely to be quick enough to hit it on the hindquarters for kicking, and trying to do so may cause the horse to dart sideways, forcing you to let go. A jerk on the head collar and a vocal reprimand will have to do.

If the horse is wearing a bridle, do not jerk the bit in punishment or you may bruise the bars of the mouth. Jerk the noseband instead.

If your horse refuses to be led forward − perhaps not wanting to leave the field or go into a stable − you must apply punishment from behind. If you carry a long, thin stick in your left hand and step back a little towards the horse's flank, you can reach back behind you and flick the horse just above the hocks. This often works the first time but then the horse realises what you are about to do when you step back and begins to run back quickly to avoid being hit. It may even begin to rear or whip round in order to get away from you.

For this reason it is better to have someone following behind to encourage the horse forward. Unfortunately, we are often alone when dealing with horses and they quickly learn that when there is no one coming up behind them it is worth trying it on!

Sometimes, if the area in which you are leading is smooth-surfaced and wide enough, you can push the horse backwards through the gateway or stable door. You will then have succeeded without a battle and without the horse realising what is happening. The horse is an intelligent animal, however, and so this method does not always continue to work.

Use methodical discipline and then only if you are sure that the horse will understand the reason for it. Realise that when you are tired or in a bad mood you are likely to be more impatient and short-tempered than usual and that perhaps you may punish the horse too harshly or even unnecessarily. Put yourself in the horse's shoes. Would you understand what is happening in the same circumstances? Would you understand what you were being punished for? If the answer is no, then punishing the horse at that moment is pointless and may make it lose confidence or become bad tempered.

Punishment when Mounted — Use of the Whip

Always carry a whip even when you think you will not need it; one day you will and it will be too late if you then have to go and pick a stick from the hedge.

Remember that a young horse may be frightened of a very long whip and that this can also be unwieldy if you are having a rough ride, when it may touch the horse by mistake. A whip just long enough for you to reach the horse behind the saddle, without taking your hand off the rein, is ideal. It must have a knob on the top so that it will not slip through your hand — a rubber martingale stop or elastic band wound round many times will do as a substitute.

If the horse will not go forward from your leg, a sharp tap from the whip will encourage it. Do not always carry your whip in the same hand. The horse must be accustomed to a tap from either side.

If the horse is reluctant to go in front when out in a group and does not respond to your leg aids, give it one sharp tap behind the saddle, enough to surprise it but not enough to hurt it. If it still does not respond, give it one more hit behind the saddle, this time hard enough to hurt, then use your legs. Remember that when you hit a horse hard it may leap forward, so sit with your centre of gravity a little further forward so that you will go with the horse and your hands will allow it to go forward. If you are not prepared when the horse shoots forward on being hit, you will be left behind the movement, your hands will go up and you will jab the horse in the mouth. The result will be total confusion for the horse: 'I was hit because I wouldn't go forward, so I shot forward fast as I was asked to do and at once got a jab in the mouth that hurt and seemed to say "Stop". I don't know what they want me to do now.'

If you hit a horse to ask it to go forward, you must allow it to do so even if it responds very quickly and goes too fast. Allow the forward movement, then steady the horse by riding it forward into a gently holding hand. Do not pull back when you have just asked the horse to go forward.

A horse may kick out in fright (self-protection) when another horse suddenly gallops past it. I do not think it is fair to hit a horse for being frightened. Try to get it used to other horses coming up behind it and passing it. If the horse is cross about other horses being close to it, lays its ears back and deliberately takes aim at another horse, it should be hit hard, maybe two or three smacks in quick succession, if possible as soon as it starts to kick and certainly immediately afterwards so that it knows why it was hit.

Remember that if your horse kicks out at another horse when you are all standing together in a bunch (as in a gateway when out hunting), you cannot hit the horse at this time because many horses really lash out as a response to being hit. The result could be another horse or rider being badly hurt by the second kick. In such a situation you can only use your voice and legs, and your hands a little.

If a horse constantly lays its ears back at another horse and dives at it trying to bite it, it must be given a sharp tap on the nose as it begins to move its head to bite. Punishment must be given quickly and be over quickly if the horse is to understand.

If a horse deliberately tries to get you off (and you are sure that there is no painful reason for its behaviour) it must be hit hard as it starts to try to dislodge you. This is easier said than done because the rider is usually so occupied in trying to stay on the horse that there is no free hand with which to hit it! Punishment at such a moment requires a very experienced rider.

If you wish your horse to go forward, do not hit it in front of the saddle. The tap, tap on the shoulder that you will often see when a horse is approaching a fence is mostly done to boost the rider's confidence! Do not hit a young horse for running out at a fence. It will have no idea why you are hitting it and may well rush at the fence in a panic next time (see page 170).

It is very easy to unintentionally touch a horse behind the saddle with the whip if it makes an unexpected move. The sudden touch of the whip is likely to make a young horse shoot forward or sideways causing the whip to touch it again. You may be completely unaware of the problem, and the horse may become difficult to control.

To try to prevent this, use a short whip and make certain you do not allow the end of it to accidentally touch the horse even when it bends its head and neck towards your whip hand (see Fig. 4.21).

TRIMMING AND APPEARANCE

Pulling the Mane

When your three-year-old will stand quietly to be groomed, you may wish to start trimming the horse to tidy it up. To pull (shorten and thin) the mane, tie the horse up or ask someone to hold it. Brush the mane out gently to get rid of tangles and then comb it. Notice the horse's reactions. Does it throw its head up? Does it shake its head about or try to run back? If the horse has been in any way awkward to groom and you have only just got over the problem, do not proceed with mane pulling unless the horse is standing quietly, quite unconcerned by your actions.

If all is well when you have combed the mane out, take six or eight of the longest hairs in the middle of the mane in one hand, run your comb right up to the roots of these hairs and wrap the long, free ends of them once round the comb, keeping hold of them in your free hand. With your other hand holding the comb, jerk quickly downwards to pull the hairs out.

Normally, one would begin at the withers and work towards the ears, but the middle of the neck is more easily accepted at first. If the horse really objects and becomes upset, stop. There is no point in having a battle or a loss of confidence in you over such a small item. All horses vary enormously in their reaction to mane and tail pulling. You simply do not know how a horse will behave until you try it. Some seem positively to enjoy it; others go absolutely frantic. Some are quite happy about their manes and hate having their tails done; others are just the opposite. Pulling certainly seems to hurt less if done after exercise when the horse is warm and the pores of the skin are open.

When you have finished (which may take several days, done a little at a time and considering the horse's comfort and patience), the mane should be the same length all along the neck, 10−15 cm (4−6 in), and of the same thickness throughout. The better bred the horse, the thinner the mane will be and the narrower will be the growing area. Many native breeds have very thick manes growing from a very wide area. If they become at all upset, these animals are better left unpulled − if they are to be shown in Mountain and Moorland classes, any form of hair trimming is incorrect in any case.

A small piece of hair, the width of the bridle headpiece, is often cropped just behind the ears so that the bridle will sit better. This will also give a

Figure 4.48 *Pulling a mane. a) The mane before pulling. b) Pulling the mane by running the mane comb up to the roots of the selected longest hairs, wrapping the free ends round the comb, keeping hold of them in your free hand, and jerk quickly downwards to pull the hairs out. c) The pulled mane.*

neater appearance when a horse is plaited up. About 5−7.5 cm (2−3 in) of hair are also sometimes trimmed off at the withers. When trimming around the head area, use blunt-ended scissors in case the horse throws its head up and the scissors come near its eyes.

If there are any long hairs on the lower jaw, they can be trimmed off with scissors to neaten the outline of the horse's head. Long hairs, or 'whiskers', on the horse's muzzle are its 'feelers' and prevent it from bumping its nose on things. Unless you are going to do serious showing, trimming the whiskers is unkind and unnecessary.

Animals that are going to live out in the winter should not have their manes, tails or heels trimmed. The mane and tail are protection from rain and wind and the long hair on the fetlocks forms a natural drainage conduit that prevents rain water from running down into the heels and washing out the coat's natural grease or 'waterproofing'. If this happens, cracks and scabs may form in the heels and these can lead to lameness and infection.

Pulling a Tail

When pulling a tail, stand to one side to avoid being kicked. Ask an assistant to hold the horse. Brush the tangles out of the tail, then comb through the hairs growing from the top of the tail. Take a few hairs from the top at one side and run the comb up to their roots. If the hairs are long enough, wrap them around the comb (as in mane pulling) and jerk quickly downwards. If the hairs are too short to wrap round the comb, hold them up with one hand while jerking the comb downwards with the other.

Work from alternate sides, looking and feeling to check that both sides are equal. Work down to the end of the dock, only removing the hairs that are not full length. Be careful not to create bald patches by overdoing the pulling out. (Some people's pulled tails look like loo brushes!) Comb the centre hairs out to the side and pull out the longer ones until the bony part of the tail has a smooth, neat appearance.

Pulling a tail may take several days, according to its thickness and the reactions of the horse. Do not upset a young horse just for the sake of its appearance.

Remember that once a tail has been pulled you cannot plait it and that you will have to go on pulling out a few hairs at a time each week to keep it neat. It will be necessary to put a tail bandage on very regularly to keep the hair lying smoothly. Be quite certain that this is what you want before you start to pull a tail − it takes a long time to grow out to a full tail again and looks quite a mess while it does so.

When bandaging a tail, use an elasticated bandage and dampen the tail, not the bandage (which may shrink and tighten as it dries). Lift the tail and begin bandaging right up at the top of the dock. On the first circuit, leave the free end of the bandage sticking up by about 15 cm (6 in) and hold on to

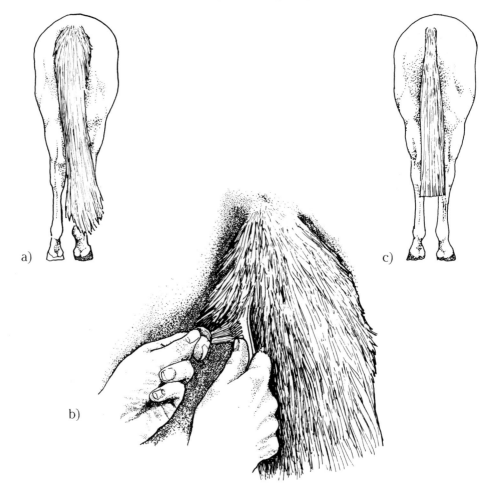

Figure 4.49 *Pulling a tail. a) The tail before pulling. b) Taking a few hairs from the top of the tail, run the comb up to the roots and, if long enough, wrap them round the comb, to pull them out. If they are too short to wrap round the comb, hold them up with one hand and pull the comb downward with the other hand. c) The tail after pulling.*

this to maintain a firm, not tight, application. On the second circuit, fold the free end down and bandage over it to 'lock' it in place. Continue bandaging firmly, not tightly, to the end of the bone, overlapping half of the width of the bandage on each circuit. The bandage may be long enough to go about halfway up the tail again. Smooth out the tapes so that they will lie flat, and tie them (no tighter than the bandage) a little off-centre so that if the horse is travelling and rubs its tail, the knot will not rub the hair. Gently bend the tail back into its natural curve.

Do not leave a tail bandage on for more than two or three hours. Check that the horse is not rubbing its tail to get the bandage off. When travelling a

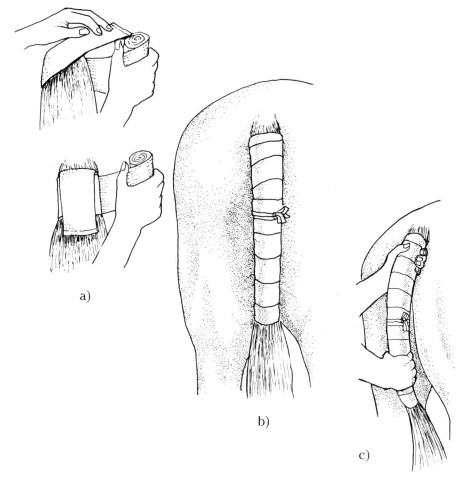

Figure 4.50 *Bandaging a tail. a) Begin bandaging right at the top of the dock. On the first circuit leave the free end of the bandage sticking up, folding it down and 'locking it in place with the second wrap. b) The bandaged tail with the tapes tied a little off centre which ensures that, if the horse is travelling and rubs its tail, the knot will not rub the hair. c) Removing the bandage by holding it firmly with both hands and sliding it off down the tail.*

horse for long distances, however, the bandage may have to be on for a long time. Make sure it is not too tight and put a tail guard on (a cloth or leather cover, kept up by a strap attached to the roller) over the bandage to protect the tail if the bandage slips. When travelling, horses will often rest their hindquarters against the wall of the box or trailer and rub a tail bandage off, giving themselves a very sore tail.

A tail bandage will never slip, and need not be put on tightly, if, as you bandage, you take a tiny section of hair from alternate sides of the tail, turn them upwards over the bandage and cover them with the next layer of the bandage as you work downwards. These tiny 'hooks' of hair will hold the bandage on and prevent it from slipping downwards. Remember to unwind the bandage to remove it as you will not be able to slide it off in the usual way. This method is not suitable if you are going to a show as the hooks of hair will remain sticking out for some time after you have removed the bandage.

Trimming Heels

If you trim the heels, the hair will grow back coarser and you will need to go on trimming regularly every few weeks. If you trim in the summer and let the hair grow again for the winter, it will be very coarse and bushy but will also protect the horse from cracked heels to some extent.

To trim the heels, either clip them with electric clippers (do not expect your young horse to accept these without a careful introduction [see page 149]), remembering that many horses do not like having their legs clipped. A horse that is stamping about and kicking can easily knock the clippers out of your hand or get a leg over the cable, so be extremely careful and ask someone experienced to help you if you are not used to working with clippers.

To trim with scissors, take a mane comb in one hand and, holding it upside down, lift the long 'feather' (heel hairs) and trim it off with the scissors. By lifting the hair in this way you will prevent a ridged line of cut hair from forming. Continue trimming until the hair has a short, neat, even

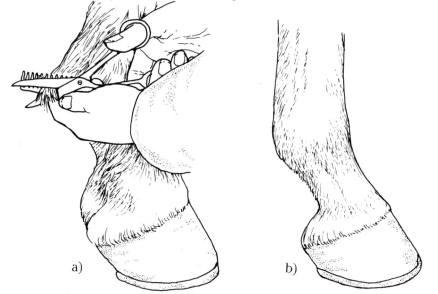

a)   b)

Figure 4.51 *Trimming the heels. a) Trimming the heel hairs (feather) by holding the hairs up with a mane comb and cutting them with scissors. b) The trimmed heel.*

appearance. Be very careful when doing the hind legs. Stand with your back to the horse's head, but remember that even here you will be in a vulnerable position and can very easily get kicked.

The pink skin under white socks is very sensitive and tiny scabs and cracks can form on the back of the pastern, just above the bulbs of the heels, even in summer. The pollen from the St John's Wort plant can cause very sore patches and large scabs on pink-skinned areas – noses, lips and heels – in the summer. A change of field and an antihistamine cream are often the best remedies. This type of sore scabbiness is not caused by trimming or wet heels.

Washing and Banging the Tail

Wash the horse's tail before banging it (trimming the long hairs at the end of the tail so that they hang level). An accepted length is 10 cm (4 in) below the point of the hocks when the horse is carrying its tail as it normally does in trot.

Young horses are often frightened of water, especially when it drips down off their tail onto their hind legs, so be careful. Tie the horse up or ask an assistant to hold it. Half fill a plastic bucket with soapy lukewarm water (use a brand of soap sold for washing horses or a mild human baby shampoo in case the horse's skin is sensitive to stronger soap). Show the bucket to the horse and let it sniff at it. Stand well over to one side of the hindquarters as the horse may lash out at the feel of the water. Gently insert the long hairs of the tail into the warm water and be prepared for the horse to clamp its tail down tightly, rush forward or kick when it feels the bone of its tail touch the water.

A small plastic bucket, only half full, is much easier to cope with single-handed. Your free hand can then rub the tail in the bucket. If you have assistance, you can stand one on each side of the horse's quarters, one holding the bucket, the other using both hands to wash the tail. Try to keep the tail over the bucket until most of the water has run off it. As you release the tail, again, be prepared for the horse to rush forward when it feels the water dripping on its hind legs.

Rinse thoroughly in the same way, using lukewarm water. (Water that is too hot or very cold can produce a violent reaction from the horse.) Dry the tail off with a towel or, if the horse is completely unworried by the whole thing so far, stand to one side and spin the end of the tail round and round with your hand (slowly at first to make sure the horse is not frightened) and allow centrifugal force to get rid of the drips.

When the tail is dry, brush it out very carefully with a soft brush, holding a few hairs at a time tightly in one hand while brushing out the tangles in them with the other. This method prevents the hairs from being pulled out by the action of the brush pulling directly on their roots and should always

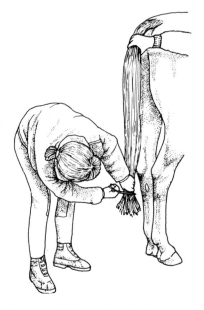

Figure 4.52 *Banging a tail. The tail is held up to the height at which the horse normally carries it at trot: the tail is then cut level with scissors about 10 cm (4 in) below the hocks.*

be used when brushing tails. If you wish your horse to have a good full tail, never brush it except after washing it and then only if you are going somewhere special. Wispy tails are caused by brushing them every day; each time a few more hairs are unknowingly pulled out by the roots.

When all the knots are brushed out of the tail, lift the horse's dock to the height at which it normally carries it in trot. Encircle the tail with your free hand and run this hand down until it is 10 cm (4 in) below the hocks. (It is easier if you have an assistant.) Cut the tail level with sharp scissors. Repeat this two or three times to make sure the cut is even.

Leg Washing

White socks may be washed before a show or special outing but do not wash them unnecessarily. The pink skin underneath white hair is more prone to chapping and cracking than dark skin and, anyway, washing removes the coat's natural oils, making the skin even more vulnerable to cracking.

Tie the horse up or ask someone to hold it. Use lukewarm water and a mild soap. Remember that a young horse may be quite frightened by this procedure and work gently, using a water brush or even just your own hand, to put only a little water on the legs at first. Once the horse is used to this, you may be able rinse the soap off by pouring clean lukewarm water gently down the legs.

Dry the legs off very thoroughly with an old towel, especially the back of the fetlocks, the pasterns and the heels. These are the areas where cracked skin is most likely to form.

Hosing the Legs

Hosing can be done to clean very muddy legs, to treat sprains or to clean wounds. Ask someone to hold the horse. Do not tie any horse up the first time you use a hosepipe near it or on its legs. Some horses are afraid of hosepipes and will pull back. If the horse does panic, you cannot simply drop the hosepipe and go to the horse's head as the hosepipe will continue to snake about on the ground, spouting water in all directions and making matters worse.

Run the hose very slowly — just a trickle of water close to the ground at first. Then allow a little water to run onto the lower leg. Some horses do not mind this at all; others dance up and down frantically. If your horse panics, abandon this method; there is no point in upsetting a really frightened horse by insisting on using a hosepipe.

To clean mud off, always use cold water so that the pores of the skin will remain closed. Warm water will open the pores and allow grains of mud to enter them. These particles of mud can then cause mud fever, a sore, scabby condition of the skin on the legs and sometimes also under the stomach.

Figure 4.53 *Hosing the legs to clean off mud or clean a wound, or to treat sprains. The hose must be held in a position which allows the water to run down the leg following the lie of the hair, and, when cleaning a wound, the water should fall from above the wound, cleaning it by flowing over it.*

Allow the water to run downwards from the top of the leg, following the lie of the hair. Do not brush wet mud or it could penetrate the skin. Even when using a water brush on non-muddy legs, still work downwards. Dry the legs off thoroughly afterwards.

If it is too cold to wash the legs off, put bandages on over a thick layer of straw or gamgee and leave them to dry thoroughly before brushing the mud off.

To treat a sprain, cold-hose the leg for 10 or 15 minutes three or four times a day, allowing the cold water to run over the affected area. Dry the legs off carefully afterwards.

To hose a wound, allow the water to come onto the leg above the site of the wound and run down over it so that it will wash away any dirt that is in the wound. While hosing, stroke the wound gently downwards with something soft and clean (not a sponge). Do not try to rub the wound clean or you may force dirt into it.

Hosing or Washing Down

After a long ride or hard work on a hot day in summer, the horse may be sweaty, particularly under the saddle, round the girth, on the shoulders and behind the ears. It can either be washed down with a bucket of water and a sponge or it can be hosed.

Begin very gradually by hosing a lower front leg and then work up over the withers and back before hosing the shoulder and neck and belly. Obviously, it is not a good idea to hose the head, so you must do this with a damp, not dripping, sponge. Do not get water in the eyes. Be aware of your horse's reactions. Some horses never accept hosing, so there is no point in terrifying them with a hose if they will happily accept a bucket and sponge.

A sweat scraper is the easiest way to get the excess water off. There are two types. One is a long, pliable strip of metal with a handle at each end. Hold it so that it forms a convex arc and pull it gently along the horse's body, starting at the neck and saddle area and pulling the water down in the direction of the lie of the hair.

The other type of scraper has one handle. There is a rigid convex metal rim on one side of the scraper and a rubber rim on the other. Use this scraper in the same way as described above. Use the rubber side on thin-skinned, sensitive horses and bony places.

After hosing or washing down you must take care that the horse does not get cold, so lead it about or lunge it quietly until it is dry. Never leave a wet horse to dry off standing in its stable except in really hot weather.

Never hose or wash a hot horse in cold weather. The cold water will very quickly lower the horse's temperature and it will soon begin to shiver and shake, which means that a chill is imminent. If this does happen, rub the horse vigorously with old towels, if possible getting someone to work with

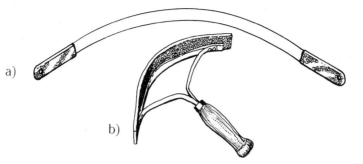

Figure 4.54 *Two types of sweat scraper. a) A pliable strip of metal with handles at each end is held in a convex arc and pulled along the horse's body to remove excess water. b) A sweat scraper with both a metal and a rubber edge; the rubber is for sensitive areas and thin-skinned horses. Both types of sweat scraper should be used in the direction of the lie of the hair.*

you on the other side of the horse while keeping the horse partly covered with a rug. When you have finished rug the horse up. If the horse is still damp, use a sweat rug under a jute rug that has been put on wrong side up. Should the horse continue to shiver, you can also thatch it, i.e. stuff handfuls of straw along its back and sides under the sweat rug, providing this does not scare the horse. Bandage the legs (not too tightly) with stable bandages over straw or gamgee. Again, be careful if the horse is not used to these. Make the straw bedding a bit deeper to increase the warmth. A warm bran mash will help to warm the horse from the inside out.

Clipping

You should not attempt to clip a young horse until you are experienced in clipping older and slightly ticklish horses. You must fully understand all the safety measures required when clipping and use well-maintained equipment. Always wear rubber boots for insulation against shocks and make sure the horse cannot stand on the cable. If you are in doubt about your ability to clip properly, you must seek expert help.

Tie the horse up and give it a haynet to prevent if from becoming bored. Remember that the horse may become cold as its coat is clipped away, so use a rug to keep it warm at the front while clipping the rear, and vice versa.

Before clipping a young horse for the first time, try, if possible, to stand it within sight and sound of the clippers while a quiet horse is being clipped. Gradually approach your youngster with the clippers running – don't suddenly turn them on when you are standing beside it. Keep your hand over the head of the clippers and allow the horse to sniff your hand, not the clippers. Put your hand on the horse's shoulder and let it feel the vibration of the clippers running through your hand, gradually making a stroking movement in the direction of the lie of the hair.

Now take smooth, short cuts against the lie of the hair on the shoulder until the horse is used to the feeling. Do a little on each side so that if you have to stop because the horse has had enough for the moment, both sides will match. Be patient and understanding. Remember to stop every so often to let the clippers cool down and to oil them frequently.

A young horse will sometimes stand quite still, rigid with fright, and then, like lightning, strike out at the clippers or shoot backwards, forwards or towards the stable door in an attempt to escape.

The lower jaw is a particularly sensitive place to clip. I think this is because when the clipper blades touch the lower jawbone, the horse feels the vibrations in its head. The nearer to the chin you get, the more sensitive the horse may seem to be, so begin near the throat and work down towards the chin, taking off a little at a time and trying not to make contact with the bone.

The other very tickly places, which many horses dislike having clipped, are around the elbows and girth area, under the stomach, the flanks, the stifles and inside the hind legs. The head, particularly the ears, usually causes most trouble and it might be a good idea to leave the head unclipped if the horse is very nervous. It does not matter if the horse will not let you clip

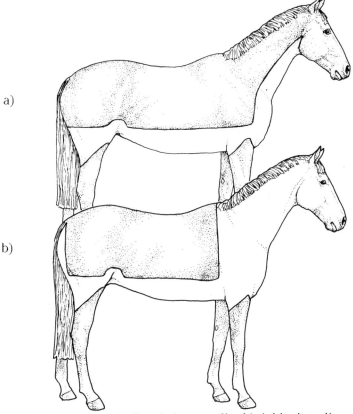

Figure 4.55   *Two types of clip. a) A trace clip. b) A blanket clip.*

its face at first. It may allow you to do more next time. You can always clip to a bridle line on the head if you don't wish to clip round the eyes or ears.

Do not use a twitch (a restrainer twisted tightly round the upper lip) as you do not want the horse to have unpleasant memories of its first clipping session. Clip as much as you can until the horse becomes restless, then do some more the next day.

For the first clip it is a good idea to do only a trace or blanket clip.

According to the amount of coat the horse normally grows, it will need clipping every three to four weeks. A common type of horse grows more coat than a Thoroughbred type and this coat also grows more quickly than the coat of a finer type of horse.

The safest type of clipper is the battery-operated kind because this has a much lower voltage than a mains clipper. It is permanently attached to your back by a belt and has a short, coiled-spring flex, so you are completely mobile and the horse is far less likely to get a leg over the cable or stand on it. You can clip a horse anywhere, inside or out, and it cannot move out of your reach. This kind of clipper also operates more quietly and horses that are upset by the mains type of clipper will often calmly accept the battery-operated type.

Figure 4.56 *Battery-operated clippers are safer than mains clippers, and give the clipper more mobility.*

Remember always to use sharp, correctly adjusted blades on a young horse. Blunt blades pulling and 'chewing' the hair will upset the quietest of horses. Have your clippers serviced regularly and the blades sharpened.

Rugs

Before you clip your horse for the first time, get it used to the sight and feel of a small blanket on its back and then progress to getting it accustomed to wearing a rug with straps or a roller.

If the horse is stabled, it will need one rug at first after clipping. As the weather grows colder, after another clip the horse may need a blanket under its rug or even a second rug. The best type of rug stays on by means of straps crossed over under the stomach and does not need a roller. Modern puffa-type rugs are lightweight and so warm that one is often sufficient. Their surcingles are also more comfortable for the horse.

Old-fashioned rugs are heavier and need a roller which must be well padded to keep pressure off the withers and backbone. You may need to place a soft pad under the roller to ensure that it fits comfortably.

The neck of any rug must not be so big that it sits behind the wither when it slips back during the night. Pressure caused by a rug digging in on or behind the wither will quickly cause a sore place.

If the horse is only doing light work and does not have a very thick coat anyway, just clipping under the stomach and up the chest and neck may be sufficient. If you want to be able to turn the horse out in a field during the day, a trace clip (halfway up the horse's sides) will be ideal. The horse will need a waterproof New Zealand-type rug that is shaped to fit the hindquarters, very well fitting at the neck and shoulders so that it does not press or rub, and has carefully adjusted straps to prevent it from slipping.

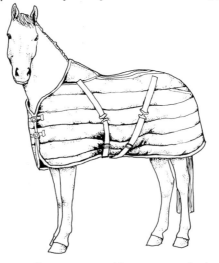

Figure 4.57 *A modern puffa-type rug with cross surcingles.*

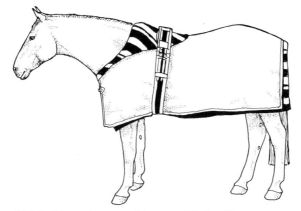

Figure 4.58 *Old-fashioned rugs with a padded roller.*

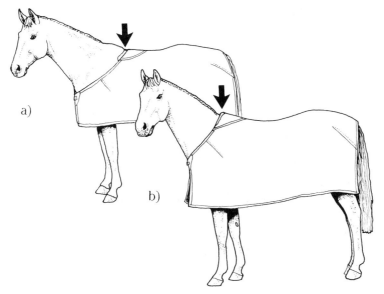

Figure 4.59 *Incorrectly and correctly fitting rugs at the wither and shoulder. a) Incorrect: the rug sits behind the wither because the neck is too big and can cause a sore place. In this position it may also rub on the bony part of the shoulder. b) Correct: the rug sits over the withers and above the bony part of the shoulder.*

There are now so many different designs on the market that you may need an experienced person to help you to choose a suitable rug and to fit it for you.

If your New Zealand rug has leg straps, these should be linked through each other before being fastened again on their own side. They should not be crossed over. The leg straps must be tight enough so that even when the horse rolls they cannot slip down below its hocks, yet loose enough to allow the horse to walk in comfort and not rub.

Figure 4.60 *A New Zealand rug showing the correct leg strap linkage.*

SHOEING

If your young horse becomes footsore, it may be necessary to have it shod all round, or in front only, according to the state of its feet and the amount of work you will be doing with it.

You can help the farrier enormously, long before he visits you, by making a habit of tapping the horse's feet with a hammer after you have picked them out − gently at first − and getting the horse used to the sound of tools clattering. If possible, get the farrier to come and shoe your youngster in its own box or in your yard the first time it is shod. Some young horses are restless if shod in a box because they are nervous of the clouds of smoke arising from the hot shoes. Stand by the horse's head and talk to it, offer a haynet or food in a bowl, and try to calm it down. If it will not settle, take it out into the yard where the clouds of smoke will not hang in the air so much. Avoid twitching a young horse the first time it is shod. Shoeing should become a quiet routine, not a constant battle.

Cold shoeing is less frightening and some farriers prefer to do this for a horse's first shoeing.

If shoeing at home is not possible, take a quiet companion to stand next to your youngster in the farrier's shop. If the horse is bored and fractious, be prepared to have only the front shoes put on, and wait for another day to have the hinds on. A battle the first time may be remembered for life, so use tact and patience and put in lots of practice at home, especially with the hind feet.

Most farriers prefer you to hold a young horse while it is being shod, rather than tie it up. Teach your youngster to stand still and behave well. Farriers can become quite irritated with a horse that fidgets, leans on them or refuses to stand still. Many farriers will, quite rightly, refuse to handle an animal that they feel is liable to injure them. In hot weather, it is a good idea to dab some fly repellent on your horse so that flies will not cause it to dance about while it is being shod thus annoying the farrier and causing him to discipline the horse himself.

Each time you pick out the horse's feet, check the shoes and notice any risen clenches (the bent-over ends of the nails which should lie smooth and flush with the wall of the hoof). If they have risen on the inside, they can cut the opposite leg. Notice if the shoe has moved or twisted at all or if the heels seem to be digging into the hoof. Keep a record of when your horse is shod and mark the calendar four or five weeks ahead to jog your memory and allow time to book the farrier.

GENERAL CARE OF YOUR THREE-YEAR-OLD

If the horse can be kept out, it will be quieter and more relaxed. Even if it is stabled at night, turn it out for part of the day if possible. The boredom of being shut in as a youngster is the root cause of many stable vices such as weaving, crib-biting and windsucking. In the summer it is better out by night and in by day because of the flies.

Feeding

When you first start to ride your horse, do not feed oats or high-protein food unless it is lazy. Grass or good hay is sufficient for the amount of work it is doing and it is important that the horse remains quiet, sensible and controllable. If all is going well, and the horse begins to do more work, gradually introduce some hard food (see page 294).

If your horse often bucks, try to find out why it is doing this. Is it just high spirits − rushing forwards or sideways with a quick cheerful kick out behind? It is possible that too much hard food and not enough work may be the cause. Many people overfeed young horses, thinking that they need to be big and strong to be ridden. If it is a lively type, a young horse is better on just grass in the summer and just hay in the winter.

Once the horse is riding quietly, a little hard food can be given and very gradually increased. Overfeeding causes many of the problems riders have with young horses − they are literally jumping out of their skins from being fed like three-day eventers!

Exercise

You cannot expect any young horse to be quiet and safe if it is only ridden at weekends. It must be ridden at least every other day and even then it must still be turned out to get rid of any freshness on the days when it is not ridden.

After a rest of several weeks, and before you recommence riding it, you must expect to spend a week lungeing it and generally preparing it for being ridden again, as you did in the early stages of breaking.

5 THE FOUR-YEAR-OLD

LUNGEING OVER POLES

Before you lunge the horse over poles, you must lunge it thoroughly on the flat (see page 36) attaching the lunge rein to the cavesson not the bit.

When the horse is going forward well and happily on the exact track you wish it to follow (which may take two or three weeks), you can introduce trotting poles on your lunge circle. Do not use side reins as they will prevent the horse from using its neck in the manner it needs to when going over poles. Use only round poles, as square-sided ones can injure heels and fetlocks. Put one pole flat on the track with a cone or smooth, low marker standing at each end of it, to help keep the horse in.

Lead the horse over the centre of the pole in both directions, allowing it to follow you and take a good look. Some horses will stop and refuse to step over the pole. If this happens, set out two poles with a gap between them like a gateway in a fence. Ask the horse to walk through the gap and then gradually close the gap until the poles form one continuous pole for the horse to step over. Never have a fight or ask anyone to chase the horse over the pole. The horse must always wish to go forward, so you must never use force. If your young horse is unsure about this new exercise, think of ways to build up its confidence gradually. Perhaps by leading it and allowing it to follow you, or a quiet pony, at walk over simple poles.

Next, lunge the horse over the centre of the pole in both directions, at walk and trot. Lay a second pole at an angle to the first, 2.7 m (9 ft) away from it at the centre and forming the beginning of a fan shape with the other pole – narrower at the inside edge and wider at the outside. This distance will allow the horse to take two strides in trot in the centre of the fan. The horse will then be less likely to try to jump the poles and will not feel trapped by a narrow space between the poles.

When the horse is coping easily with the 2.7 m (9 ft) distance and you have checked that its footfalls land evenly on either side of the second pole (proving that the distance is correct), then you can add a third pole between the first two. If, according to the horse's footfalls, the distance seems too long or too short, adjust the poles. The hind foot should come exactly in the centre of the gap between the poles. If it is too close to the

156

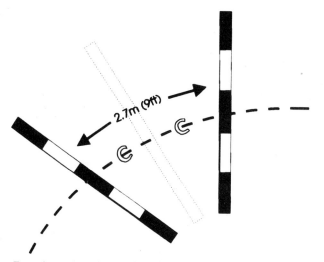

Figure 5.1 *Fan-shape trotting poles, first stage. Two trotting poles with two trot strides between them. The dotted-line pole shows where the third pole will go.*

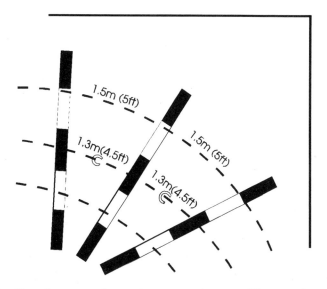

Figure 5.2 *Fan-shape trotting poles, second stage. Three poles with one trot stride between them.*

second pole, open the poles out by about 15 cm (6 in). If the hind foot does not even fall halfway to the second pole, close the distance a little.

This judgement must be made when the horse is following a true circle, passing exactly over the centre of each pole. Put markers at each end of every pole to make it easier for the horse to keep on a true track. A small pony may need only 1.15 m (3 ft 9 in) between poles; a big long-striding horse could need 1.45 m (4 ft 9 in).

To make the horse work and use itself a little more, drive it forward and out onto a slightly larger circle, so that it will go over the poles where they are 1.5 m (5 ft) apart. If you build up enough impulsion, you will see the horse really push itself forward and use itself at this distance. The hind foot must step exactly in the centre of the gap between each pole. If this does not happen, think: 'Am I asking for too much at this stage? Has the horse enough impulsion – is it really going forward?'

Only do this exercise if you can lunge accurately and control the horse so that it goes over the same part of each pole, thus ensuring that the distances are the same for each stride. If the horse goes to the centre of the first pole and then cuts in towards you, the distance between the second and third pole will become too short and the horse will hit the poles or trip over them and may lose confidence.

If you do not wish to use a fan shape and can move forward with the horse, you can lunge it over poles placed parallel to each other so that your lungeing circle now has one straight side where the poles are. Begin with one pole, then use two, 2.7 m (9 ft) apart, before putting one in the centre so that there is a gap of 1.3 m (4½ ft) between them.

Never walk over poles set at the trotting distance of 1.3 m (4½ ft) because the strides will be wrong; the horse will knock the poles and may become upset or stumble.

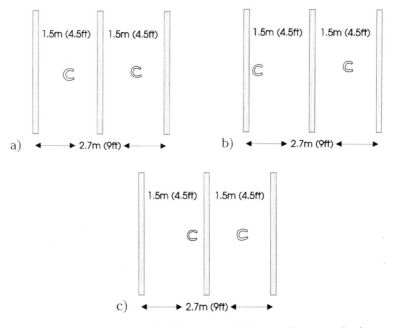

Figure 5.3   *Parallel trotting pole distances. a) Correct distance: the hooves should fall in the centre of the space between the poles. b) Too close: the second hoof comes down too close to the last pole. c) Too far apart: the second hoof falls too short of the last pole.*

LUNGEING OVER JUMPS

If you have never done this before, you must practise on an older horse.

Use the same tack that you would use for normal lungeing, but attach the lunge rein to the cavesson not the bit, and do not use side reins or bridle reins looped behind the stirrup leathers, because they would prevent the horse from using its head or neck and rounding its back freely. Overreach and brushing boots must be used and are particularly important here, where a mistake can cause a knocked joint or a tendon injury.

Build your jump against a high fence or hedge, making sure there is no barbed wire for the horse to run into. If the field fence itself is low, raise it where your jump is to be, making it safe to approach in both directions. Have an upright at each side, with long, sloping poles on the inside, as wings. These must be smooth enough for a lunge line to run over them. A plastic bag wrapped round the tops of the poles where they meet will create a smooth curve. Make sure the lunge line cannot catch on anything.

At first, just set up the uprights but do not put any poles on the ground between them. Lunge your horse on a normal circle, then work towards a track that runs through between the wings and get the horse going happily through the gap in both directions, first at walk, then in trot.

Progress to one pole lying on the ground, then to low cross poles. These will encourage the horse to go straight for the centre of the fence, which will be the lowest part. Next, you can build a small parallel and add branches, cones, plastic bags and anything else that is safe and will keep

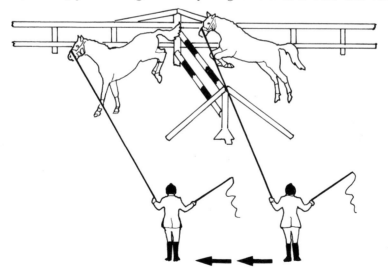

Figure 5.4 *Lungeing over a jump showing how the trainer must move forward with the horse to ensure it has total freedom of movement at all stages of the jump.*

the horse interested. If the horse rushes, lay down three trotting poles 1.3 m (4½ ft) apart, followed by a gap of 2.7 m (9 ft) and then your jump: the poles will slow the horse down and make it think.

A jump of 46−61 cm (1½−2 ft) is high enough at this stage. The horse must want to go. If it appears at all worried, lower the fence.

You must be ready to move forward quickly with the horse and must maintain a supple, allowing hand so that there is never any pull on the horse's head in the approach, in the air or just after landing. The horse must always feel that it has the freedom to use its head and neck and round its back.

If the horse runs out, extend the length of the wings with more cones and poles. Your fences should be so low that the horse can be encouraged to go from a standstill if it stops. It is important that a young horse should learn to go first time. So many young horses are allowed to 'look' and then go the second time round and this easily becomes a lifelong bad habit. Work on both reins, reorganising the jump as necessary. Do not be tempted to see how high the horse can jump, but rather how many different, small, solid-looking obstacles, including ditches, it will go straight over first time, calmly and willingly.

None of this work should last for more than twenty minutes. Two or three short sessions a week are far better than one long lesson. Always end on a good note with the horse still wanting to jump and calmly enjoying it.

RIDING OVER TROTTING POLES

Again, use only round poles, as square-sided ones can injure heels and fetlocks.

Shorten your stirrups a couple of holes, as you will then find it far easier to sit in balance and go with your horse. Work in rising trot, because you will be able to feel and maintain an even rhythm more easily and your horse will find it easier to round its back and lower its head. Sitting trot can often produce a raised head carriage with a hollow back and the hind legs left behind − the last thing you want when jumping.

Set up a pair of jump stands by a wall or fence, leaving a clear, wide outside track. Remove the jump cups as these are dangerous and should never be left on unless occupied by a pole. Work in rising trot between the empty jump stands.

Next, put a single pole on the ground between the stands. Walk, then trot, over it, being careful to stay in balance and keep an even rhythm. It is best to have an assistant to organise your cones and poles, etc.

Two poles, 1.3 m (4½ ft) apart, will tend to make a horse try to jump both; three poles, 1.3 m (4½ ft) apart, can look alarming and make a horse rush and muddle through, so it is best to use two poles 2.7 m (9 ft) apart for

Figure 5.5 *Two four-year-olds (a bay and a chestnut) ready for a jumping lesson after a ride round the farm to settle them. The riders have their stirrups at jumping length.*

Figure 5.6 *Trotting over three poles. The bay four-year-old is working calmly and confidently. Note the straight line from the rider's elbow through to the horse's mouth and the softness of his shoulder, elbow and wrist, but his heels could be a little lower. His gently controlling but 'allowing' hand lets the horse go forward with confidence. He is sitting quietly in balance with the horse.*

the average 14.2–15.2 hh horse and 15 cm (6 in) wider for 16 hh horses. This arrangement is too wide to jump and has enough space between the poles not to worry a youngster. Put a cone at each end of every pole.

When the horse is going quietly over these, put in a middle pole so that they are all 1.3 m (4½ ft) apart. If the poles are the correct distance apart, the horse's hind leg should step exactly in the centre of the gap between the poles. If the footfall is correct in the first gap, but beyond the centre of

Figure 5.7 *Trotting over three poles. The chestnut four-year-old has met the first pole wrong and consequently slowed down suddenly because of a loss of confidence. The rider has lost her position, but has still managed to keep a light even contact on the reins.*

the next, you will need to move the poles a little further apart — by about 7.5–15 cm (3–6 in). If the footfall is correct for the first gap, but falls before the centre of the next two, you will need to shorten the distance a little. Before you alter the distances, however, make sure your trot is a good one. A slow, lazy trot can make it seem that the distance is too great. A long, hurrying stride can make the distance seem too short. Never walk over poles set at trotting distance. The stride is wrong for walk, so the horse will knock the poles and become worried.

If possible, have an assistant to alter the poles for you and to replace any that are knocked out of place. Both you and the horse will lose concentration if you are constantly dismounting to move the poles about.

Approximate Distances for Trotting Poles

hh	metres	feet
12.2	1–1.14	3½–3¾
13.2	1.14–1.2	3¾–4
14.2	1.2–1.37	4–4½
15.2	1.37–1.45	4½–4¾
over 15.2	1.45–1.5	4¾–5

The correct distances also depend on the build and length of stride of your horse. Cobby types tend to be short-striding, Thoroughbreds long-striding.

If you are alone, constantly getting off to alter poles can be very annoying, so build them in a fan shape, approximately 46 cm (18 in) apart at the narrow end and 1.8 m (6 ft) apart at the outside. You can now walk over them on the inside at 61 cm (2 ft) apart, then trot at the centre and lengthen the stride and make the horse work towards the outside. When you do this it is essential that you come over exactly the same part of each pole or the distance will be wrong, so work on an accurate circle. Coloured poles painted with the same length of stripes are excellent for this work as you can then aim to go over, say, each red piece. If you only have plain poles, tie coloured strips of material round them and aim for those.

If your horse rushes, come into your poles off a circle. Do not hold the horse back or it will rush even more. Plan your approach so that the horse will have very little time in which to see the poles in front of it. Ask yourself, 'Is this horse rushing because it enjoys this work and is excited, or because it is frightened and wants to get it over with quickly?' These are the two main reasons for rushing.

RIDING OVER JUMPS

Before you begin this work, you and the horse should already be familiar with trotting poles.

Put your stirrups up a couple of holes for trotting poles and jumping. This makes it easier to stay in balance with your horse.

Use three parallel trotting poles, set 1.3 m (4½ ft) apart, and trot over these in both directions.

Next, set up two crossed poles approximately 2.7 m (9 ft) beyond your last trotting pole and work in rising trot.

Now convert the cross poles into a small parallel. Put a ground line or small 'filler' in. All your fences must look solid and as if they 'need' jumping.

Figure 5.8 *The first jump. The bay's first attempt at a small cross poles fence with a trotting pole 1.3 m (9 ft) in front of it. The horse is uncertain how to cope, shown by the position of its head and ears. The rider is sitting in balance and maintaining a light contact on the horse's mouth.*

Figure 5.9 *The first jump. The chestnut's first attempt shows a little more confidence than the bay's. The rider is sitting in balance with the horse.*

Soon you will be ready to build several small, solid-looking fences, still working in rising trot and still aiming to keep an even rhythm in the approach and after landing. If the horse canters the last few strides, sit quietly in balance and allow it to do so, then ride forward into your hand and onto a circle after landing to re-establish balance in rising trot. Try to keep the horse in trot during the approach, because then it will have to round its back more and make a better shape when jumping.

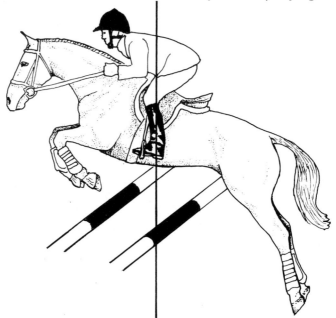

Figure 5.10 *Sitting in balance over a fence.*

Never pull back; always ride forward into a gently checking hand to steady a horse. Do not work over several jumps in a grid if your horse rushes. Work coming in off circles and on changes of direction. You cannot stop a horse from rushing by holding it back – it will only get even more excited or worried. If this happens, approach the jump from a very short turn in (from walk if necessary) and just allow the horse to go forward into the fence; don't hold it back. Keep the work simple until the horse is calm and confident.

To keep your horse round and well balanced, it is best to work on circles. In your approach, take care not to go beyond the centre line of the fence or you will unbalance the horse. If your first jump is approached on the right rein, ride one or more circles on the right rein until the horse is going calmly in an even, active gait, then jump the fence, thinking 'right' in the air and having more weight in your right stirrup, and, as you land, go away on a circle to the right. It is easier to keep a horse balanced if you jump every jump on the same rein at first, always circling the same way and using your circles to rebalance the horse before the next jump. Then jump them all on the other rein in the same way.

As the horse progresses in its work, you can change directions smoothly, jumping one fence from a circle left and the next from a circle right. Always be ready to use an extra circle to rebalance the horse when necessary. Aim for a smooth, flowing performance, including some circles, before you attempt to jump a full course in the normal way. *Never* jump the next fence until your horse is calm, balanced and in rhythm again.

Figure 5.11 *This rider is left behind the horse's movement and is hanging on by the reins causing the horse to open its mouth in pain.*

Figure 5.12   *This rider has also been left behind — she is sitting at the back of the saddle — but has managed to push her hands forward to ensure she is not pulling on the horse's mouth.*

If your horse rushes or gets overexcited at any time, go back to trotting-pole work on circles. Then walk into a fence, turning in very short, so that the horse has perhaps just two strides of trot before popping over the fence. Turn away on the same circle and come forward to walk again. Do not hold the horse back, just use the short approach to calm it down, then there is no time for it to get excited. You must be very supple to get forward and go with the horse where it jumps from a slow gait. Push your hands forward to follow its head. Never, never pull on its mouth. If you get left behind, slip the reins.

Always have an upright at each end of the fence to guide the horse in. Introduce solid fences by leaving a wide gap in the centre for the horse to go through at first and then gradually closing it. Walls and brush fences usually come in two sections so this is easily done. The same thing applies to barrels, but with these remember always to have a pole on the ground on each side of the barrels to prevent them from rolling if hit. Without these poles they can easily bring a horse down. Do not put poles on the centre of a straw bale or barrel when using these as supports. The poles can roll and bring a horse down. Put the poles on the edge where they can fall off easily. Do not pile up straw bales or cavalletti. This is dangerous.

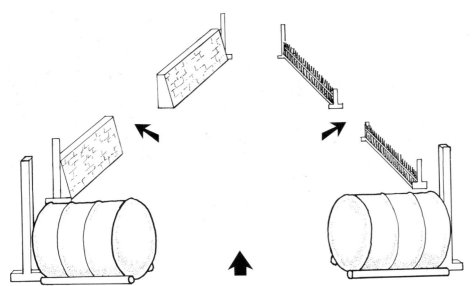

Figure 5.13 *Introduce solid fences by leaving a wide gap in the centre for the horse to go through at first, and then gradually close it.*

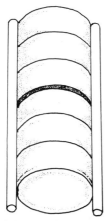

Figure 5.14 *Jumps using barrels as fillers must have poles or bars each side to stop them rolling if hit by the horse.*

Figure 5.15 *A home-made jump utilising barrels and discarded containers with the anti-rolling poles on either side of the jump.*

If you have a refusal, you have asked too much too soon, you have not prepared the horse in time for the jump or you have worried it by catching it in the mouth, flying in the air or bumping down on its back. You may have kicked the horse on the way in (making it think back to you instead of forward to the jump) or upset it by being out of balance in the approach. Try to sit in balance and get a good working trot with plenty of impulsion to bring the horse's hocks underneath it so that it is easy for it to jump, then ride quietly forward, allowing the horse to concentrate on the jump and work it out for itself. Any sudden movement from you in the last few strides will make the horse think back towards what you are doing so that it will lose its concentration on the jump. Keep an even contact on the reins in the approach because suddenly dropping the contact makes a horse lose balance and confidence. Have supple shoulders and elbows so that your hands will follow the movement of the horse's head as it jumps. Its mouth must *never* be pulled as it jumps.

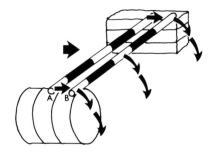

Figure 5.16 *When barrels or straw bales are used as jump supports do not put the pole in position A, the centre of the jump, but in position B, on the edge of the jump. A centrally placed pole can roll if hit and bring a horse down, but a pole placed on the edge will simply drop off the jump.*

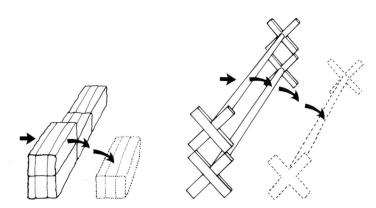

Figure 5.17 *Do not pile up straw bales or cavalletti when building jumps; if they are struck by the horse, they can tumble into its path and possibly make it trip or fall.*

Again, when approaching a fence do not allow your track into it to take you beyond the centre line of the fence or you will unbalance the horse.

You do not want your young horse to learn to run out or refuse and it will not if you plan carefully and think ahead all the time you are riding it.

At this stage keep the jumps small enough to jump from a standstill so that the horse will learn to go first time. Too many young horses (and older ones) develop the habit of stopping the first time then jumping the second time round. Do not overface the horse and thus teach it to stop at a fence. Keep your fences small and solid but inviting and encouraging.

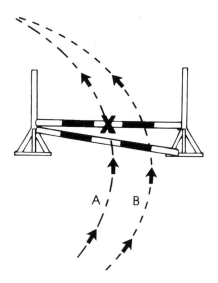

Figure 5.18 *Always aim for the centre when approaching a fence. Line A is correct with X marking the centre of the fence. Line B is incorrect; if a horse is allowed to wander away from the central approach it will become unbalanced and might learn to run out.*

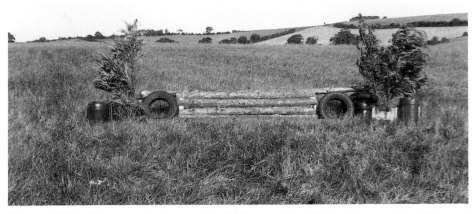

Figure 5.19 *Home-made jumps should be small, solid looking and inviting, and encourage the horse to look and jump centrally.*

Running Out

If the horse runs out to the left, correct it by turning it to the right, and vice versa.

Do not hit a young horse for refusing or running out. It will not understand why it has been hit and, in any case, it is usually the rider's fault at this stage. Have you asked too much too soon? If so, make the fence easier — anything to avoid a second refusal — you must encourage the horse to want to jump again. Your aim is to produce a horse that will jump any small fence calmly and confidently, wanting to go forward over its fences.

A horse usually runs out because:
1. The fence is not inviting enough — a good, big upright, or wings, to lead the horse's eye into the fence are necessary.
2. It has been asked to jump too high too soon.
3. It is frightened of a new fence.
4. The rider is nervous and is holding the horse back, communicating this fear to the horse through the reins.

In none of these cases will hitting the horse do anything but harm.

If the young horse refuses a small, inviting fence that it is used to jumping and the rider has put it at the fence in balance, at a suitable pace and with an allowing hand, the horse probably does want hitting, once, hard. This should happen, however, not as the horse is turning away from the fence (which will only confuse the horse), but as it is being ridden towards the fence and is four or five strides from it. If you hit the horse any further away from the fence, it will have forgotten about it by the time it reaches the jump.

Figure 5.20 *A bad fence: it has no ground line, no uprights, is uninviting. A fence of this kind might encourage a horse to run out.*

If you hit a young horse any nearer than four strides from the fence, it will look and think back towards you as you hit it and may not have time to think forward towards the fence again and organise itself to jump it. In this case it will refuse again because it was not ready to jump, and this time, the refusal will be your fault, not that of the horse.

Anyone jumping a young horse must be an experienced and capable rider. They must have a secure seat, independent of the reins, and must have a sense of rhythm and stride and an allowing hand. They must not be even the slightest bit apprehensive about jumping the youngster. If you do not come up to these high standards you should not jump young horses even over tiny jumps because a 'green' horse can suddenly leap four feet high over a one-foot fence.

Steady Progress

Do not do too much jumping on a young horse. A short session twice a week is enough, and six or eight jumps in each session are also enough as a young horse tires quickly and that is when it begins to land awkwardly or bang its legs out of carelessness. Change and vary your small fences as much as possible or the horse will soon become bored and careless. Always end on a good note, with the horse going well and enjoying the work.

Introduce doubles by putting jump stands and a pole on the ground 9.8 m (32 ft) − two non-jumping strides − before a small fence, then gradually build this up to make a small fence. Always make the first fence of a double slightly smaller than the second. Shorten the distance by approximately 61 cm (2 ft) when working indoors, in heavy going or uphill.

When your horse has been jumping doubles with distances of 9.8 m (32 ft) and 6.4 m (21 ft) − one non-jumping stride − calmly and confidently for several weeks, set up a grid which will eventually comprise three small fences approximately 3.6 m (12 ft) apart.

Begin with a small fence (approximately 45 cm [18 in] high) and place a single pole on the ground between a pair of jump stands 3−3.6 m (10−12 ft) in front of it. Come in at a steady canter a few times.

Change the pole into a small fence 45 cm (18 in) high and place a single pole on the ground, between jump stands, about 3−3.6 m (10−12 ft) in front of it. Come in in canter again a few times, then change this pole into a jump of the same height as the other two.

Your horse must come in in canter as these fences are bounce distance apart − jump, land, jump, land, jump, land. You must come in with enough impulsion for the horse to be able to cope with three jumps one immediately after the other. If built up in this way, this exercise should give the horse confidence enough to cope with what is being asked of it. These three bounce jumps in quick succession will encourage the horse to round its back correctly and use its hocks.

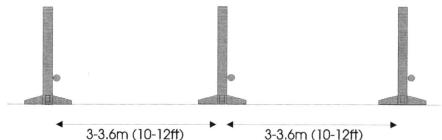

3-3.6m (10-12ft)   3-3.6m (10-12ft)

Figure 5.21 *Three small fences set at 'bounce' distance apart.*

If at any point the horse seems to be losing confidence, go back a step in your preparation for the exercise and do not try to complete it all on that day. Always finish on a good note.

BUILDING A JUMPING COURSE

Your course must be inviting and encouraging for a young horse. All the turns must be flowing curves. There must be plenty of room between fences so that if your horse becomes unbalanced, hurries or lands awkwardly, you will have room to ride a rebalancing and steadying circle before putting it at the next fence. The first fence should be towards home or towards other horses and should be low and simple.

If your horse lacks confidence, open any fillers and leave a gap to trot the horse through before you set off to jump the course with the fillers in place.

If the horse is a little unsure of doubles (and many are) ride a circle and come in on a curve to jump the second part of the double only. Then, when you jump both parts of the double, the horse will know the second part is

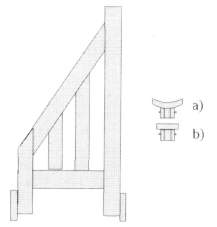

a)

b)

Figure 5.22 *A sensible jump stand with two types of jump cups. a) Shallow curved jump cups should be used for poles. b) Flat cups should be used for gates and planks.*

'safe', having already jumped it, and will be more likely to concentrate on the first part of the fence and jump it properly. Refusals at the first part of a double are very often caused by the young horse staring at the second fence for so long that it arrives at the first fence quite unready to jump. In the approach to a double, the horse needs time to look at the first fence, look at the second fence, then look at the first fence again and prepare to jump it.

A height of 46−61 cm (1½−2 ft) high is sufficient at first. All your fences should look solid and as if they need jumping properly. Flimsy, gappy fences encourage a young horse to be careless. Use upright wings, which will lead the horse's eye into the fence. The poles should be smooth and rounded and should rest in shallow, curved cups. Gates and planks should rest on flat cups from which they can be easily dislodged. All cups not in use should be removed from the uprights as they could prove dangerous to horse or rider.

A horse judges its take off from the ground line of the fence, so make this obvious to the horse, perhaps by placing a pole on the ground underneath the fence.

Figure 5.23 *A simple design for a good, solid home-made jump stand.*

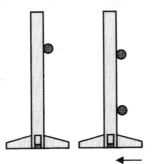

Figure 5.24 *An untrue parallel; the second rail is one hole higher than the first rail. This ensures that a young horse sees the second pole.*

At first do not make your spreads more than 61 cm (2 ft) wide and always use only a single pole to give the fence width so that the horse cannot get caught in a tangle of poles. Do not build a true parallel; make the second rail a hole higher so that the horse can see it clearly.

At first, set out a ground pole a little in front of a gate or planks. A young horse can easily take off too close to a true upright and lose confidence through hitting it.

Work in rising trot in a steady rhythm to encourage the horse to use its hocks and round its back. At first jump your double with a distance of 9.8 m (32 ft) between the two fences, which will give your horse more time to think it out.

Distances for Doubles

Horse at Trot
One non-jumping stride — 5.5 m (18 ft) to 6.4 m (21 ft)
Two non-jumping strides — 9.8 m (32 ft) to 11 m (36 ft)

Horse at Canter
One non-jumping stride — 7.32 m (24 ft) to 7.93 m (26 ft)
Two non-jumping strides — 10.36 m (34 ft) to 11 m (36 ft)

A shorter striding cobby type will be more comfortable with less distance between fences than a longer striding Thoroughbred type, so get an experienced person to advise and help you from the ground the first few times.

Jumping a Course in Trot

At first, jump a course in trot. Before you begin any jumping exercise, remember to take up your stirrups at least two holes shorter than you would ride on the flat and check your girth.

Look at the plan of the simple jumping course (Fig. 5.25). As you will approach and leave the first fence (1) on the right rein, your preparatory circle should also be on the right rein. Use this circle to get your horse going forward in a good rhythm, well balanced and with enough impulsion (bringing its hocks well underneath it to push itself forward). As you are circling right, have a little more weight in your right stirrup, think right and look right. Use half-halts, riding forward into your hands to steady and balance the horse, and when you are happy with the way the horse is going, trot in to fence No. 1. Sit quietly, with your upper body a little forward, ready to go with the horse.

Do not interfere with the horse as it approaches the fence, but if it seems hesitant in the approach, squeeze it forward in rhythm with its stride. If you kick and flap and wobble about on the horse's back in the approach, it will

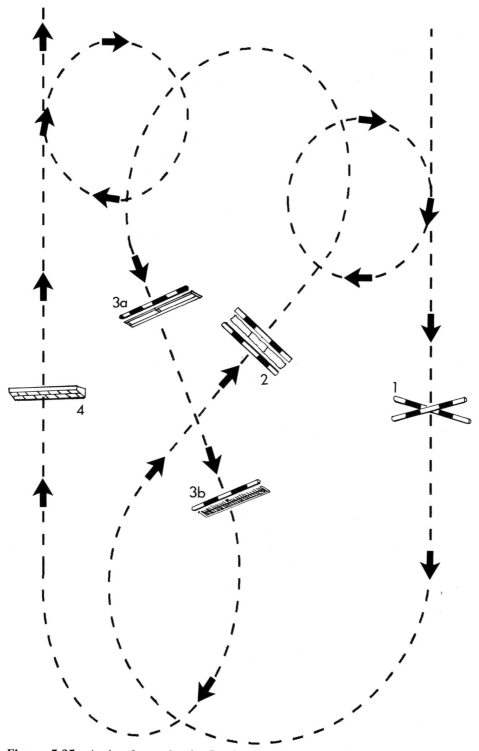

Figure 5.25 *A plan for a simple, flowing jumping course for a young horse.*

think back towards you instead of concentrating on and looking at the fence and it may well refuse for this reason.

Land after fence No. 1 with a little more weight in your right stirrup. Look right, think right, ride right and ride your horse forward into your hand using half-halts to steady and rebalance it through the turn and in your approach to fence No. 2. On landing after this fence you will be going left, so in the approach to this fence you must slowly and carefully move your weight more into your left stirrup as you ride your half-halts. Before the horse takes off at fence No. 2 you must be looking left and thinking left and be ready to ride onto a smooth curve to the left on landing. Your change of weight and thought must be so smooth and gradual that it does not in any way disturb the horse's balance or distract it from thinking forward.

Your third fence is the double, to be ridden on the left rein on the approach, so keep your weight a little more in your left stirrup and ride a smooth curve left, going out far enough for your horse to have plenty of time to see and think about the two fences in a row. Keep looking left at the two fences of the double and come in on a smooth curve so that, as you approach them, the centre of the first fence is exactly in line with the centre of the second fence. If you turn in too soon, the horse will see the first fence and then, directly after that in its line of vision, it will see the gap to the right of the second fence and will very likely follow this obvious track and run out to the right.

If you overshoot the correct line of approach, you will unbalance the horse by having to bring it back further left to get to the first fence, and you will also place the horse so that it will not see the second fence of the double but, instead, will see the gap to the left of that fence and, following its line of vision, will be likely to run out to the left. It is vitally important to line up the two fences of a double as you approach the fence in order to help a young horse to understand where you wish it to go and what you wish it to do.

You approach the first part of the double on the left rein, so you will have slightly more weight in your left stirrup, but you are going to curve to the right after the second part of the double. As you land after the first part of the double, transfer more weight smoothly into your right stirrup, look right, think right, ride right and ride forward smoothly and in rhythm with the stride to encourage the horse to jump the second part of the double.

Sit with more weight in your right stirrup, ride forward into your hands and use half-halts to prepare for fence No. 4. Keep your weight more in your right stirrup because, as you land, you must gently steady the horse in a smooth curve on to a circle right.

Slow down to a walk, give the horse a long rein, walk on past the entrance or other horses and then leave the jumping area. Never let the horse stop at the entrance or at other horses or it will make a habit of trying to do this.

It is better to ride the course in rising trot because the horse is more likely to remain calm and round its back to jump correctly than if you are in sitting trot. Also, it is easier in rising trot for you to feel the horse's rhythm and stay with the movement when the horse jumps.

If the horse lands in canter, do not pull back to slow it down. Instead, ride forward into your hands and use half-halts. Never jump a fence if your horse is unbalanced or too onward-bound. Use one or even two circles between fences to regain balance, rhythm and calmness before you proceed to the next fence.

If your horse refuses, try to work out why this has happened. Did something distract the horse so that it was not even looking at the fence when it got to it? Was it frightened and unsure of jumping? Did you do anything to upset the horse's balance or distract it and make it think back towards you instead of forwards to the fence in the approach? Did you jab it in the mouth at the previous fence?

Quietly ride a circle and squeeze the horse firmly in to the fence once more, allowing with your hands so that the horse feels that it can use its head and neck and has the freedom to jump. (It is far, far better to hold onto the mane or to a neck strap than to risk jabbing a horse in the mouth.)

If you have a second refusal, you must alter the fence and make it so low that the horse can, if necessary, get over from a standstill. Whatever happens, it must not be allowed to stop a third time. Circle it calmly and take it over the smaller fence two or three times until it is going smoothly and confidently. Only then should you think of putting the fence up to its original height and asking the horse to jump that.

If things go wrong, keep calm and make it easier for the horse. Do not have a fight or hit a young horse for refusing. It must like jumping. It must want to jump and it is up to you to think and plan ahead so that this does happen.

A young horse will often jump awkwardly and screw over it if it meets a fence incorrectly. If it thinks the fence looks spooky, it may jump higher than 1 m (3 ft) over a 45 cm (18 in) fence, so you must have a firm seat and supple body to cope with these variations. If you cannot do this, you should not be jumping a young horse, even over very low fences. If you are out of balance or in any way unstable on the horse's back, it will soon lose confidence in jumping and start to refuse or to rush to get this frightening moment over quickly.

Jumping a Course in Canter

When you jump a full course in canter you must change and use your weight in exactly the same way as described for jumping the course in trot.

Using the same jumping plan (Fig. 5.25), approach fence No. 1 in canter with the off fore leading and keep more weight in your right stirrup so that the horse will learn that this means you are going to continue on the right rein after landing. If your weight and balance are correct, the horse should not change leg in the air, but should land still on the off fore lead. In this case you can continue in canter, riding forward into your hand and using steadying half-halts to rebalance the horse ready for fence No. 2.

If, however, the horse does change legs in the air and lands with the near fore leading, you must not continue in canter and expect the horse to curve to the right or it will become very unbalanced and may even cross its forelegs and get into a real muddle. In this case, use half-halts and ride forward into trot, get a slight right bend and prepare your horse for canter with the off fore leading. Put your left leg behind the girth to ask for the first step of canter and your right leg on the girth to keep the horse going forward. As the horse becomes more educated, you will need only a few strides of trot before re-establishing the correct canter lead.

Fence No. 2 is approached in canter with the off fore leading, but as you are going to curve to the left on landing, you would like the horse to change legs in the air so that it will land with its near fore leading, ready for the left rein approach to fence No. 3. As you approach fence No. 2, smoothly move your weight into your left stirrup, look left, think left, bring your body slightly to the left and, as the horse takes off, give the canter aids for near fore leading (right leg behind the girth, left leg on the girth).

If the horse does change legs in the air and lands with its near fore leading, you can continue in canter. If it does not, ride half-halts once more, ride forward in trot, prepare and rebalance your horse and ask for canter with the near fore leading.

The horse should approach fence No. 3 (the double) in canter with its near fore leading. You must remain with your weight in your left stirrup and change your weight and balance smoothly between the two parts of the double, ready to give the canter aids for the off fore to lead as the horse takes off for the second part of the double. If the horse lands with the off fore leading, it will then be ready for the right-rein approach to fence No. 4.

If the horse changes legs over the first part of the double and is already leading with its off fore as you approach the second part, you must change your weight and balance smoothly to the right to coincide with the leg the horse is now on so that you will both be ready for the right-rein approach to fence No. 4.

On landing after fence No. 4, keep your weight more to the right and ride smoothly onto a circle to the right, using half-halts to ask for trot, then walk on a long rein and give a word of praise and a rub on the neck for a good round.

YOUR FIRST SHOWS

As a four-year-old, your horse can be taken to small shows to compete in show classes and minimus jumping. On your first visit to a show, lead the horse around to see the sights, wearing saddle, bridle, cavesson and lunge rein, so that you will have plenty of rein to hold the youngster with if it gets very excited. Keep away from the practice jump where dozens of ponies or horses will be belting up and down, because the youngster may become frightened and kick out. When the horse has settled, mount up and ride in the quieter areas of the showground.

I have always found it better to take a young horse to a show alone. If it goes with a companion, it invariably screams and yells to it and gets in a panic if they lose sight of each other. Then the horse will not concentrate when it is in the ring, because it is looking for its friend all the time. It is probably better just to ride about to see how your horse will react and not to compete on the first occasion.

Figure 5.26 *A four-year-old's first show. (above) The youngster is lunged on the showground to help it settle. (left) The horse is ridden round the showground to get used to the sights and sounds. (right) In the ring for its first class.*

If you are in a hunter class or show pony class for the first time, try to follow a quiet, sensible animal, give yourself plenty of room and keep well away from anything that is misbehaving. If you are asked to gallop in a hunter class, don't; just canter, as you do not wish your youngster to hot up and get overexcited on its first few outings. It is good manners to explain to the judge why you ignored the request to gallop – obviously, you will be penalised, but this does not matter at this stage.

If you are hoping to get placed in a show class, enter the ring between two not so good-looking horses and give yourself plenty of room between them. Keep your horse going in an even rhythm no matter what anyone else does. If someone is having a problem, pass them (if possible on the outside) and find another clear space for yourself where your horse can be seen and has room to show itself off.

Do not think the horse will point its toes more if you trot really fast, because it will only become unbalanced.

Do not change a young horse's bit simply because you are going to a show. If it normally goes well and happily in a snaffle, ride it in its usual bit. Many young horses are upset and spoilt by having a pelham or double bridle put on too early and without enough preparation at home first, just for the sake of a show.

Cantering a Figure of Eight with a Simple Change Through Trot

Always ride your preparation circle in trot on the same rein that you intend to ride your first canter circle. Choose the rein on which your horse goes best for your first circle.

Remind yourself of the diagonal aids for canter. (Put your weight a little more onto the inside seat bone. Bend the horse in the direction it will be cantering, asking for the bend with your inside rein. Keep your inside leg on the girth and use your outside leg behind the girth to ask for the first step of canter.)

First impressions are very important. Think of your figure of eight as having a 'straight' middle (i.e. two circles with a straight line where they meet). As you approach the straight piece towards the end of your first canter circle, ride several half-halts to bring your horse's centre of gravity further back and so lighten its forehand in preparation for coming into a trot that is as collected as possible. Straighten the horse, think of keeping the trot short and balanced, change your weight and change your leg position. Do not rush. Get the new bend in the horse before asking for canter on the other rein.

Again, at the end of the canter circle, ride half-halts so that your horse will come into a light, balanced trot on completing the figure of eight.

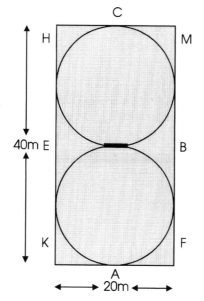

Figure 5.27 *Figure of eight showing the straight section where the circles meet.*

Running up in Hand

If the class is asked to take their saddles off and run their horses up in hand, give your horse a quick brush and polish with a stable rubber to remove any saddle marks. Take the reins over the horse's head and lead from the near side. Hold both reins in your right hand, knuckles upwards, and with the reins divided by your fingers so that you can use each rein independently to guide the horse by turning your hand to the left or right. Have your right hand at least 30 cm (12 in) from the horse's mouth so that the horse can move freely. Carry your showing cane (more correct than a whip in showing classes) and the free end of your reins in your left hand.

When it is your turn to bring your horse out in front of the judge, walk briskly out and stand your horse sideways on to the judge, at least 3 m (3⅓ yd) away so that the judge can stand back and look at the picture of the whole horse. As you walk the horse forward and prepare to halt in front of the judge, watch the horse's legs and try to halt so that the foreleg nearest to the judge is a little further forward than the other foreleg, and the hind leg nearest to the judge is a little further back than the other hind leg, so that the judge can see the horse's 'longer' side.

If this does not work out quite right, stand in front of the horse and push it back a step to correct it. Remain standing in front of the horse unless it is very nervous, in which case you should stand a little to one side. Offer the horse a small titbit, holding your hand up and a little in towards its chest so that it will keep its head up, arch its neck and look its best.

Watch the judge, who should look at the back of the horse next. As the judge moves round to look at the off side, quickly push the horse back a step so that you are again showing the judge the 'longer' side of the horse.

Next, you will probably be asked to walk the horse away from the judge and trot back. Walk *directly* away from the judge and turn the horse round at walk by pushing its head away from you so that you have to walk round the horse, not the horse round you. Choose level ground, use your vocal aid for trot and run briskly, level with your horse's shoulder, straight back towards the judge and straight on past when he or she moves sideways out of the way. The judge will then stand behind the horse to see its back view at trot.

Walk back to your place and put the saddle on again. In case the judge wishes to ride the horses in the show class, ensure that your stirrup leathers will lengthen sufficiently for long legs, and that the stirrup irons are big enough to take a man's foot.

Jumping

If the minimus jumping course is fairly solid and well built in a decent-sized ring, with room between the fences, it could well be an ideal school. (If it is a flimsy course in a small ring it will do more harm than good.) Your horse will have no idea why it has gone into the ring and will not be concentrating, so choose a low course that can be jumped almost from a standstill if necessary. It is a good idea to ask permission to jump two consecutive rounds without leaving the ring as in the first round the youngster will be looking at the crowd, watching other horses outside the ring and just not thinking, whereas in the second round it may begin to look at, and concentrate on, the jumps and might go quite well.

Aim for calm, clear rounds; do not be tempted to do too much too soon because the horse is going well. Jumps off against the clock are not for you yet. Do not take a young pony into 'Chase me Charlie' jumping, where the competitors follow each other round, jumping one fence that is raised each time. This is how ponies learn to rush, stop or run out. Do not enter pair jumping classes when you have to ride side by side with a partner. Youngsters find another animal beside them alarming and distracting. They will often run out because they feel there is not enough room for them. By all means go in a pair if your youngster needs confidence, but get your partner to give you a lead by going on in front of you.

Do not enter one class in the morning and another in the afternoon or the horse may become bored by waiting about and be tired or stroppy by the time your second class begins. Two classes are quite enough at this stage and, if possible, these should be fairly close in time and within an hour or so of your arrival at the show. Remember that several short days out are better than one long one, especially if you have a long drive home.

Do not feel you must compete in a class just because you have entered for it. Use your own judgement. If your horse is very excited about being in this new environment, it may become unmanageable in the ring when other horses begin to canter. This experience will do it more harm than good, so be guided by your horse's behaviour on the day.

Remember that you are trying to give your horse experience, and winning is not important at this point. Concentrate on producing a youngster that behaves itself at shows, knows what it is supposed to do in the ring and honestly tries its best.

A day out is tiring mentally and physically so give your horse a rest or an easy time the next day after trotting it up to check for stiffness or lameness.

Plaiting Up

You must pull your young horse's mane (see page 139) to an even length and thickness before you can make neat plaits. There should be an odd number of plaits down the off side of the horse's neck (normally nine, seven or eleven), the single plait in the forelock making it an even number.

Look at your horse with a critical eye. Has it got a short, thick, fat neck? If so, you should put in eleven long plaits about 5–7.5 cm (2–3 in) long. The large number of plaits will make the neck seem longer and long plaits will help to disguise the thickness of the neck.

a)

b)

Figure 5.28 *Plaiting the mane to make the horse's neck look thicker or thinner. a) A greater number of longer plaits to disguise a short thick neck. b) Fewer plaits set in 'racing knobs' on top of the neck give the neck more height and depth.*

If your horse has a long, thin neck, put in seven or nine rolled plaits (racing knobs) to make it seem shorter. Before you begin to plait each section on a thin neck, lift the hair up a little to make the neck appear deeper. When you have plaited to the end of each section, roll it under into a round knob and set these knobs on top of the neck to give it more height and depth.

Having decided on the style that will suit your horse best, damp the mane with a water brush and divide it up into the required number of sections, all of equal thickness, and secure them with elastic bands.

Thread a blunt plaiting needle with doubled, strong thread the colour of your horse's mane and put a knot in the end. (If at any time you are not holding on firmly to this needle, do not put it in your mouth but pin it firmly to your shirt or top so that it cannot fall into your horse's bed. You will never find it if it does and it could prove very dangerous.)

Plait the first section to the end and double the end over twice. Stitch the end securely so that it is neat and the plait cannot unravel itself.

To make a long plait, double the plait under once and put the needle in under the plait to come out on top of it close to the neck and roots of the mane. Stitch a left loop and then a right loop to keep it all secure at the top and then stitch the plait together downwards, working so that the thread is hidden in the gaps between the three sections of hair. Finish off with several stitches out of sight under the end of the plait.

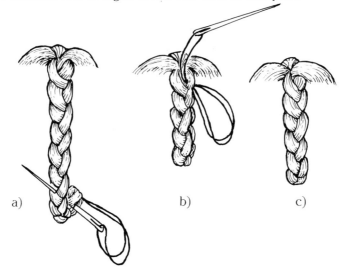

a)   b)   c)

Figure 5.29 *Making a long plait. a) Plait the first section to the end, double the end over twice and stitch the end securely. b) Double the plait under once and put the needle in under the plait to come out on top close to the neck. Stitch a left, then a right, loop to keep it secure. c) Stitch the plait together downwards with the thread hidden in the gaps between the three sections of hair. Finish off with several stitches under the end of the plait.*

To make a rolled plait to sit high on top of the neck, double the end over twice and stitch it securely as before. Now lift the plait upwards and roll it towards you into a neat ball, starting at the tip. Put in a few stitches as you go to hold it all in place. Finish off with a holding loop to the left and another to the right so that no wisps of hair will escape, and then put in some neat stitches underneath.

Undo your plaits carefully with scissors, taking care not to cut the hair. Do not leave plaits in overnight or they may irritate the horse and cause it to rub its mane badly.

Practise plaiting your youngster's mane so that the horse learns to stand still for you and so that you know how long it takes. This will make life easier for you and should prevent the horse from getting worked up as it may do if it is only ever plaited up before going out to do something 'exciting'.

I do not feel that it is really necessary to subject a young horse to having its tail plaited. A plaited tail for shows is not essential, and it is just one more thing for which the youngster has to stand still. If you wish to plait the tail, leave it until the horse is a little older and more experienced.

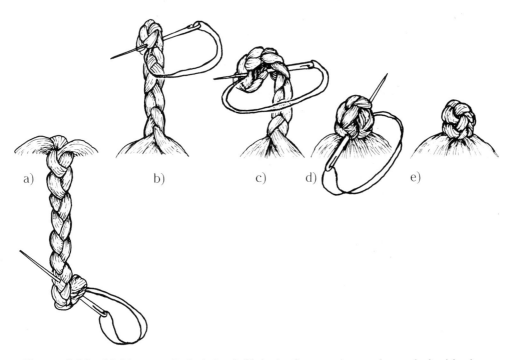

Figure 5.30 *Making a rolled plait. a) Plait the first section to the end, double the end over twice and stitch the end securely. b) and c) Lift the plait up rolling it towards you into a neat ball starting at the tip. d) Stitch a holding loop to the left and then to the right to secure hair. e) Finally, put in some neat stitches underneath.*

PONY CLUB OR RIDING CLUB RALLIES

Tell your instructor at the start of the rally that you have a young horse or pony that has never been to a rally before. If the horse feels tired, ask if you can get off and rest it and just watch the others. Two hours of going round and round is far too much for a youngster. Do not attempt anything more advanced than you have done before.

Riding Out

If you are riding out in a group, your youngster will be quieter if you keep up with the others than if you hold it back by itself where it will think it is being left behind. However, it is better to ride with one or two sensible friends than to join a rather wild group.

Choose your companions carefully. Ride with people who understand young horses who will give you plenty of warning before they change gait or direction and will ask you if you are ready before they do so. Otherwise, your young horse will soon think that merely shortening your reins means trot *now*. Make sure the other horses are good in traffic or yours may learn bad habits from them. Their pace and rhythm must suit your horse, because, if it has to bustle along to keep up with the others, it will become unbalanced and on its forehand.

When in a group, always trot until the horses are calm and settled before going forward into a steady canter, keeping an even rhythm. A horse rarely gets out of control suddenly. It usually gets into a longer and longer stride of canter first, so gently check your horse with the rhythm of *every* stride so that each stride stays the same length as the one before. Have your reins short enough before you *start* to canter, because, if you shorten them while cantering, you will lose the steadying rhythm and give the horse the opportunity to shoot forward fast. It is essential that the group you are riding with also keep a good steady, *controlled* canter rhythm. You cannot hold a youngster in a steady canter if everyone else takes off in a flying gallop. Discuss this beforehand with your companions and do not ride out with people who lose control in canter or who want to gallop.

YOUR YOUNGSTER'S FIRST DAY WITH HOUNDS

Cub-hunting

If at all possible, go cub-hunting first to give your horse an introduction to hunting, and have a friend on a quiet, experienced hunter with you. Hack on or unbox some way from the meet to give the youngster a chance to settle down. At first, keep it walking on a circle and then, as it settles, ask it to stand still for short periods. Remember that a young horse may kick or strike out at hounds out of fright, so keep your distance from them. Other horses coming up behind you, or throwing up mud as they canter past, may upset your youngster. A green ribbon on your horse's tail will warn others that this is a 'green' young horse needing room and consideration. If your horse is liable to kick other horses out of bad temper, place a red ribbon on its tail.

Many people approach a gateway and then let their horses go full gallop as soon as they are through it. This encourages a horse to get overexcited and hot up before gateways. To avoid this, when you have gone through the gate, turn left or right and trot quietly until the horse has settled, then allow it to canter. *Never* gallop a young horse; at this stage it must not be allowed to find out it has a 'top gear'.

Even if you do not usually use a running martingale, it is probably a good idea to put one on the horse, but do get the horse used to it at home first. If the horse gets very excited, the martingale will help to keep its head in a more controllable position and you will also have a neckstrap to hold on to if you need one.

Hunting

Choose a quiet, mid-week day to take a young horse hunting. Avoid Saturdays and 'fashionable' meets if possible. Unfortunately, nowadays people out hunting on young horses are not shown very much thought or consideration by the rest of the field. The green ribbon on your horse's tail should help but, these days, many people do not seem to know what it means and allow their horses to tread on the heels of the horse in front. This behaviour soon teaches a young horse to kick in anticipation of having its heels trodden on, so, before this happens, politely tell the person behind you that you are on a young horse and ask them to give you plenty of room.

If you were unable to go cub-hunting, take your youngster out for the first time on the second half of the day's hunting. Ring the hunt secretary and ask permission to come out late, explaining why. There will be fewer people and any overfresh horses that might have upset your horse should have settled by now. Again, try to take a sensible horse for company. Ride out a little to one side of the 'field' so that your horse can see and hear without feeling surrounded. If hounds turn and want to come by quickly, turn your horse's quarters away from them and close to a hedge if possible, so that no hounds can go behind you and get kicked. Play with the reins a little, moving the bit in the horse's mouth to distract it and prevent it from striking out at them in front.

When jumping, get in behind (but not *too* close to) an experienced horse that you know will go. Allow your horse to see the jump. Do not jump nasty, trappy places or overgrown ditches where the youngster may frighten itself.

Give it confidence in itself and in you by putting it only at sensible fences, and do this at the speed and angle of approach that are easiest for it to cope with.

Hunting is hard work, especially if it is muddy, so only keep your horse out for a short time — little and often is ideal. Many youngsters will have done enough by the Christmas of their first season's hunting, so it is a good idea to give them only a trace or blanket clip so that they can then be roughed off for a rest.

RIDING CROSS COUNTRY OR AT HUNTER TRIALS

Where possible, practise at home over ditches, small hedges, rails and pallets, all of which you may find on a cross-country course. Practise jumping up and down hills and at angles. Practise small doubles at angles or with sharp turns in or out. If you have nothing suitable at home, many people will let you hire their fences for an hour's schooling. Always walk round and look at the fences before you try to ride them.

Never jump when you are alone. Always have someone with you to advise you and help if there should be an accident.

To begin with, get the horse going in a good rhythm in trot, and jump just one fence at a time from trot. Walk between fences so that the horse remains calm. You may need to jump a fence two or three times before your horse goes calmly and confidently.

Figure 5.31 *The author at Everdon Horse Trials, sitting in balance, allowing the horse freedom to use its head and neck while retaining a contact on its mouth, and looking ahead to the next fence.*

If any fences seem a little too demanding for your horse, miss them out. The horse must want to jump. It must be looking and thinking forwards and wishing to go and it is up to you to plan and ride so that the horse enjoys the work and is calm and confident.

If all has gone well so far and you feel the horse is ready, jump four or five fences one after the other, always being ready to circle wherever necessary to steady and rebalance the horse, or to revert to walk if the horse becomes excited. Some fences can be jumped from canter but you should still trot into the trickier ones so that the horse has more time to think and organise its legs.

Remember that if you are jumping uphill you must ride on more so that the horse has enough impulsion to make the extra effort necessary to jump.

Going downhill, steady the horse in the approach but allow with your hands soon enough so that the horse feels you are going to let it use its head and neck when jumping. At this stage the horse should learn just to 'pop' over a downhill fence. Most horses will tackle a drop (without a fence) from one level to another with no problems, but all drop fences worry inexperienced riders. If you dislike, or are nervous about, any fence, do not attempt to jump it on your young horse. The horse will sense your nervousness in the approach and will be very likely to refuse. You must be 100 per cent certain that you want to get to the other side and that you and the horse are both capable of doing so. If you are in the least uncertain, the horse will know. A young horse needs a rider with experience and a confidence that it can feel to encourage it to undertake something new.

Figure 5.32 *Jumping confidently and happily across country. The rider is in balance, and maintaining contact while allowing the horse its head.*

Figure 5.33 *(left) Down the steps. The rider has slipped her reins to allow the horse to use its head and neck, but has maintained contact.*

Figure 5.34 *(right) Into the water. The horse jumps confidently into the water, and the rider slips her reins, but, again, maintains the contact.*

Figure 5.35 *Horse and rider working well together, with the horse showing complete confidence.*

You are holding your horse with legs and hands in just the same way that a mother will hold a child's hand. The child can tell from the feel of her hand whether the mother is tense and anxious or if she is feeling calm and encouraging, thus giving a feeling of safety and security to the child.

When you approach a hedge with a small ditch close to it on the landing side, you know that the ditch is there but the horse does not. You must ride on more at this type of fence so that the horse will clear the ditch easily. If you go so slowly that the horse drops a hind leg into the ditch, it will lose confidence in you and in jumping unknown places.

A ditch on the landing side should cause fewer problems than a ditch on the take-off side. On seeing the ditch at the last minute, many young horses will try to turn away from it. They may then slip sideways down into the ditch and really frighten themselves, quite possibly for life. A horse has a very long memory and its first impression of something new usually sticks.

Once a horse has stopped at a ditch before a fence it is extremely difficult to get it to go over because in the approach it will be looking to left or right in an attempt to avoid negotiating this (to the horse) very frightening obstacle. No horse will jump until you can get it to think and look ahead to the landing side of a fence, so school thoroughly over ditches by themselves until the horse is really confident. A pole directly over the ditch can then be introduced before attempting a ditch when riding to or away from a fence.

Remember that the terrain between fences will unbalance a horse if it is up- or downhill or if it is a bit boggy. The state of the take-off and landing must be considered. If it is deep and muddy, the horse has to make more effort to clear an obstacle and if the height of the obstacle is judged from the firm going below the mud from which the horse actually takes off, the fence may be considerably higher than it appears at first sight.

If it has rained after a dry spell, the ground may be slippery — greasy for the top centimetre but hard underneath. While your horse is still learning about cross-country work, do not put it in a position where it may experience problems or frights. At this stage your aim must be for the horse to gain confidence in itself and in you.

Some doubles are built at an angle so that there is more distance between the two elements at one side than the other. Think about this when you walk the course on foot. Stride the jump out and decide which distance, and thus which point for take-off and landing, will suit your horse best. Think of your approach and, if possible, choose an angle whereby the horse's eye is led from the first fence to the second and not to a gap to the left or right of the second fence.

When jumping a double the horse has to make two efforts fairly quickly, so you must approach the fence with more impulsion and, the second you land after the first part, you must ride on for the other part of the jump.

You must be experienced enough to get your distances right so that the horse will arrive at the second part of the double on the correct stride for an easy take-off. If the horse arrives at the second part totally wrong, say much too close to the fence, it may stop because it does not have the experience to reorganise its balance quickly and jump off its hocks.

A young horse coming in on a long stride may stand back and jump but is more likely to put in an extra, short stride which will bring it too close so that it may end up leaning forwards against the second element of the double, unable to jump it.

Practise doubles and distances at home with an experienced instructor. Work out and practise the distances and ways of approach that suit your horse best before trying to jump solid fences.

When riding cross-country fences, aim to ride in a steady rhythm, teaching your horse to lengthen and shorten its stride when asked, according to the terrain, the going and the type of obstacle at which you are riding.

At your first competition, or if you are schooling in the company of other horses, you may find that one of the most difficult things is to get the horse to forget about the other horses and look and think where it is going.

At first, when being asked to go over a jump in a fence, a young horse may think it is a barrier between fields, something it already understands, and may not realise at all that it is to be jumped. In the approach the horse will look to right and left and not forward and on. A lead from another horse is the easiest way to overcome this problem. The same method will give confidence to a horse that is frightened of ditches or water crossings.

If no other horse is available, many horses will follow a person on foot if that person first goes up to them, talks quietly and rubs and scratches them for a minute or two. The assistant must not lead the horse, however, as this

Figure 5.36 *A young horse being given a lead across country by a schoolmaster, and being given enough room to see the fence.*

will usually make it run back. The rider must ride the horse forward and encourage it to follow the person on foot. This person must realise that the horse may attempt to follow exactly where they go and land just where they are standing, believing that they have chosen the only safe spot!

Your horse must be fit before you take it round a cross-country course. A tired horse that is puffing hard will become uncoordinated and will make mistakes. If you can feel this happening, retire and walk back.

Competing in a Pairs Class

Many competitions begin with this class to encourage young horses or novice riders. By all means take your young horse round, if possible choosing as a companion a horse that is known to yours, but never attempt to keep level or to jump abreast. A young horse is often distracted by another horse beside it. It can also be frightened by the proximity of another horse in the approach to a fence and over it and may stop or run out to avoid the horse when it would not normally do this.

In a pairs round, always make a young horse follow in single file, allowing a four- to six-horse length gap between you. Choose a lead horse that you know will never refuse, ridden by a rider who understands the way a young horse should be ridden round a small course.

A keen horse can soon become overexcited, strong and on its forehand going across country. If this even begins to happen, go back to trotting into one fence at a time and walking afterwards. Teach your horse to relax and walk on a long rein (see page 210) whenever you have finished doing anything exciting. Then, as soon as you drop your reins, the horse will know that the excitement is over. This is a very useful lesson and well worth the time you will need to spend perfecting it.

SCHOOLING

On the Bit

When a horse is 'on the bit' it is pushing itself forward from behind into the contact of your hands. Its back behind the saddle is slightly raised but soft and supple. Its neck is gently arched and its head is carried so that the front of its face is perpendicular to the ground and steady, with a soft lower jaw. The general overall impression should be of a convex arc, and the footfalls should be quiet, showing that there is no tension in the horse.

Possible faults are:
- The mouth opening through too much use of the rider's hands and not enough leg.
- Stiffness and tension in the rider, making the horse hollow its back and leave its hind legs out behind it.

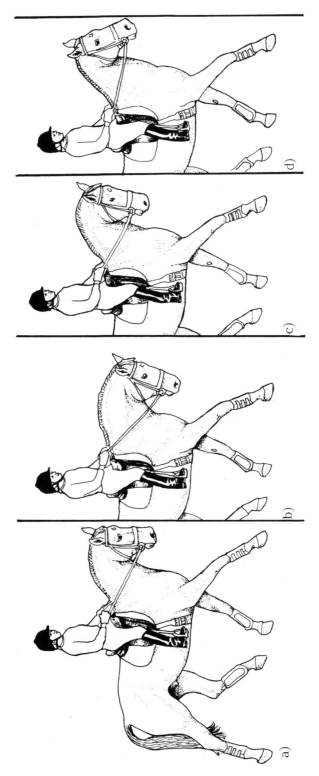

Figure 5.37 *a) On the bit. b) Overbent. c) Behind the bit. d) Above the bit.*

- Hollowing of the neck so that the horse comes up above the bit (caused by the two problems already outlined above).
- The horse is overbent. (The neck is arched and bent but the front of the face is behind the vertical and the head is carried low, often leaning on the rider's hands.) This is usually caused by the rider having a very strong contact on the reins so that the horse tries to avoid the discomfort in its mouth.
- The horse going behind the bit, with arched neck, the head fairly high and the front of the face behind the vertical, trying to avoid any contact with the bit. The more the rider tries to take a contact, the more the horse backs off from the bit. The horse is afraid of the contact of the bit in its mouth and tucks its head in more and more to avoid the pressure from it. This problem can be caused by too severe use of the hands, a sore, bruised mouth or too thin a bit for a sensitive mouth.
- If the horse is constantly tossing its head, reaching and diving with its head or carrying it crooked when the rider has a contact on the reins, it could be feeling pain from its teeth. This could be caused by pressure on the inside of the cheek from sharp edges on the outside of the teeth in the top jaw, by pressure of the tongue against sharp edges on the teeth on the inside of the lower jaw or pain from a wolf tooth (a small, extra tooth sometimes found in the top jaw just in front of the first molar).
- Pain could also be caused by a pinch of the lips, caught between the bit and the noseband if this is incorrectly fitted, i.e. too low.
- Carrying the head to one side can also be caused by a rider constantly sitting crooked.

Do not attempt to put a young horse on the bit unless you have taught several older horses to go on the bit and have the experience, tact and feel to know exactly what effect you are having on the horse. You must be capable of keeping your reins in a straight line and maintaining an even contact on the horse's mouth. It may be a good idea to have an experienced person on the ground to observe and help you if you are not absolutely sure of your capabilities.

Only ask a horse to come on the bit if it is going forward happily and freely in a rhythmical stride and is in balance and supple on both reins and happy in its mouth.

Ideally, work on a 20 m (22 yd) circle in rising trot and ride your horse forward into more contact on both reins. Do not pull the front end back to you; ride the hindquarters forward into slightly holding hands. There must be a straight line from your elbow through your forearm and hand to the horse's mouth. There must be no stiffness in your shoulders, elbows or wrists; these joints must feel 'oiled'. If you use both hands equally and just 'hold', the horse will tend to lean against you.

Get the horse correctly bent equally through its neck and body, and while riding it forward into your outside hand, make tiny movements of the bit with your inside hand by just feel, feel, feeling with the third finger of your inside hand as if you were saying 'Please, please, please give a little with your lower jaw'. These tiny movements, so slight that no one can see them, should prevent the horse from leaning, and encourage it to move and relax its lower jaw instead of setting against your hand. When you feel the horse give to your hand, ride forward with your legs a little more and keep a quiet contact on both reins. Your legs should now be riding the horse forward into your hands.

The horse will probably come above the bit (the most usual first reaction) after one or two strides. Quietly repeat the tiny movements with your inside hand and when the horse gives again (sometimes you will feel the horse nod its head slightly as it gives), ride forwards again into a quiet contact with both hands. Gradually, the horse should remain on the bit for more and more strides.

The reason for getting a horse on the bit in trot is that if you do it in walk you are very likely to shorten the horse's stride. If you have no success in trot, however, try in walk on a 20 cm (22 yd) circle, using exactly the same method but being very careful not to shorten the stride.

Your hands must definitely be there for the horse to give to, and then accept, the contact. The contact must not be strong, however, nor should you attempt to pull or hold the horse down onto the bit. When the horse will stay on the bit in walk for several minutes, try to keep it on the bit when you ride forwards, still on the circle, into rising trot. If the horse comes up off the bit, return to walk and begin again.

Work equally on both reins and allow the horse to rest and stretch its neck down by giving it a loose rein at walk between short periods of work (about 10 minutes). When the horse will happily stay on the bit in trot on a circle, you can try changing direction.

Allow plenty of time for straightening the horse and change your weight and the horse's bend very smoothly and with perfect co-ordination. Use half-halts and keep riding forwards. Think about and try to feel what is happening underneath you. Success is made up of a delicate balance between leg and hand and the 'feel' to enable you to know when a touch more leg or rein is necessary.

If the horse always comes above the bit in the change of direction, try this in walk first, then, when you succeed and the horse understands what you want it to do, work in rising trot again.

Next practise upward and downward transitions on the bit, using walk, trot and halt only. Establish circles and serpentines in these gaits plus staying on the bit through transitions, before you attempt canter on the bit.

In downward transitions, notice if you are stiffening your knees, pressing against the stirrups, stiffening your back, shoulders, elbows or wrists, or pushing down with your hands as you ask the horse to slow down. These are all very common faults and there are very few people who do not have a single one of them!

Any one of these faults will be noticed by the horse which will then be likely to hollow its back and come above the bit. It often helps to think of lifting your hands a little as you ride forwards in downward transitions in case you have unconsciously stiffened in some way, thus making the horse come above the bit.

Some horses naturally have a wet, soft mouth and will begin to froth at the mouth when worked in this way. Others may have less sensitive, drier mouths and be less responsive to your efforts. A Polo mint, tied to the centre of the bit by plaiting thread passed through the hole in the mint, can have a truly magical effect on this type of horse. (The thread is tied to the centre joint of a snaffle bit. The mint eventually dissolves and comes off the thread which remains tied to the joint of the bit. The thread is very short and causes no problems.)

Try to maintain an even, light contact on the horse's mouth. Only work for a few minutes at a stretch so that the horse does not become uncomfortable when using 'new' muscles. The horse must understand what you are asking it to do and be happy in its work. If there is resistance and resentment, you are probably tensing your fingers, wrist, elbow or shoulder on one or both sides and trying to pull the horse down onto the bit. Or it could be that you are going on for too long, perhaps becoming cross or rough because you are not succeeding.

Work equally on both reins but do not expect too much too soon. At first the horse will be on the bit for one stride, then two, three, four, five. Be very careful not to shorten the stride in walk. You must ride forward and think 'Walk on', and you must not allow your hands to drop below the line of elbow, hand, bit or you will be stiffening against the horse's mouth and so making it resist your hand.

Ten minutes' work at a time is sufficient at this stage, but it could be done twice a day.

Turns

Use an easy turn left across the BXE line of the arena or school to start with.

Work in walk on the left rein, on the bit, with the horse bent slightly to the left on corners. Just after F ride a half-halt (close your legs and ride forward into a very slightly holding hand; think 'Whoa!' for a second) to warn and prepare the horse, get its hocks under it a little more and lighten its forehand ready for the turn. Move your weight a little more into your left seat bone (think left knee forward). Think of pushing the horse out to the right a little by using your left leg, and so prevent the horse from falling in with its left shoulder. Your left rein asks for the left bend, your right rein controls the pace and the amount of bend in the neck (which should never be greater than the bend in the rest of the body). Your left leg is on the girth, riding the horse forward; your right leg is quiet behind the girth, controlling the quarters and helping to ensure that the hind legs follow in the tracks of the forelegs. Here, as in all riding, both legs should always be in contact with the horse's sides, ready to be used. You should be able to feel the warmth of the horse's sides coming through your boots.

As you approach X, your rein contact should be even and your leg pressure even and level. The horse should be straight and your weight should be equal on each seat bone. Ride a second half-halt. On the centre line prepare the horse for a change of direction to the right by changing your weight onto your right seat bone. Ride a third half-halt. Move your weight more into your right seat bone, begin to change your aids smoothly and with co-ordination – right rein asking for the bend, left rein controlling pace and bend in the neck, right leg riding the horse forward, left leg quiet behind the girth, controlling the quarters. Just before you come to your turn to the right onto the track, ride a fourth half-halt to ensure the horse uses its quarters through the turn and remains light in front.

As soon as possible, progress to the same exercise in trot.

Work in walk to start with because there is a great deal to do and think about in even a simple change of direction. The rider must learn to make all

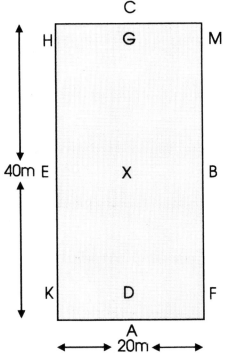

Figure 5.38 *A dressage arena.*

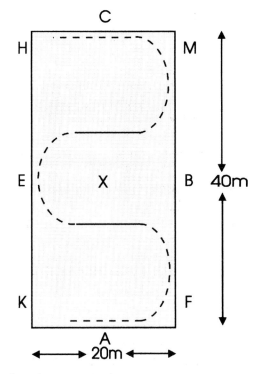

Figure 5.39 *A three-loop serpentine.*

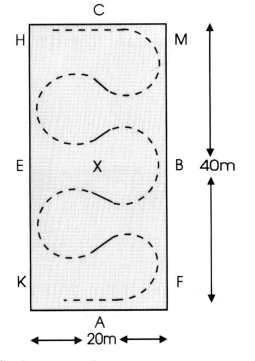

Figure 5.40 *A five-loop serpentine.*

these preparations and changes smoothly and with co-ordination so that the horse will learn to keep the same rhythm, be supple and stay on the bit throughout the movement.

Progress to serpentines and any other smooth, well-planned changes of direction you choose to use, always putting in the same preparation and co-ordinated change of aids. Think: 'Is the pace staying the same? Is the horse working from behind and really using its hocks? Are its ears often pricked, thinking forward and understanding my aids for changes of direction so that it carries them out smoothly?' Or, 'As I go across the centre line and approach the other side of the school, do its ears flick back and does its weight change from one side to the other and back again because it is becoming increasingly confused?' Its body should be straight and parallel with the short sides of the school as you cross the centre AC line.

Practise transitions up from the completion of a circle and transitions down onto a circle. This will help to keep the horse round and light in front by encouraging it to step under with its inside hind leg and lift the part of its back just behind the saddle. Lifting your inside hand slightly will encourage the horse to step under its body.

When cantering on the bit many horses start to lean and become un-balanced. Work on a circle of at least 20 m (22 yd) in diameter. If the horse leans on your hands, try cantering only 5 m (5½ yd) then trotting again, then canter 5 m (5½ yd) then trot. After a few minutes the horse will realise

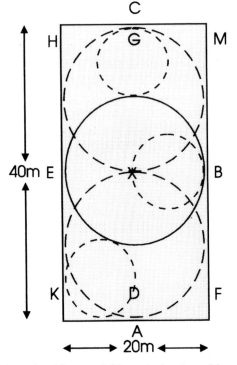

Figure 5.41 *Positions for 10 m and 20 m circles in a 20 m × 40 m arena.*

there is no point in getting on its forehand and leaning as it is going to trot again almost immediately, so, with any luck, it will keep its forehand light and its hocks under it, ready to trot again. If this works, gradually vary the number of strides of canter until the horse can cope with a full circle without leaning. Never hold on to the horse or it will lean even more and get even more on its forehand. The horse must learn to carry itself. Use frequent half-halts to keep the horse light in front and encourage it to keep its hocks under it.

Cantering with a slightly shorter stirrup and working on a circle with your weight out of the saddle can improve the ease and roundness of canter. No weight on the back helps to remove tension and stiffness. As the canter improves, very gently sit in the saddle again.

Cantering with your weight out of the saddle can also help a horse that is inclined to go disunited in canter. (With a disunited canter the horse's legs go out of sequence and the rider feels a sideways, rocking motion.)

If the horse constantly goes disunited and seems to find canter really difficult on one rein, it may have back trouble. Check this in rising trot. Does the horse feel the same on both diagonals? On one diagonal, instead of being thrown forward when rising, do you feel you are being thrown slightly sideways and does your seat seem to sink and drop to the opposite side as it goes down into the saddle? If so, the horse very probably has a painful problem and its back should be checked by the vet or an equine back specialist.

Other signs of possible back trouble are: the horse drags just one hind toe; it has difficulty turning in one direction and carries its hindquarters a little to the outside so that the hind legs are not travelling in the same track as the forelegs; and, a once willing, confident jumper, suddenly consistently refuses in the very last stride for no apparent reason.

Stand behind your horse when its hind legs are square and level and see if its projecting hip bones are at equal height and if the muscle on its hindquarters is equal on both sides. If you can see a difference, the horse's pelvis may be out of true. This can happen if a horse suddenly slips up sideways, twisting its back, when it is galloping and bucking in the field, for instance. It can also happen if the horse falls awkwardly, perhaps putting a foot in a hole or falling over a fence.

Leg Yielding

You must be able to ride this movement correctly on older horses and also have taught several older horses to leg yield before you try to teach leg yielding to a young horse.

Leg yielding is the most natural lateral movement for the horse because, when it shies at something, it naturally moves sideways away from the frightening object while still looking towards it and away from the direction of movement. When riding out, leg yielding is useful for moving the horse away from wire or holes or away from another horse that is about to kick yours. It can be used to move a horse over towards a gate so that you can open or shut it or to move a horse over onto the verge when traffic is coming up behind you on the road.

The movement helps to make the horse supple and active in the quarters. Leg yielding can be taught as soon as the horse will go forward freely, willingly and in a good rhythm on straight lines and big circles. The horse does not need to be collected. Its body should be straight and there should be just a very slight bend in the neck and head, away from the direction of the movement.

If your horse already understands about moving away from your leg and is fairly supple on turns and circles, leg yielding should be no problem. If you feel you need to use force or strength to try to make the horse perform the movement, you have not done enough early training on turns, circles and half-halts.

When ridden correctly, the horse should move forward and sideways with its body straight and parallel to the side of the school and a slight bend of the neck away from the direction of the movement (see Fig. 5.42).

At first a smooth, flowing forward and sideways movement with no change of rhythm is more important than keeping the body straight. Turn down the three-quarter line and ride forward and sideways towards the

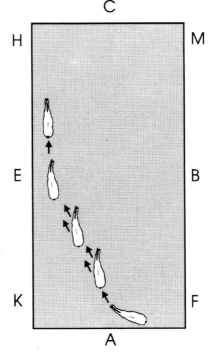

Figure 5.42   *Leg yielding.*

outside track (see Fig. 5.42). Progress gradually a few steps sideways then a few steps forward before you expect the horse to go in one long continuous movement of forward and sideways.

The horse's fore and hind legs cross over one in front of the other. It moves on two tracks, the forelegs on one track, the hind legs on the other track.

Use only a little inside hand to ask for the bend in the neck. Do not drop your hands as you ride forward into a half halt with your outside hand or the horse will think you are trying to stop the forward movement. Your horse must feel that at all times your hands are allowing some forward movement but just politely checking it for an instant before asking it to move sideways with your inside leg as the horse's inside hind begins a step. Your outside leg quietly controls the hindquarters and encourages the forward movement.

Think, 'Forward, half-halt and sideways' in a steady rhythm.

As you progress you can ask your horse to work towards and away from the sides of the school, giving it plenty of time to go straight before you change the bend and the direction of movement.

Get the movements correct at walk before progressing to working in trot.

Problems often occur because the rider's aids are too strong, so do less and you may have more success. Working from the three-quarter line towards the wall of the school or manège seems to draw the horse naturally in the direction you want to go. If you work so that the horse is going towards the entrance of the school, this will also encourage forward movement.

Leg yielding can also be ridden from a 10 m (11 yd) circle by spiralling outwards gradually, making the circle bigger while maintaining a very slight inward bend. Because you are on a circle there will be some bend in the horse's body too.

Do not do too much leg yielding because a horse can learn to move sideways and away from your leg in order to evade it and can begin to swing its hindquarters out on turns and circles so that its hind legs go out onto a wider track than its forelegs, rather than following in the same track.

Turn on the Forehand

This exercise develops feel and co-ordination in the rider. Most problems are caused by the rider giving aids that are too strong. Again, you must be able to ride this movement successfully on an older horse before you can attempt to teach it to a young horse.

Have your reins short enough to ride the movement. Ask for the first turn in the direction that the horse will want to go, i.e. towards home. The horse's forelegs should pick up and put down on the same small area; its hind legs should describe an arc round the forelegs, with one hind leg stepping in front of, and slightly across, the other. In a turn to the right the horse's head will bend slightly to the right but its quarters will move to the left.

Quarter-turns

Begin with a quarter-turn. Walk your horse straight towards a wall or solid fence and halt facing it. If you are going to do a quarter turn to the right, do not use your right rein or the horse will move its forehand. Very gently, steady the horse with your left rein (to stop the forehand from moving to the right). Very quietly and gently ask for a tiny right bend while continuing to steady the forehand with your left rein. Keep your left leg still on the girth and use your right leg behind the girth to ask the horse to move its hindquarters over to the left.

Your left leg controls the number of steps the horse takes and is ready to be used to ride the horse forward in walk as its body begins to come parallel with the wall or fence at the end of your quarter-turn. Using the leg nearer to the wall or fence to ride the horse forward helps to prevent the hindquarters from collapsing outwards and unbalancing the horse as it finishes the turn.

Take the movement very slowly, one step at a time, at first. Think about and try to feel what is happening underneath you. If you feel the front of the saddle lift up slightly or if the horse begins to raise its head, it is going to take a step forwards with a foreleg. As you feel this begin to happen, feel very gently on your left rein (which is controlling the forehand) to stop the horse stepping forward.

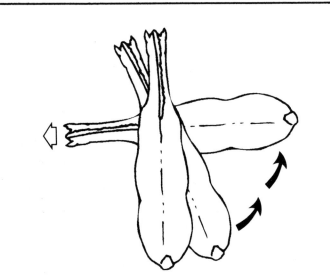

Figure 5.43   *Quarter-turn on the forehand.*

If you feel the back of the saddle lift more, the horse is going to step backwards, so very gently close both legs and fractionally ease your reins to prevent this from happening.

Aids that are too strong will make the horse go from stepping forward to stepping backwards and then getting really upset, so be very calm — just 'think' your aids and praise the slightest attempt to understand and obey you.

If you are having difficulties, an assistant can hold the bridle gently in their right hand to stop the horse from walking forward and, with their left hand just behind the girth, nudge the horse's hindquarters over away from them.

Half-turns

When the horse can do quarter-turns in both directions calmly and smoothly, you can begin to introduce half-turns.

This time halt parallel with the wall or fence but on an inside track to allow room for your horse's head to turn, and have a slight bend, towards the wall. The horse's hindquarters will move inwards, away from the wall.

Have your reins short enough before you begin. If you are going to do a half-turn to the left, steady the horse gently with the right rein and quietly ask for a slight left bend with your left rein. Keep your right leg quiet on the girth and, using your left leg behind the girth, nudge the horse's hindquarters over one step at a time.

When the horse is at right angles to the wall, it will instinctively want to step forward and left away from the wall it is now facing. Anticipate this and, as the horse begins to come at right angles with the wall, feel gently on your right rein to prevent it from stepping forwards.

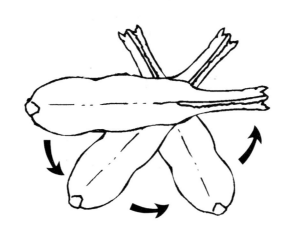

Figure 5.44 *Half-turn on the forehand.*

Think of the half-turn as two quarter-turns and take it slowly. As the horse completes the half-turn and the off (right) side of its body begins to come parallel with the wall, ride forward with your right leg.

Aim for slow, careful, 'thinking' turns. Only do a few in each schooling session and always end on a good note. Do not go grinding on and on hoping to get it better, because you will not − you will only upset and worry your horse. If the horse does become upset, this is a sign that you are asking for too much too soon or that your aids are too strong or too uncoordinated.

Turn on the Haunches

You should not attempt this movement on a young horse until you can do it calmly and successfully on an older horse.

This movement should really be done while maintaining the normal rhythm of walk but it is sometimes easier for you and the horse to go forward almost to halt and then take the movement very slowly to begin with.

Make your first turn in the direction that the horse wishes to go. The hind legs describe a small arc; the forelegs describe a larger arc around the hind legs, crossing one in front of the other.

Quarter-turns

Begin with a quarter-turn and, to make it easier for the horse to understand what you want it to do, ride towards a corner. To ride a quarter-turn to the left − the direction to which the horse's head will go − ride parallel to a

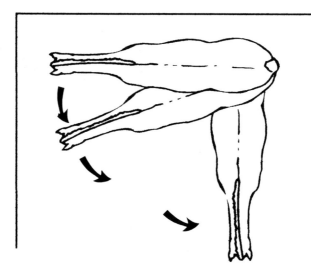

Figure 5.45 *Quarter-turn on the haunches.*

wall on the horse's off side. As its head approaches the corner, with the end wall straight in front of it, keep your left leg quiet and still on the girth and your right leg quiet and still behind the girth. Do not 'use' your legs actively, just feel that they are 'holding' the horse's hindquarters.

Put more weight into your left seat bone. Your right hand steadies the horse so that it will step forward only slightly, just enough to enable it to describe an arc with its hind legs. Your left hand asks for a very slight left bend.

The horse is asked to move its forehand in an arc to the left by a slight feel on the left rein and by slight pressure of the right rein on the off side of its neck. You must maintain a light hand and must think 'Up and over' with the forehand. Any stiffness in your hands, elbows or shoulders, or your hands held too low, will make the horse step backwards.

Work on quarter-turns in both directions.

Half-turns

When the horse is executing quarter-turns quite happily and in a regular rhythm in walk, half-turns can be introduced. With a half-turn, the forehand moves inwards, away from the wall.

Again, begin with a turn in the direction in which the horse will find easier.

Ride parallel to a wall in walk. Ride a gentle half-halt, thinking 'Whoa' for just an instant. For a right turn, the wall will be on your left, so, as you ride the half-halt, have your right leg on the girth and your left leg behind the girth, holding the horse's hindquarters, but do not use your legs actively.

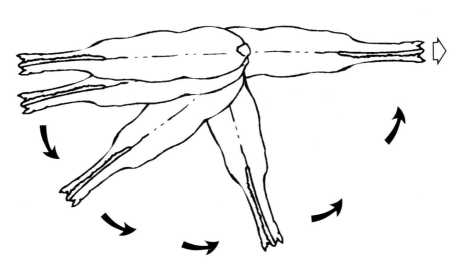

Figure 5.46 *Half-turn on the haunches.*

Gently steady the horse with your left rein and, also with the left rein, put slight pressure on the near side of the horse's, neck, while at the same time asking for a slight right bend with your right rein. Put more weight into your right seat bone and think 'Up and over' to the right with the forehand.

Aim to make the half-turns forward-going, calm and smooth and in the same rhythm of walk throughout the movement. Think of keeping the forehand light and of slightly lifting your hands to keep them light, so that the horse will be less likely to step backwards, which is the commonest problem in this movement.

Rein-Back

Teaching Rein-back

Your horse should already have learnt to go back in hand in its early training. If this has not been done you must teach it now by standing in front of the horse and pushing it back while using the vocal aid 'Back!'.

Once this has been learnt successfully, you can begin the mounted training.

At first you will need an assistant to stand in front of the horse as you, the rider, say 'Back!'. If the horse does not respond, the assistant can just touch alternate coronets with their toe to encourage the horse to pick its feet up.

Figure 5.47   *Rein-back in hand.*

Riding Rein-back

It is essential that you are able to ride rein-back properly on an older horse before you try to teach it to a youngster.

You must make sure that your reins are short enough before asking for rein-back. It is no good halting first and then reeling in the reins!

To make it easier for the horse to understand what you want it to do, work alongside a fence or wall and lay a pole on the ground about 1.5 m (5 ft) away from, and parallel to, the wall so that you are backing down a 'corridor'.

Ride forward into a normal halt but instead of easing your hands as the horse halts, maintain the contact, moving your fingers a little to ask the horse to step back. Do not use your legs; just hold them on the horse's side to keep it straight.

A horse must raise its back behind the saddle to take backward steps and it will find this easier if you sit lightly in the saddle, bringing your weight forward a little.

Two or three steps backwards are enough, then ride forward into an ordinary halt so that the horse will not learn to run back when it is only being asked to halt. If your young horse is inclined to run backwards as a form of disobedience, do not begin to teach rein-back at this stage, and always be very quick to give with your hands as the horse begins to halt.

Rein-back is in two-time, the legs moving in diagonal pairs as in trot. If you wish to rein back an accurate number of steps, close your legs and gently ride forwards as the horse begins to take the last backward step.

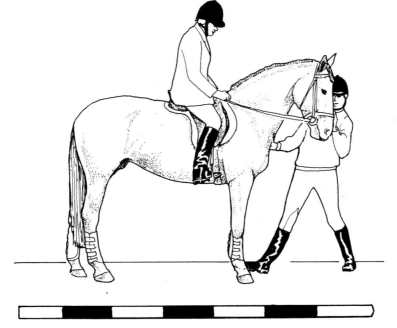

Figure 5.48 *Riding rein-back.*

TEACHING YOUR HORSE TO RELAX

As soon as your young horse will walk forward well and go in a straight line when you have a light contact on both sides of its mouth, you can start to teach it to walk straight and freely forward on a longer rein, stretching its neck gently and lowering its head a little as it does so. Your legs will keep the horse straight as you ride it 'on a long rein'. This term means that although both your reins are in a straight line, the horse is allowed to stretch its neck and lower its head as much as it wants to.

If your horse is calm and sensible, you can now teach it to walk 'on a loose rein'. This term means that the reins are hanging loosely and your only contact with the horse's mouth is through the weight of the rein. (Do not, however, have the reins so long and loose that there could be a danger of the horse getting a leg over them.)

If you train your horse to relax in this way and walk homewards on a long or loose rein, it will teach it to relax mentally. Horses ridden on a contact by a rider slightly holding them back often learn to fuss and jog on the way home.

Figure 5.49 *Teaching the horse to relax on a) a loose rein, and b) a long rein.*

Regularly walking home on a long or loose rein tells the horse that the more exciting part of its exercise is over and it can now relax, lengthen its neck, lower its head and swing along in an easy walk. This training will also relay the same message to the horse after cantering or jumping. Even an excitable animal will learn to respond to this training if it is done thoughtfully and consistently. It is very useful to be able to get a horse to 'switch off' when you want it to.

THE FIRST DRESSAGE TEST

Arrive in plenty of time so that you can ride about quietly and settle the horse down before you attempt to put it on the bit and work it in. There is absolutely no point in starting to do this until the horse has settled and will listen to you. Until you know how your youngster will behave, it is difficult to judge how much work it will need before the test. The horse must be quiet enough to respond to your aids, yet cheerful enough to go forward freely in the test.

In your practices at home, do not ride straight through the test many times or the horse will learn it by heart and start to anticipate the movements. Work on individual movements, out of sequence, to keep the horse attentive.

At home, whether schooling or out on exercise, always work the horse in a rhythm so that eventually you will almost be able to hear a metronome when you ride it.

Remember that first impressions are important, so practise a straight entrance up the centre line, using half-halts to prepare for your square halt. Do not hurry. Halt, wait, salute, wait. Move off. Half-halt before you turn at C, warning the horse in plenty of time, so that it knows in which direction it is going to turn. Prepare for the correct bend in plenty of time. Ride forward through the turn and immediately half-halt again because the next turn (at the corner) comes up very quickly. Ride the horse through this, then use another half-halt, because all horses tend to quicken and get on their forehand on the long side of the school. Prepare for changes of gait and direction early enough; be certain you have the correct bend on all circles and corners. Be accurate on your markers, having learnt at home how far before each marker you need to prepare and warn the horse in order that the transition will be exact.

Find out whether your youngster goes better in sitting or rising trot. Sometimes it is easier to ride up the centre line at the beginning and end of the test in sitting trot. Because you are closer to the horse, you then have more control and can keep it straight. A 'wavy' entry gives a bad first impression. For the rest of the test, the horse may be 'rounder' and easier to keep on the bit in rising trot.

Remember your half-halts before and after every change of gait and change of direction. Think well ahead so that you have plenty of time to prepare your horse and co-ordinate your aids smoothly.

Try not to tense up or your horse certainly will. If things go wrong, do not get cross or become rough with the horse or it will remember and, at the next test, worry and tense up even more. Expect only a little, stay calm and try to enjoy your ride.

Afterwards, read through the judges' marks and remarks and try to improve on the worst points in your schooling. Do not worry if you ride the same test under a different judge the next time and get worse marks — different judges do mark to a different standard. Remember, the more you worry or fume, the worse things will get. Be kind but definite in your requests when you ride your horse and do not school it if you are cross, tired or tense — go for a hack instead!

SECTION TWO

Working with
Young Horses

6 ASSESSING AND HANDLING YOUNGSTERS

Like people, horses are born with very varied characters and nervous reactions. Their intelligence and willingness to learn also vary. As you begin to handle your young horse, try to assess its character. Is it a bold and pushy type of horse prepared to use its strength to shoulder you out of its way? If so, it must learn to respect and listen to you, so, if necessary, give a jerk on the headcollar, which the horse will feel on its nose, or a thump with your fist just above the point of the front of its shoulder to emphasise your vocal commands when you ask it to stand still. If it still ignores you, a sharp rap with a stick on its nose may be needed. Always begin gently and only increase the force of your aid if the horse ignores your requests.

When handling any horse, but especially a young or stroppy one, be careful never to put your hand, fingers or thumb in such a position that they could be caught in the Ds or rings of the headcollar or lead rope if the horse should run backwards or forwards suddenly or even rear up. Never wrap the lead rope round your hand as this could break the bones in your hand if the horse pulls hard. You could even be dragged along the ground, unable to disentangle yourself from the rope if the horse took off. Wear gloves and a hard hat when leading, to avoid rope burns and head injuries from kicks. Wear strong footwear with a good heel so you will not slip.

You cannot proceed with any form of training until the horse will listen to your commands and understands what you are asking it to do. When giving vocal commands, do not chatter on to the horse or you will confuse it; use the words of command only. Halt and praise the horse frequently when you are first leading it in hand. A gentle voice and a scratch or rub on the neck or forehead are all that are needed.

Is your horse very nervous? A frightened horse is tense and its quick, nervous reaction is quite often the very opposite response to the command you have given. If this happens, do not shout at, or hit, the horse because it has not obeyed you. At this point its mind will be totally unreceptive through fear. You must have the patience to calm this horse and get it to relax and trust you before carefully and clearly repeating your request.

Reward good behaviour with gentle scratching on the shoulders, neck, withers or forehead and a quiet praising voice.

214

Does your horse like people and enjoy attention? A horse that always seems pleased to see you, pricking its ears and whickering as you approach, is a pleasure to own. It will enjoy the attention of handling and grooming. However, even a young horse of this trusting nature can be upset by being handled by several different people with varying voices and methods of working, so a nervous horse may never gain confidence in anyone if it is treated in this way.

Most horses are better handled and worked by only one person for the first few weeks. The constant repetition of the same voice and methods will help the horse to understand what that person wishes it to do, and will have a calming effect.

RESTRAINING AND TWITCHING
Restraining

The importance of training a horse to accept being tied up will be realised when you have to bathe, dress or bandage a wound, which may unavoidably hurt the horse. No person is strong enough to hold a horse that wants to get away from pain. If you know the horse will panic and fight the rope, it may well have to be held by someone. Passing the rope twice through a ring or round a post without actually tying the rope will give extra purchase but if the horse does run back be careful that your hands are not drawn into the tight part of the rope near the ring or post.

If the near foreleg is injured, your assistant should pick up the horse's off fore. Their left hand should hold the wall of the hoof near the toe and pull it up tightly, close to the horse's elbow, while their right hand holds the leg just above the knee and pushes downwards. If they put some of their weight against the horse's shoulder, this helps to keep the horse's weight on the near fore. The horse may try to hop forward, so your assistant must be prepared to hold on firmly and not release the leg.

If a hind leg is to be treated, the foreleg on the same side as the injured hind leg must be held up in the same way as described above.

The person treating the injury must stay close to the horse, facing towards the tail to avoid being kicked. Do not squat down low to treat a wound – it takes too long to get up or move out of harm's way. Bend as little as possible and keep your own legs as near to the horse's forelegs as you can. A horse can kick out behind but it can also bring its hind leg forward (cow kick) to hit you. Having brought it forward, the horse can then swing it out at you, so remember that the hind legs of a horse are dangerous and have a long reach!

Do not 'dab' at the injury. Hold the leg firmly with one hand and work gently but positively with the other. The hand holding the leg will feel the muscles contract and this will give you an 'early warning' signal if the horse is going to kick.

Figure 6.1 *Holding up a foreleg to restrain a horse when treating an injury on another of its limbs.*

Twitching

Never use a twitch unless you or your assistant are very experienced in using one. Sometimes simply holding the top lip in a firm hand grip and giving little twisting movements will be sufficient to distract the horse. Only when all else has failed and what you have to do to the horse is essential should you resort to a twitch.

The two most common forms are a round wooden stick about 76 cm (2½ ft) long with a hole at one end through which is threaded a piece of rope thicker than a pencil and about 25 cm (10 in) long in total. An assistant holds the horse and a second person puts their hand through the loop of rope and draws the top lip into it, being careful not to include the nostrils and also keeping their hand and fingers well clear of the rope.

The assistant then quickly twists the stick to tighten the rope on the top lip and holds the stick with their two hands well apart to give greater strength. If the horse tries to move, a quick little twisting movement of the hands − felt on the nose − may distract it. Do not let go of the twitch because a twitch attached to the nose of a panicking horse can damage you badly before it is shaken off.

The other form of twitch commonly used is made of two bars of metal or wood, about 45 cm (18 in) long and hinged together at one end, which can be closed by means of a strap or a piece of cord at the other end. The top

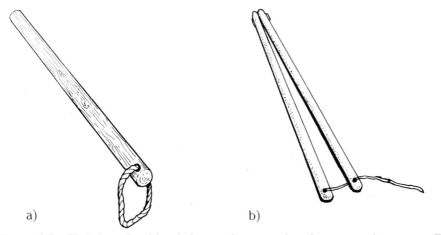

a)   b)

Figure 6.2 *Twitches should only be used to restrain a horse as a last resort. The two most common forms are a) a wooden handle with a rope loop through which the upper lip is placed, the stick is then twisted to tighten the rope on the lip, and b) two bars of metal or wood, hinged at one end and closed by a strap or cord at the other end which tightens the twitch once the top lip has been placed between the two bars.*

lip is put between the two bars and they are then tightened on the lip by the strap or cord. This kind of twitch is less likely to damage the horse's lip and also less dangerous to work with.

Sometimes it is necessary to twitch a horse when an injury has to be treated. Some horses may also require twitching when being clipped. With a young horse, avoid this by not clipping the sensitive areas the first few times, then gradually attempt to get a little more hair off.

A horse that really objects to being shod may have to be twitched but this is often because not enough time and trouble were spent on teaching the horse to stand and have its feet picked up when it was young.

Try to avoid using a twitch if you can, but if you do have to use one, keep it on for as short a time as possible – just a few minutes. Try to regain the horse's confidence afterwards and get it used to having its lip and nose handled once more. Horses soon learn when the twitch is coming and will do almost anything to avoid it.

KICKING

If your young horse constantly threatens to kick you when you approach it, it may retain bad memories from its past. A horse can react differently to the approach of a man or a woman. Very many horses, and ponies in particular, are really frightened of men. They may have been very roughly handled by them at some time, perhaps having been hit, shouted at, chased or treated brutally when being loaded. Vets are still more likely to be men than women, so the pain and fright caused by castration or injections will be associated with men. Most women are quieter, more patient and less bullying with horses than men tend to be.

When approached aggressively, some people will fight back; others will retreat and only attempt to defend themselves if cornered. The same is true of horses, but very few horses are born with a trait of aggressiveness towards people. Usually, harsh treatment is the start of this behaviour.

Has your horse learnt to be aggressive, does it actually dislike being handled? With ears laid back will it sometimes make the first move and reverse towards you intending to kick you before you have even begun to approach it, or threaten you by making little dives at you? Does it, again with ears laid back, nip or turn its back on you, present its hindquarters and threaten to kick?

There can be two reasons for this behaviour. The first is aggression. An aggressive horse is trying to frighten you and, if it succeeds, can easily learn to dominate you, so you must not step back away from the horse if it comes at you, nor show fear in any way. If you are nervous, the horse will know and take advantage of this fact, so it is far better to admit your feelings at once and decide that this is not the horse for you. If you continue with this type of horse when you are afraid of it, the situation will only get worse. If taken over by an experienced person who is very calm and confident and whose voice and manner instantly command respect, this same horse may give no more trouble. The characteristic will remain, however, and if at a later date this same horse is handled again by a nervous, ineffective person, it may well try to dominate them once more.

The second reason for this behaviour is fear. The frightened horse is not going to attack you. It is just trying to keep you at what it considers to be a safe distance. It presents its hindquarters and threatens to kick but very rarely lays its ears back. It is protecting itself, not attacking. With this sort of horse you must make yourself seem less threatening, so turn sideways on to the horse; do not look it in the eye; droop your shoulders; bend down lower; look submissive.

Do not approach the horse. Talk quietly to it and carry some delicious-smelling food in a bowl or in your hand. Wait for the horse to approach you and keep very still when it does eventually come up to you. Allow it to sniff you to reassure itself that you are not a danger. Let the horse make all the advances, gradually allowing you to stroke and handle it. Position a small feed and some hay in such a way that the horse has to come right up to you to reach them and will thus gain in confidence.

It is better to leave a headcollar on a horse that is very nervous in the stable. Always go in with some titbits in your hand and wait for the horse to come to you. Do not grab at the headcollar; gently slip your hand onto it and take a feel, not a pull. As many times as possible each day, attach a rope to the head collar and tie the horse up so that you can handle it, gradually becoming less gentle but always being careful not to frighten the horse. As it gains confidence, dispense with the titbits.

It is absolutely essential for a nervous horse to be brought into, or kept in, the same stable to ensure it feels safe there. Likewise, it should only be handled by one person so that it will have confidence in them. New people must be introduced gradually when the horse is tied up nearby or is held by its normal handler. Keep children and dogs well away from it.

Does your horse accept you when you handle it briefly and efficiently but show signs of bad temper if you caress it or make a fuss of it? Many mares fall into this category. They seem to be thinking. 'Do the job if you must, but get on with it and don't mess me about!' Respect their wishes and behave accordingly. This type of horse must allow you to do the essentials, though. For instance, if it does not want its legs brushed, you must tie it up and, using just your hand at first, then a soft brush, work on the shoulder before moving down the forelegs. Keep your hand or the brush in contact with the horse whatever it does, until it learns to accept this. (Obviously, you should begin with the forelegs for reasons of your own safety.)

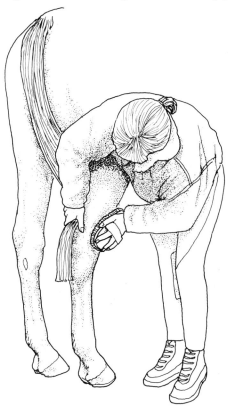

Figure 6.3 *Holding the tail in the hand nearest the horse, and placing the hand just above the hock when brushing a horse's hind leg will enable you to feel an 'early warning signal' if the horse is about to kick.*

When the horse accepts the brush in front, start on the hind legs in the same way. Stand sideways on to the horse, facing the rear, with your back towards its head. Keep your shoulder and side close to the horse's side. Stay as near to its shoulder as you can, only going just near enough to the hind leg to enable you to reach it. In this position you are much less likely to get kicked.

Never, never approach any horse, particularly a young horse, from the rear and bend down facing its head to handle a hind leg or pick up a hind foot. In this position you make a perfect target if the horse should kick.

Start handling or brushing the hindquarters first before the leg. As you move lower down the leg, have your free hand on the hindquarters in order to feel if the horse's muscles tense up in preparation for a kick. If the horse does try to kick, stay very close to it and step towards its shoulder. In this position you will be out of kicking range even if the horse 'cow kicks' (kicks forward under its belly). You can then quickly restart brushing the hind-quarters again before trying to brush the hind legs once more. Revert to using only your empty hand, if necessary, so that the horse at least accepts something touching the legs.

Another 'early warning signal' that the horse is going to kick is found just above the back of the hock. With your back towards the horse's head, hold the hair of the tail in the hand that is nearer to the horse and rest this hand just above the back of the hock. Use the other hand to brush the horse's leg. If the horse even thinks about lifting that leg to kick, you will feel the movement of the tail and the contraction of the muscles in the leg.

If the horse is only going to pick its leg up in protest, the movement that you feel will be small and you can quietly keep hold until the leg is put down again. If, however, the movement is very strong, the second's warning that this gives you will allow you time to move quickly towards, and close to, the horse's shoulder to avoid the kick.

If, at any time when you are grooming, the horse tries to swing its hindquarters quickly towards you, do not step out past them to get away from the horse or you will put yourself in a perfect position to get kicked. Instead, step towards the shoulder, keeping really close to the horse and resume grooming immediately.

SENSITIVE AREAS

Learn which spots are your horse's tickly places. The most common ones are the elbows, round the girth area, up between the forelegs, the stifle, the flanks, up inside the hind legs, under the stomach, under the dock, the sheath with geldings and the udder with mares. When you acquire a new horse, especially a young one, avoid these places at first, then gradually handle them one at a time, noting and memorising your horse's reaction

Figure 6.4 *Sensitive areas: the chest region between the forelegs; elbows; round the girth area; stomach, sheath/udder; stifle; inside the hind legs; flanks; dock.*

to each one. Use your empty hands at first, applying them firmly and rhythmically, then a soft brush. Do not dab tentatively at the horse or it may think you are teasing it.

Many horses are nervous about having their ears touched, so gently rub and stroke them. Never attempt to restrain a horse by twitching an ear or even by holding on to an ear, or the horse may become head shy. Use only your hand or a soft brush on the face. At this stage the accent is mainly on handling rather than on grooming.

Always include picking out the feet, as this will help the farrier when the horse has to be shod. Initially, pick each foot up just a little way off the ground and for a very short time. Before you begin, make sure the horse is standing on level ground. Run your hand from the shoulder or quarters down to the foot and always use the same word of command each time, such as 'Up' or 'Lift', when you ask the horse to lift its feet. Push the horse's weight over onto the leg opposite to the one that you want to pick up. If the horse fights you, try not to let go but as soon as it is calm again, allow it to put the foot down. Let go of the foot gently.

As you lift each foot hold it near to the toe so that the horse will not try to lean on you. While you hold it, tap the wall first with the hoof pick and later the hoof, with a hammer, to prepare the horse for the feel of being shod. Always pick the feet up in the same order and eventually you will find that the horse lifts them almost without being asked.

Figure 6.5 *When picking out a youngster's feet do not lift the foot too high, and hold it near the toe so that the horse will not try to lean on you.*

BITING

There are several reasons for biting or nipping.

1. Aggression − when the horse dives at you and attacks you with ears laid back and mouth open. If you are going to succeed with this type of horse, you must show it you are not afraid of it and it must learn to respect you.

   You must slap it, once only, very hard on the nose, then move quickly as it may well whip round and lash out at you, whereupon you must hit it again, once only and very hard, on the quarters.

   Sometimes, having realised that you are not frightened of it, the horse will not continue with its attacks on you. It may now even be a little frightened of you. (**Warning**: this type of horse is *not* suitable for inexperienced people and only an experienced handler should try the tactics described above.)

   Now you have to encourage the horse to like you. Give it no food or water other than that which you offer it − over the stable door at first if necessary. Make sure you offer this frequently, especially water, but insist that the horse takes everything from you. As soon as possible, get a head collar on the horse with a short length of rope (about 46 cm [18 in]) hanging down that you can get hold of easily when the horse approaches you for food or water.

Always tie this sort of horse up really short when handling it. Reprimand it with one sharp slap on the nose if it tries to bite. If it continues to snap at you as you are trying to groom it, hold a metal curry comb out towards its nose all the time and let it bite at that while you continue grooming. This is an uncomfortable object to bite and because there will be no reaction from the curry comb, the horse will probably soon lose interest in it.

Figure 6.6 *When grooming a horse that bites, hold a metal curry comb out towards its nose and let it bite at that while you continue grooming.*

2. If you are handling ticklish or sensitive places thoughtlessly, you may cause an animal to nip or kick in protest.
3. If the horse has previously been fed too many titbits by hand − or is now being fed too many by you − when, for once, you do not bring anything for the horse, it may get cross and bite you. It is better not to feed titbits other than when catching a horse in the field, attempting to load it into a horse box or trailer or getting the confidence of a nervous horse. If it nips, tap it smartly on the nose, once.
4. Jealousy is another reason for nipping. If you are feeding another horse as you catch it in the field, you may be bitten by your own horse to get your attention. This is normal behaviour, but should still be discouraged with one sharp slap on the nose. You, of course, can try to avoid the situation by being tactful when catching one horse out of a group.

I have constantly said that you should hit the horse once only. This is because punishment must be quick and last only an instant. It must be a short, sharp shock to make the horse think. Beating a horse might relieve your irritation with it, but the reason for the beating will very rarely be understood by the horse which will only become confused and cross or frightened, according to its character, and you will have taken a backwards step in your relationship with the horse and in your ability to make it trust you.

Obviously you must take care that any horse that is apt to bite or nip should not take chunks out of unwary visitors, vets or farriers. If in doubt, use a plastic 'bucket' muzzle when the horse is being shod or handled by strangers. Accustom it gently and slowly to this new contraption, and realise that, if the horse is left in the muzzle, it is likely to try to rub it off and may get it caught up on any projecting fittings.

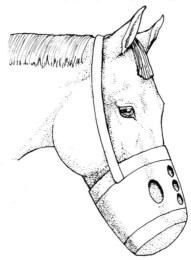

Figure 6.7 *A 'bucket' muzzle for a confirmed biter.*

CHEWING

Some young horses will chew everything that they can get hold of. The halter rope, lunge rein or bridle reins will be in their mouths in seconds and chewed through very quickly. Once, as I was slowly and carefully doing up its girth, a horse turned its head round and chewed through the offside stirrup leather, allowing the stirrup iron to fall to the ground!

For a persistent offender, the halter rope may need to be replaced by a smooth, fairly thick chain when tying the horse up. (A thin chain could damage the horse's mouth if it ran back while chewing it.)

I do not think that constantly hitting the horse for chewing is a good idea. It could make it jumpy or cross, depending on its temperament. Remove whatever it is chewing from its mouth, say 'No!' in a very cross voice and give a quick, sharp jerk on the noseband, head collar or cavesson so that the horse will feel discomfort on its nose.

Try to anticipate exactly when the horse will begin to chew and forestall its action by saying 'No!' when it starts to think about it. You will slow it down in this way, but given the opportunity many young horses will continue to chew, possibly up to the age of five.

A horse that chews and snatches at things can cause accidents by, for example, grabbing at the strap of a running martingale and getting this stuck across its mouth. If this happens, get off immediately, because the horse can very easily run back, lose its balance (its head being tied down by the strap across its jaw) and go over backwards on top of the rider.

If the horse is not in a panic and relaxes for a second, you can get the strap out of its mouth, otherwise you must undo the girth to slacken the tension and remove the strap in this way.

If the horse constantly snatches at the martingale straps, use a bib martingale, which has a solid piece of leather filling the normal V-shaped gap down between the two martingale rings.

Geldings have been known to snatch at a martingale strap and get one of the rings caught round a tush on their bottom jaw. (The tushes are teeth that grow in the gap between the molars and the incisors in the upper and lower jaws of male horses.) If this happens, dismount very quickly as the extreme pain caused by this can make the horse rear and fall over backwards. When the horse relaxes for a second, unhook the ring. If it does not relax, you must undo the girth first and free the pressure.

Horses that chew and snatch have even been known to grab at a stirrup left hanging down, getting it stuck in their mouths with disastrous results. Always run up your stirrup irons, even if you are standing holding the horse, and be aware of the accidents that can happen.

Some young horses will constantly try to get the lower cheek of a cheek snaffle bit in their mouths. If this is a problem, you must go back to using a ring snaffle.

Horses that chew and tear at rugs can be fitted with a head collar and bib attachment. This looks like a long plastic scoop which prevents the horse from getting hold of the rug in its teeth. Horses can drink in these, but cannot eat with a bib attachment on.

PAIN

It is very difficult for a horse to express aches and pains in a way that will enable its owner to recognise the problem.

Carrying the rider's weight, plus the unaccustomed pressure of saddlery, can cause strains, aches, rubs and bruises that often cannot be seen because they are covered by the horse's coat. Think how you might feel when carrying a heavy back pack or after moving bales of hay for several hours. You might be really stiff next day, as would a young horse when first being ridden.

Think of the rubs and pinches that a pair of new shoes have given you. The pressure of the saddle and girth can have the same effect on a young horse whose back and skin are not used to them. The sensitive skin at the corners of the mouth and over the bars inside the mouth can become painful too.

Watch for any change in your horse's reaction to being saddled, bridled, mounted or ridden and always, every day, check the areas I have mentioned for any sign of damage.

Feel the legs for any sign of heat or swelling. If the horse begins to go gingerly over stony ground, its soles may be bruised. If it is unshod, it will need shoeing to give it protection against the rough ground. If it has been shod already, it must be kept on softer ground as much as possible.

If the horse suddenly begins to eat less and to half chew a mouthful of hay before stopping and spitting some out (quidding), it may have sore gums from teething or some of its loose milk teeth may be uncomfortable. (You should be constantly aware of the stage of development of your youngster's teeth and be able to confirm your suspicions by checking its mouth — if in doubt, read the chart on page 237.) If this problem has not resolved itself within a few days, consult a vet, as it could be caused by the outside edge of sharp back teeth in the top jaw hurting the inside of the cheeks, even in a very young horse.

Head Shaking

If the horse suddenly begins to fuss with the bit or to toss its head when ridden, discomfort through teething is the most likely cause. Head tossing can become a habit, so it is better to rest the horse for a few days, or ride it in a small, enclosed area in a mild type of bitless bridle.

If the head tossing is caused by pain in the mouth, a tight martingale is not the answer and will only make matters worse as the horse will fight the additional pain caused by the restrictive action of the martingale. Bad habits can easily be formed at this stage.

Sometimes, at the beginning of summer, a horse will start to toss its head violently up and down when ridden. It may rub its nose on its knees or even on the ground. The head tossing may become so violent that the horse is unbalanced by it, and it may be more noticeable close to trees or hedges than in an open field. Fields of rape or beans in flower may produce a really violent bout of head tossing, always with an up and down movement, never sideways.

Horses that behave in this way suffer from an allergy and the head tossing will only occur between May and September. There seem to be two types of allergy. In one, the sensitive area inside the nostrils is affected by pollen. In the other, this area is affected by minute insects and this allergy will be most obvious when the horse is close to trees and hedges. Some horses are affected by both types.

In the autumn and winter, the horse will behave perfectly normally in every way but, unfortunately, the condition will recur every summer and if you wish to use your horse all summer, neither of you will have any pleasure. A fine-mesh net over the horse's nose or an antihistamine treatment from your vet may help in some cases. However, it is honestly better to sell a horse that has this allergic problem than suffer the constant frustrations and disappointments this condition will bring for you both. Someone who only wishes to hunter trial, hunt or hack through the autumn, winter and early spring months would have no such problems with a horse like this, although you might well find that the horse's selling value would reflect this problem.

Sideways head shaking is completely different and can be caused by something in the ear (the head may be carried tilted towards the uncomfortable ear, which may itself be held at an outward and downward angle), or, more usually by pressure from the bridle on the roots of the ears, a browband that is too tight, or a piece of hair being pulled by the bridle.

To recap, discomfort near the ears produces sideways shaking of the top of the head. Discomfort from the bit usually makes the horse put its head up and move its nose sideways. Allergic reaction in the nostrils makes the horse toss its head directly up and down, sometimes carrying it very high or very low for several seconds.

SIGNS OF TIREDNESS

Watch for signs of tiredness when you begin training your youngster. It is important that you do not work the young horse too long as muscle fatigue can lead to long-lasting problems in the future.

1. A horse that has previously had a normal or high head carriage and a willing, forward-going stride, begins to trail along with its head down and go slower than usual.
2. The horse may seem lethargic and may trip and stumble.
3. The horse may seem more unbalanced than usual and more difficult to ride in a straight line.
4. If your horse is getting tired it may start to 'brush' and actually go lame for a few strides if it hits the underside of its fetlock joint with the opposite shoe (see Fig. 8.10). There may even be a small cut on the fetlock joint. Brushing is more common behind and is most likely to occur when circling and schooling, in deep going, or when the horse is tired. Brushing in front is mostly caused by the faulty action of a horse which stands toes out.

It is no good *just* putting on brushing boots as the horse will continue to knock its joints through the boots and, because the boots stick out, will do so even more. The farrier must use corrective shoeing. The inside of the shoes can be set slightly under the hoof so that the hoof protrudes a little beyond the shoes. The inside of the shoes can be 'chamfered', (rounded off so there is no edge to catch the opposite joint) or a ¾ shoe (see Fig. 6.14) can be used. A feather-edged shoe which is narrow and rounded off on the inside may stop the horse brushing. This shoe has only one nail hole beyond the toe clip on the inside and often has an extra clip on the outside to prevent the shoe moving. Boots will still be needed to protect the joints.

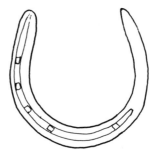

Figure 6.8 *A feather-edged shoe may stop a horse brushing.*

5. The horse may buff (knock the inside of the top of the hoof near the coronet with the opposite hoof or shoe, making a white line just below the coronet). This is also more common behind.
6. The horse may click or forge (both terms mean that the horse catches the toe of its front shoe, as it is picking the foreleg up, with the toe of the hind shoe, as the hind leg is going down).
7. The horse may drag its hind toes.

Figure 6.9 *Clicking or forging; the horse catches the toe of the front shoe with the toes of the hind shoe as it is picking the foreleg up.*

8. If the horse stands in the stable resting the diagonally opposite hind and forelegs at the same time, then shifting and resting the other two legs, the horse is 'leg weary'.

Note: 4, 5 and 6 above could also be happening because the horse has long feet and needs shoeing or because it is generally lazy and is being ridden in a slack or slovenly way.

A horse that has been in work for two or more weeks and is showing these symptoms is in need of a rest of at least two weeks and probably a month. However, if you simply turn out a jumpy, nervous horse and leave it in the field, it is likely to lose some of the confidence it had in you, so, continue to bring it in, handle it and lead it about quietly every day. A placid type will be quite all right left out but, of course, it should still be looked at and checked over each day.

There are no set rules for how long a young horse should be worked before it has a good rest. It depends entirely on the physical and mental state of the individual horse. If in doubt, ask the advice of an experienced person who saw the horse during its first few days of being ridden and will therefore be able to see if there is now a difference in its way of going.

A young horse is less likely to get tired if it is worked for two fifteen-minute periods a day rather than one longer one. Avoid going up or down steep hills but if you do come to one, dismount and lead the horse. Deep, muddy tracks or uneven going are trying for a young horse, as is being asked to travel along a straight, narrow wheel rut. Remember that even an older horse in a very narrow rut (less than 46 cm [18 in] wide) is likely to knock its fetlock joints continually with the opposite foot. A young horse may trip and, if unable to get its foot out of the rut and regain its balance, could very easily fall over.

LAMENESS

Remember to check your horse carefully the day after strenuous work. First note how the horse is standing when you enter its box. Is it standing square, with its weight evenly distributed on all four feet? Is it favouring one leg slightly? This means that there will be slightly less weight on one leg (forelegs always give more trouble than hind ones because they carry the weight and take the strain while the hind legs propel the horse forward). A bad leg may tremble slightly and if you tap it behind the knee, the horse will nearly fall because it has had very little weight on that leg.

A horse that is lame in front drops its weight more heavily onto its sound foreleg so it appears to nod its head down as the sound foreleg goes to the ground and raise it slightly as the lame leg goes to the ground. Watch the horse led at trot on level ground. It must be held loosely so the action of its head is not interfered with.

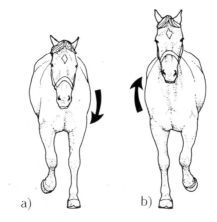

Figure 6.10   *Lame in front. a) A horse lame on its off fore nods its head down as the sound near foreleg goes to the ground, and b) raises its head as the lame off foreleg goes down.*

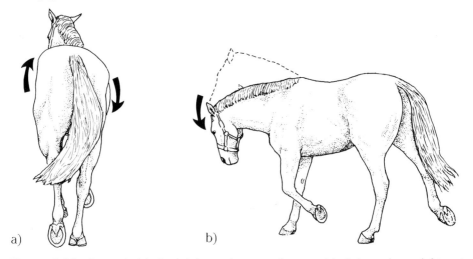

Figure 6.11   *Lame behind. a) A horse lame on its near hind drops its weight onto the sound off hind leg and carries the hip of the near hind leg, and b) as the lame near hind leg goes down, the horse's head nods down as it tries to take the weight off the near leg and transfer it to its forehand.*

A horse that is lame behind appears to drop its weight onto the sound hind leg and slightly carry the hip of its lame leg. There is some nodding of the head but in this case the horse nods its head down as the lame hind leg goes to the ground because it is trying to put more weight on its forehand to save the lame hind leg.

Lameness in front is more obvious when the horse comes towards you or goes past you. Hind lameness is more obvious when seen from the rear.

Feel the legs for heat, swellings or small cuts, feel the feet for heat always comparing one leg with the other and one foot with the other, slowly and carefully with your hand. Check that there are no stones in the foot. If the horse has been shod in the last 48 hours, it is possible that a nail is pressing on the sensitive part of the hoof and causing discomfort.

Watch the suspect foreleg carefully and, even if the horse seems sound, give it a day's rest. Examine the leg again next day. If the horse is still favouring it, do not ride it, but get some expert advice. Many serious problems could be prevented if owners are quick enough to spot the earliest, tiny signs of trouble brewing.

Possible causes of a horse favouring one leg are:

1. Splints   Five-year-olds often throw splints when first worked hard. A splint is a bony growth that usually forms at the junction between the cannon bone and the two pencil-like splint bones at the back of the leg. These run from the top of the cannon bone to about two-thirds of the way down them, tapering off as they go. A high splint can affect the action of the knee. A splint forming to the rear of the splint bone can affect the free movement of the tendons. While forming, a splint causes pain and inflammation. Once it has settled down, hardened and cooled off, it rarely causes trouble unless it protrudes on the inside of the leg where it can be knocked by the foot of the opposite foreleg.

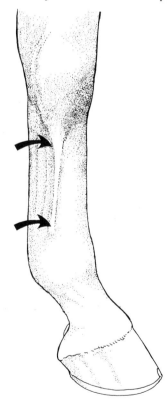

Figure 6.12 *A splint bone; the arrows indicate the length of the bone.*

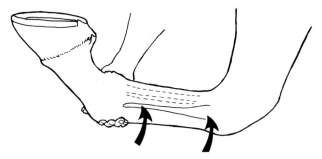

Figure 6.13 *Feeling for a growing splint. When the foreleg is picked up and the tendons have relaxed pinch the splint bone between your fingers and thumb moving all the way down the bone starting at the knee. If the horse flinches a splint is forming.*

To feel for a growing splint, pick up the foreleg and, when the tendons have relaxed, feel for the two splint bones, one at a time, with your fingers and thumb. Starting at the top, near the knee where the splint bone is widest, pinch firmly all the way down the bone. If the horse flinches, repeat the process and see if it flinches again at the same place. If it does a splint is almost certainly forming.

If the horse is not lame in walk but is lame in trot, you can continue to work it quietly in walk. The splint may take a month or more to cool down and harden off. You can then, very gradually, resume normal work. If you turn a horse with a growing splint out for a complete rest it will probably come sound, but as soon as you start work again the splint may well flare up once more and cause trouble on and off for a long time.

2. Sprain   This may be so slight that you cannot find it, so get an expert to look and feel for you. The horse will need to be rested, maybe for a week or even longer. Obvious heat and filled legs need much longer rest. Ask for expert advice immediately and again before you next attempt to ride the horse. Check the place for heat or swelling after recommencing riding the horse.

3. Pulled shoulder muscle   This is very difficult to detect. It may be more noticeable on turns when the horse may take a shorter stride and appear to trail the leg slightly. It may also show on slopes. An experienced person could lift the foreleg forward and slowly outwards and back to see if the horse flinches at any point.

4. Bruised sole   The horse will probably have trodden on something sharp – sometimes a white mark can be seen where perhaps a flint has caused the trouble. A few days' rest on soft ground will usually put this right. If it happens very often, your horse may have thin soles (you would have the same discomfort if you wore thin-soled, soft shoes on sharp stony ground). The horse may need to be shod with wider-web shoes to protect more of the sole, or to be fitted with a protective leather pad placed under the shoe and covering the sole. In any case, avoid sharp stones with this horse.

5. Corns   A corn develops under or near the heel of the shoe. This can be caused by uneven pressure from the shoe or if the shoe, having been left on too long, has begun to dig into the foot so that the hoof has grown round the heel of the shoe. Seek advice from your farrier before removing the shoe. If the trouble is a corn, a surgical shoe can be fitted.

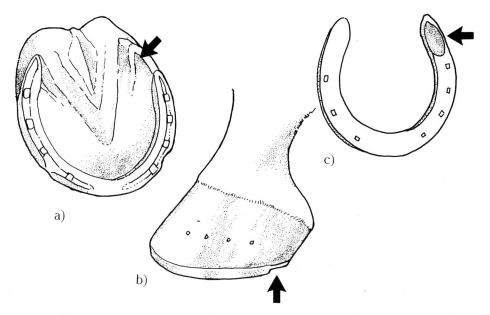

Figure 6.14   *Shoes designed to relieve pressure on corns. a) A three-quarter shoe; b) a set-heeled shoe; c) a seated-out shoe. The arrows show where the pressure is being relieved over the seat of corn.*

There are three shoe types specifically for this problem:

  i) A three-quarter shoe   The area of the corn is not covered by the shoe so there is no pressure from it, but stony ground must be avoided.

  ii) A seated-out shoe   The shoe is hollowed out over the seat of the corn; it looks as if a thumb had been pushed into the shoe to make the little hollow. Bits of grit can sometimes work their way into this hollow and cause discomfort.

  iii) A set-heeled shoe   This shoe is cut away at the heel on the road-surface area. The corn is protected but the pressure is taken off it by the cut-away section.

There are many other causes of lameness but these five are the most likely ones.

[7] DEVELOPMENT

Thoroughbred horses mature quickly and many are raced as two-year-olds, which means that they are often backed when barely two. The jockeys are very light but, even so, the young, soft, immature wings of the spine are often bent and deformed by being asked to carry weight too soon. These horses often end their racing careers at four or five years of age, whereas you will hope that your youngster will remain fit and well for 15 to 20 years.

For this reason, do not put heavy weights on any horse before it is five years old and do not work it hard as a youngster — long hours, heavy going, steep hills. When you buy a young horse that is not fully grown, make sure it is going to be well up to your weight. If in doubt, get expert advice on this.

A very narrow horse, with both forelegs and both hind legs set very close together, does not have the frame to carry weight. This horse will grow up tall and narrow.

A weight-carrying type may go through a bony, gawky stage as a yearling or two-year-old but it will have a strong framework to grow into as it develops and fills out. It will be broader in the hips, rounder through the rib cage, its two forelegs and two hind legs will be further apart from each other and it will have a greater measurement of bone (measured round the cannon bone and tendons below the knee).

Small, neat, short-backed horses and most ponies tend to be better balanced and stronger as youngsters. Horses that are going to grow to 16.2 hh or more are often slow in maturing and are unbalanced as youngsters. They outgrow their strength and are sometimes not fully mature until they are eight years old. If you buy a very big youngster, you will have to be very patient indeed, and it may well need to work a year behind its age in your training schedule.

Young horses grow in fits and starts and some parts of their bodies seem to grow more quickly than others. A young horse may grow higher behind than in front and become unbalanced. The saddle will then sit quite differently on it and more weight and pressure will be placed on the shoulders. The horse may begin to trip or stumble. It is better to rest a horse that has suddenly grown a lot higher in its quarters and wait until its forehand catches up.

234

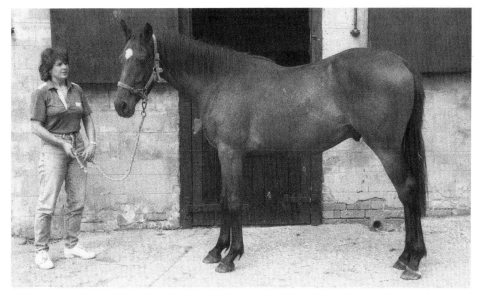

Figure 7.1 *The erratic growth of a two-year-old; the horse is higher behind than in front, and should be rested until the forehand catches up.*

Such uneven growth may go on until the horse is four or five years old.

The wither also changes shape with age. A two-year-old may have no wither at all, just a round, flat back, so that the saddle may rock and roll about and need a fairly tight girth to keep it in place. The saddle will sit quite far forward at this stage because there is nothing to keep it back in place. Between three and five years, the wither will gradually grow up and the saddle will sit progressively further back. You will feel that you have more horse in front of you and more length of rein.

The saddle that fits a two- or three-year-old when you back it is unlikely to fit the same horse when it is mature. Even a mature horse's back changes shape from winter to summer or from when it is fit and muscled up to when it is unfit and soft, so check the saddle carefully and frequently and do not expect a numnah to put right the damage a badly fitting saddle will inflict. Expert advice on saddle fitting is essential if you are not experienced in this matter.

TEETHING

The first set of teeth your foal will grow are its milk teeth. These are smaller and whiter than adult teeth. They are shallowly rooted and will fall out over a period of time as they are pushed out by the growing adult teeth. Teething can be an uncomfortable business for the young horse. You should be aware of the stage of growth of your youngster's teeth and watch for signs of discomfort. If the horse is obviously teething, be prepared to give it a day off or loose-school it to avoid working it in a bit if its mouth is sore.

When you go to buy a young horse, you should be able to estimate its age from the stage of growth of its incisors (front teeth). This can be done fairly accurately up to the age of nine or ten and a little less accurately for a horse in its teens. The following chart shows the development of the teeth over the years.

0−1 A full set of milk teeth (six in each jaw) but the edges of the corner teeth will not meet completely.

1−2 A full set of milk teeth with the corner teeth meeting.

2−3 The two centre teeth in each jaw will be replaced by adult teeth.

3−4 The two lateral teeth in each jaw (between the central teeth and the corner teeth) will be replaced by adult teeth.

4−5 The horse will have a full set of adult teeth but the edges of the corner teeth will not quite meet.

5−6 The edges of the corner teeth will meet.

6−7 There will be a small hook on the edge of the corner teeth in the upper jaw.

7−8 The hook will disappear and there will be increased wear of the tables (flat surfaces) of the teeth.

9−10 A groove will appear at the top of the middle of the corner teeth in the upper jaw. This is called Galvayne's groove. By the age of 15 the line reaches approximately halfway down the tooth, by 20 it reaches the whole way down, by 25 it has disappeared from the top half of the tooth and by 30 it has disappeared altogether. Some horses do not appear to have a Galvayne's groove because no dark line can be seen, but you should be able to feel a shallow groove if you run a finger down the tooth.

As the horse ages, the teeth also grow at a more sloping angle and there is increased wear of the tables. In shape the tables become less oval and more triangular.

It is very difficult to age a horse of over 10 years accurately.

A mare has a total of 36 teeth, a gelding or stallion has 40. The male horse's extra four teeth are called tushes. The tushes appear in the gap behind the incisors between the age of four and five.

Wolf teeth are tiny, shallowly rooted teeth that appear in the upper jaws of some, but not all, horses of both sexes. They grow in front of the molars but not as far forward as the tushes in male horses. If your horse has wolf teeth, the bit may interfere with them, causing the horse to fuss with its mouth. It is a simple operation for your vet to remove the wolf teeth.

Between the age of three and four you may see large lumps on the outline of the horse's lower jaw. These are produced as the new back teeth grow up

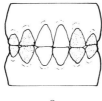
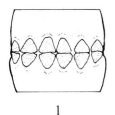
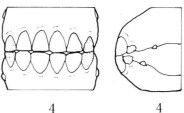

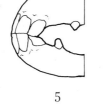
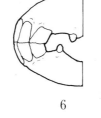

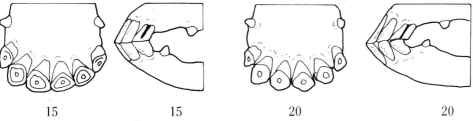

Figure 7.2 *A dentition chart from one year old to 20 years old. The milk teeth are shaded.*

and can be made sore if the horse's head collar or noseband is too tight so check the fitting of these.

If your horse begins to fuss with its mouth or has difficulty in eating, check to see if the outer edges of the upper molars are sharp and cutting into the inside of the horse's cheeks as it chews. If this is the case, ask your vet to rasp the horse's teeth.

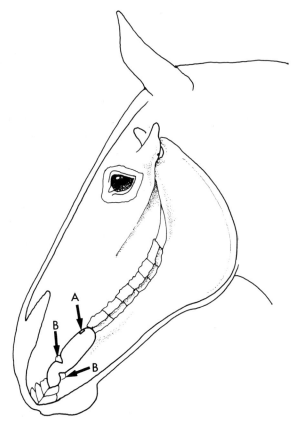

Figure 7.3 *Wolf tooth (A) and tushes (B).*

WORK SCHEDULE

Just as with human children, whose schooling is split up into terms and holidays to give them a time of mental rest, so the horse should be given rest periods. The younger the horse, the shorter the 'term-time' of schooling should be because the youngster is physically and mentally incapable of coping with more.

The two-year-old should be handled and shown the world. It should never be worked so much that it becomes tired. Lungeing or loose-schooling should only be done in walk or with only a very few minutes of trot. This type of work should be done only two or three times a week. If the horse is a big, unbalanced, overgrown animal, lungeing or loose-schooling should not be done at all as this horse is not physically ready to carry itself on a circle. Horses of this type need a lot of time to grow and mature and are often better kept a year behind in their education. Remember this when buying a youngster.

The three-year-old may stand three weeks of quiet daily riding for a total of one hour per day (again, two half-hour sessions would be better). The horse should never be worked so hard that it is physically or mentally tired unless it is very obstreperous and you feel you must work it a little more in order to cope.

If you are working a three-year-old for longer than the above schedule and asking it to do more energetic work so that it is quiet enough for you to ride, you must remember that you are putting more physical strain on its bones, tendons and muscles than they are ready to take. Many young horses have sprains, big fetlock joints (from brushing), windgalls and filled tendons by five years old − all caused by being worked too hard too soon. Being ridden every other day is sufficient for many three-year-olds.

A four-year-old should cope with an hour a day and can begin to carry you up and down different gradients. It should be able to work for six to eight weeks without a rest but watch out for any signs of tiredness in the horse and be ready to rest it sooner.

If the horse is going through an obvious period of growth − it is suddenly much higher behind than in front or the withers are changing shape quickly − the horse is better rested whatever age it is. Horses become unbalanced during a time of sudden growth and physical change, just as children do, and the horse is best left to cope with this without the extra problem of a rider on its back.

The four-year-old should be able to learn to jump up to 90 cm (3 ft), approaching in trot at first. Two short periods of jumping a week, for not more than twenty minutes each time, are enough for most four-year-olds. Remember, the aim should not be to see how high the horse can jump but to have it calmly and happily clearing many different solid-looking obstacles.

The five-year-old should be able to start on a programme of regular work and may need clipping if it is going to be hunted or do any competing during the winter. This young horse will never have been fit before so it will need a long, slow fittening programme to avoid strains, sprains and knocks. Plan to take at least 10 to 12 weeks to get a five-year-old fit. Do mostly walking and a little trotting for the first three weeks. Next include hill work in walk and trot, then short canters and some jumping. After eight weeks, if the horse feels well and strong, some long, slow canters and more strenuous uphill work can be included.

Never gallop a young horse for two reasons.

1. Gallop is a four-time gait and therefore each leg has to carry the entire weight of the horse for a second or two. The young horse is still easily unbalanced. If it becomes unbalanced in the gallop, the muscles and tendons of one foreleg may not yet have fully tensed up ready to take the weight of the horse before the foot touches the ground. The result may be a very badly sprained tendon. This is particularly true on uneven ground where more strain can be put on one part of the leg.

2. At this stage the horse must not find out that it has another 'gear'. It it gets going too fast it will not be able to stop itself because it is very likely to get on its forehand. You will not be able to stop the horse and it will quickly learn that it can take charge and tank off with you.

You must keep a young horse in a steady rhythmic canter, each stride being the same length as the previous one. Even when hunting or competing, the horse should only canter during its first season if you want, eventually, to own a well-mannered, well-balanced, sound older horse that will last you for many years.

After a long or hard day's work, give the horse a rest out in the field if possible. Remember, however, that to turn a fit, excitable horse out in a field when it has not been out for weeks is asking for trouble. It is said that more horses are lamed or damaged through galloping wildly about the field than anywhere else. If the fit, stabled horse is going to be turned out, this must be done regularly so that the horse goes out in the field most days and this is seen by the horse as an accepted part of its usual routine.

Boredom

A young horse soon becomes bored when shut in a stable with no occupation, so try to turn it out into the field as much as possible. If the field is sheltered and the horse does not have a particularly fine coat, it will be calmer and happier living out with suitable companions. All young horses are happier in company; a natural requirement for a herd animal.

If you do put a New Zealand rug on, remember to introduce it properly in the stable (see page 152). Start by putting on a small blanket and then progress to an ordinary rug. Once the New Zealand rug is on the horse, let it wear the rug for an hour or so inside the stable (or until the horse is quite calm), then lead the horse about in the rug before releasing it in the field.

(Young horses have been known to panic and gallop through fences when they first see a well-known companion in a New Zealand rug, so let them get used to this sight first in the stable yard.)

In the stable, giving hay little but often will relieve boredom, as will a thick piece of rounded chain hanging up or a sturdy plastic toy dangling on a strong piece of rope, which can be nuzzled and played with.

If you always school the horse in the same place, it will become bored and will show this by becoming less willing, less responsive and perhaps reluctant to enter the schooling area. To maintain the horse's interest, school anywhere suitable – out on a ride, in and out of trees for instance – and vary the sequences of your school movements when working in your school area. Too much schooling bores any horse, so try to vary its work as much as you can.

Do not expect a young horse to work regularly in the field in which it is turned out. The horse associates this field with freedom and can often resent having to work there while it will work quite happily in another field. Vary the place, pattern and method of exercise and schooling as much as possible. Put yourself in the horse's place. Would you enjoy the work or would you be bored stiff or even grumpy? Think and plan ahead to make life pleasant and interesting for your young horse while progressing with its education.

A Training Schedule for Young Horses

This is a very approximate guide because horses vary enormously in physical and mental development.

Foal to one year old
- Lead.
- Tie up.
- Handle.
- Pick up feet.
- Feet trimmed.
- Standing still.
- General obedience.
- Walk and trot in hand.
- Regular daily handling.
- A short time stabled and tied up most days.

One to two years
As for foal to one year old, plus:
- Loose-schooling at walk and trot for two fifteen-minute sessions per day, or lead out on alternate days.
- Lungeing at walk and trot for short periods wearing saddle and bridle. Two fifteen-minute sessions per day, or lead out on alternate days.
- Backing if strong and mature enough. (Begin bareback.)
- Regular handling and disciplining, including some time stabled and tied up.

Three to four years old
As before, plus:
- Long-reining.
- Lungeing in side reins (optional).
- Loose-schooling in canter.
- Lungeing in canter.
- Backing if not done previously.
- Riding in enclosed area in walk and trot.

- Riding out in company in walk and trot.
- Starting canter ridden.
- Trotting poles.
- Loose jumping.
- Progress to one hour's work a day, preferably in two half-hour sessions, or ridden work on alternate days with loose-schooling/lungeing/long-reining on other days.
- If the horse seems tired or is obviously growing, do not ride it for two to six weeks but continue to handle it and do a little loose-schooling/lungeing/long-reining.
- Turn the horse out as much as possible.

Four to six years old
- Loose jumping.
- Jumping on the lunge.
- Jumping ridden.
- Schooling on the flat and over a variety of terrain and fences.
- Shows.
- Hunting.
- Dressage.
- Regular, steady work for eight to 12 weeks (unless the horse seems tired) for one hour to one and a half hours per day. Give an easy day after an outing or a harder working day.
- Give complete rest, turned out, as necessary.
- If the horse is tired, work it loose or lunge it instead of riding.
- Turn the horse out as much as possible. If it is fully stabled, get it out for two sessions a day and do not just leave it in the stable on rest days.

8 BUYING A YOUNG HORSE

If you are buying a youngster just because you want to learn how to break and school for the first time, I would suggest that you buy a sturdy pony. For your first attempt, a smaller animal is easier to control and cope with in every way. It is also cheaper to buy and should be fairly easy to sell on if you do a thorough job.

If you want something to keep for yourself, think carefully what you intend to use it for and what facilities you have for winter care. Will your horse be stabled or will it have to live out? On the whole, geldings are more amenable in temperament than mares, so I would suggest that you choose a gelding for your first experience of breaking. Consider your own height and weight and look for an animal that is capable of carrying you but will not grow too big or strong. Remember that the horse you buy at two years old will grow and also fill out! If you are only five feet tall you will not be giving yourself a fair chance if you pick an Irish Draught cross that is going to make 17 hh.

CONFORMATION

If you are buying an unbroken youngster you can only assess it from the ground. You must look carefully at its conformation and see how it moves.

An intelligent head and a large kind eye are assets. A neck that grows up from in front of the withers and is naturally convex in the top line will give a good natural head carriage. A big, heavy head, neck and shoulder and a low head carriage will bring the horse's centre of gravity too far forward and the horse will be on its forehand.

If the horse's natural head carriage is very high and it has a concave top line to its neck (and often a big bulge of muscle underneath the neck), this is called a ewe neck. Because of this conformation the horse will have a natural tendency to throw its head up and back when excited or when having a difference of opinion with its rider. Unless dealt with very carefully from the beginning by an experienced person, this conformation fault tends to get worse, so it is best avoided in the first place.

Figure 8.1   *A ewe neck.*

A thickness where the neck joins the head can cause two problems. The horse may find it difficult to flex at the poll when, eventually, you ask it to come on to the bit. The thickness may also cause a restriction when breathing. The horse may 'make a noise' − a slight whistling sound when breathing in. This is classed as an unsoundness and would affect the horse's value.

A flat, wide forehead is considered a sign of an honest, generous temperament, whereas horses with a 'bumpy' forehead have the reputation for being nappy.

To be a good ride, any animal you choose must have a good, sloping shoulder behind which the saddle will sit well back. To assess the shoulder, draw an imaginary line from the highest point of the withers to the ground. If this line comes well behind the forelegs, you should feel that there is plenty of horse in front of you when you eventually sit in the saddle.

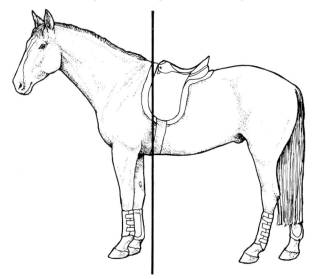

Figure 8.2   *A good sloping shoulder; the saddle sits well back.*

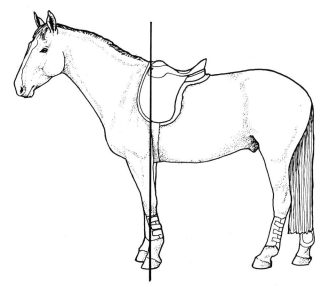

Figure 8.3   *A straight shoulder; the saddle sits too far forward.*

If this imaginary line comes from the wither straight down the foreleg, you will probably feel that you and the saddle are sitting over the horse's forelegs and that there is nothing in front of you − a most precarious position. A straight, upright shoulder also produces a shorter, more stilted stride which is less comfortable to sit to, especially in sitting trot. A horse with a sloping shoulder has the freedom to swing along.

The horse should be a comfortable ride, so look for a sloping pastern to give a soft, springy step. A short, upright pastern gives a more jarring, jolting ride because it is not such a good shock absorber. A cobby type of horse will usually have a more upright pastern than a Thoroughbred type. One is built for strength; the other for speed.

Figure 8.4   *Correctly sloping pasterns and shoulders produce a long, low springy action giving a comfortable ride.*

Figure 8.5 *Short, upright pasterns and straight shoulders produce a short, round action, giving a jarring ride.*

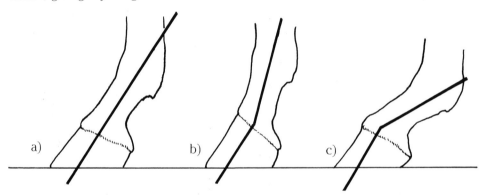

Figure 8.6 *a) A balanced foot with the same angle through the hoof and pastern. b) An unbalanced foot; the angle is broken back. c) An unbalanced foot; the angle is broken forward.*

There should be the same amount of slope on the hoof as on the pastern. Your imaginary line through the centre of both hoof and pastern should be straight and unbroken. A horse is said to be 'back at the knee' when the front of the foreleg, viewed from the side, appears to have a backwards curve. This puts additional strain on the tendons and is best avoided.

Looking at the horse from the front, there should be a good width between the forelegs; they should not look as if they both come out of the same hole. An imaginary line should go straight down through the forearm, the centre of the knee, cannon bone, fetlock, pastern and hoof.

A twisted or crooked foreleg is a weakness. It puts extra strain and jarring all down one side of the leg.

Toes turned out mean that the horse will be likely to brush − knock the opposite fetlock joint with its hoof or shoe as it brings its leg forward. Toes turned in mean that the horse is likely to dish − swing the forelegs outwards below the knee. This is not as serious as brushing as, unless it is extreme, it is merely ugly, not troublesome.

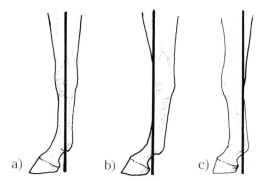

Figure 8.7   *Foreleg conformation – lateral view. a) Good. b) Back at the knee. c) Over at the knee.*

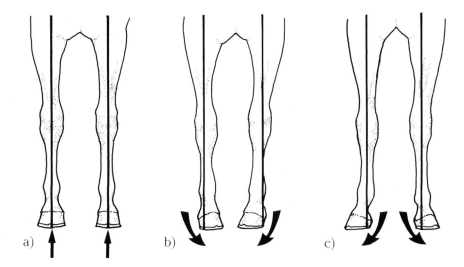

Figure 8.8   *Foreleg conformation – front view. a) Good. b) Toes in. c) Toes out.*

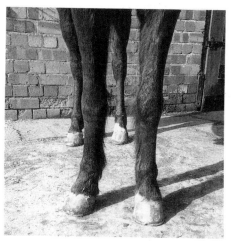

Figure 8.9   *Pony with marked toes-out conformation.*

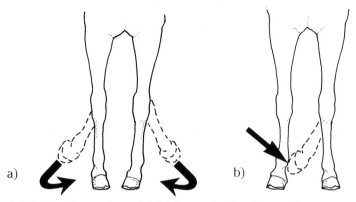

Figure 8.10 *Foreleg action. a) Dishing — the forelegs swing outwards below the knee. b) Brushing — the forelegs knock the opposite fetlock joint with the hoof or shoe.*

'Bone' is the measurement taken around the cannon bone and tendons below the knee. A big, heavyweight hunter may have more than 23 cm (9 in) of bone, whereas a small Thoroughbred could have only 15 cm (6 in). The horse should look as if its legs 'fit' with the rest of its body.

Look at the place where your girth will lie. Is the horse deep through the girth? If there is a sharp, uphill slope under the horse's belly just behind the girth, the horse is said to be herring-gutted. On a horse of this type the girth will slip back and take the saddle with it, so you would need to use a breast girth or breast plate. The ribs should be deep and well rounded to give plenty of room for the heart and lungs.

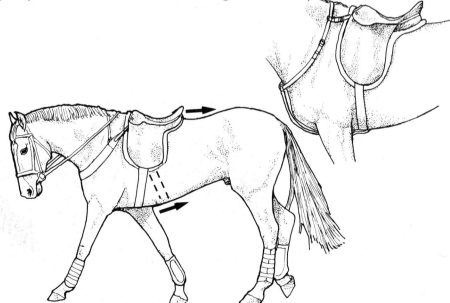

Figure 8.11 *A herring-gutted horse needs a breast girth or (inset) breast plate to stop the saddle from slipping back.*

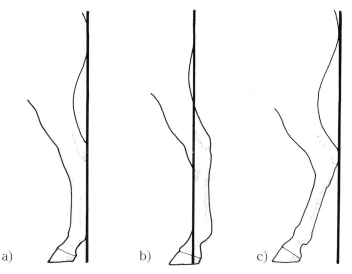

Figure 8.12 *Hind leg conformation − lateral view. a) Good. b) Out behind. c) Sickle hocks.*

The horse must have the strength to carry its rider forward, so look at the hind legs from the side. Draw an imaginary line from the back of the hindquarters to the ground. This line should run from the point of the hock via the back of the fetlock joint to the ground. A horse whose hocks and fetlock joints are behind this line will not be as strong in its hind legs. It will be more difficult to get the horse to step under its body with its hind legs and to make it really use itself. It may tend to hollow its back and 'leave its hind legs behind' when it moves.

If the hock is slightly in front of your imaginary line, and the fetlock joint even more so, the horse is said to be sickle hocked. In this case there is a

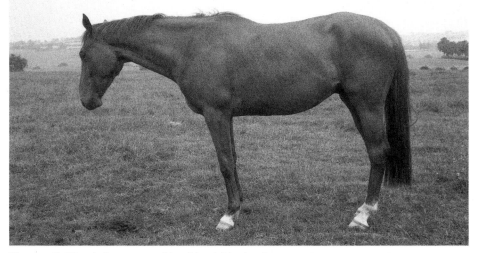

Figure 8.13 *A four-year-old with sickle hocks.*

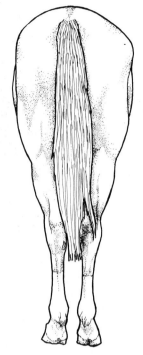

Figure 8.14 *A tilted pelvis; the right hip bone is lower than the left.*

great strain on the back of the hind leg from the hock downwards and this horse may, with work, develop a curb – a sprain 10–15 cm (4–6 in) below the hock.

Stand behind the horse and look at its hindquarters. When it is standing square with both hind legs level, are its hip bones at the same height and level? Is there a straight line through the centre of the hock, cannon bone, fetlock joint, pastern and hoof?

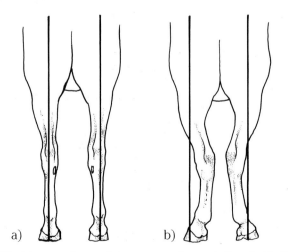

Figure 8.15 *Hind leg conformation – rear view. a) Good. b) Cow hocks.*

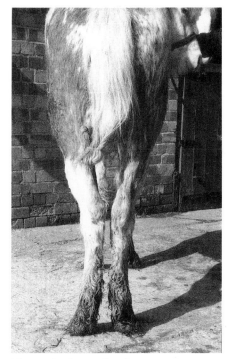

Figure 8.16 *Pony with marked cow hocks.*

If the hocks turn in towards each other and the feet turn out, the horse is said to be cow hocked. This is also a weakness because the joints that support the horse and propel it forward do not lie underneath each other. If the toes turn out, the horse may also brush behind.

The feet should be round, with wide, open heels and a well-developed frog to act as a cushion to prevent jarring. The sole should be slightly concave and the weight should be carried on the walls of the hoof. A flat sole can make a horse very sensitive on stony ground and lead to bruising of the sole.

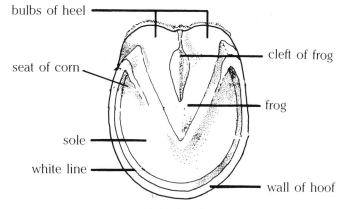

Figure 8.17 *The ground surface of the hoof.*

TEMPERAMENT

Temperament is going to be of prime importance to you so watch the horse's ears and eyes. Are the ears moving slowly backwards and forwards? Is the horse calm and relaxed in its eye or are the eyes very wide open, perhaps with the whites showing?

As you approach, does the horse prick its ears and stand calmly, or does it back off with raised head and ears flicking quickly backwards and forwards? When you handle it, does it ever lay its ears back? Is it nervous or jumpy with people or sudden noises?

Lay your arm across the horse's back and gently lean against it. Does the horse look back at you in a tense way with a raised head? You should hope to find that the horse is totally unworried by your action. You are looking for a calm, confident horse that has been well handled. A nervous, jumpy or bad-tempered animal is not for you.

MOVEMENT

If the horse will trot out in hand, you can stand behind it to see if it moves straight and then stand in front of it to watch it coming towards you. As it goes past you, stand to one side to see if its action is long and low or round and high.

If the horse will not lead, it may be possible to see it loose in the field. Here, as it stops and turns, you can also see if it is naturally well balanced.

Remember that a young horse still has a lot of growing to do. Some youngsters look gawky and awkward, just like growing children. At one time their withers look higher than their rumps, at other times their quarters will be higher than their withers. Try to look at the skeleton under the coat and skin to make sure it is straight and strong. If you are unsure of your own judgement, ask a knowledgeable friend to accompany you and also consider having the horse checked by a vet if you are going to spend a lot of money on it. Do not forget to ask the breeder about the youngster's dam and ask to see her if you can. Consider her temperament which she may well have passed on to her foal. Does she have any hereditary problems? What sort of work has she done? Has she won any competitions? Ask the same questions about the sire and, if possible, get his stud card.

WHAT AGE TO BUY?

If you buy a weaned foal or yearling, you must teach it to lead and be well mannered. Follow all the procedures described in the sections on the foal and yearling.

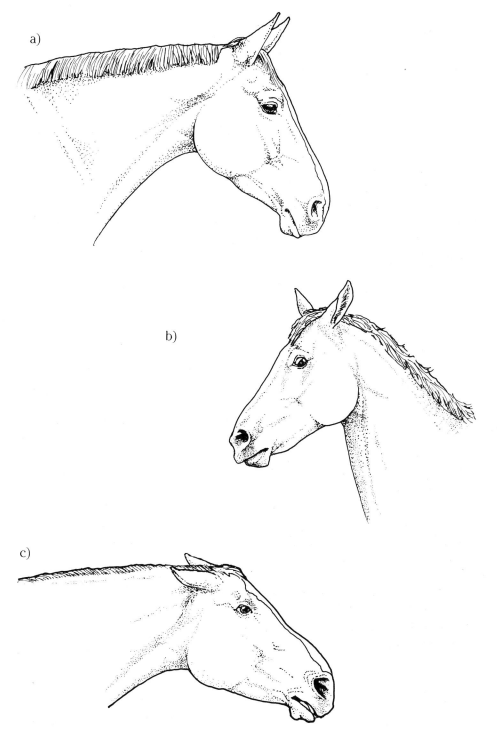

Figure 8.18 *Expression of temperament. a) Calm and confident. b) Nervous and worried. c) Bad tempered.*

Physically and mentally, a two-year-old is only capable of working for very short periods. Like a young child it can only concentrate for a short time and it tires quickly. It may be slow-thinking and rather unbalanced. Be prepared to give it several weeks' rest in between short spells of education to allow time for the new knowledge to sink in. A two-year-old may not be strong enough to back and you should not try to push things too far too fast at this stage.

Even if it is alert, well balanced, mature in appearance and strong in the back, you should still not ask it to do more than a few minutes' work a day. Little and often is much better than long, tiring sessions.

If you buy a three-year-old, you should be able to progress further. If, after three or four weeks of gentle work, the horse is showing no signs of brushing, clicking or forgeing − hitting the toe of its hind toe/shoe on the toe of its front toe/shoe − dragging its hind toes on the ground or showing general signs of tiredness or boredom, it can be kept going quietly for a few months, not necessarily being worked everyday.

A four-year-old should be capable of gradually building up to an hour's work a day − preferably divided up into two sessions − and may be strong enough to be worked continually for several months.

If you are buying a three- or four-year-old that has been recently broken and ridden out a few times, go and see it in its stable first. Notice how it reacts to its owner or rider. Is it calm and confident when they approach? Or does it stiffen, tense up and move away from them? Does it look pleased to see them or cross, with ears laid back? These signs will give you a guide to the sort of treatment it has received and its feelings towards people in general.

Check the points on good conformation covered on page 243 and see the horse walk and trot in hand to study its action (see page 252).

Next watch the horse being saddled and bridled. Is it relaxed and confident or nervous and apprehensive? See its owner or regular rider on it first. Does it stand still to be mounted or does it move away and look back at the rider, tensing up as they prepare to mount?

Will it walk and trot quietly towards and away from home in an open field? If possible, see it ridden in the field with another horse and note if it will go towards and away from its companion without arguing and whether it behaves sensibly when in company.

See it ridden out alone up a road and several times past the entrance to its home in both directions to see if it is nappy. Not wanting to leave the home yard or to pass the home gate is a very common problem with young horses and will not show up if they are only ridden in a field or enclosed area.

Note how the rider sits and how obvious their aids are. See if the horse appears to be much stiffer on one rein than on the other.

Next, ride the horse yourself, first, if possible, in a small, enclosed area.

Notice its reactions when a stranger mounts and rides it. Is it relaxed and looking forwards or is it tense and worried, looking back at you with apprehension?

Now ride it in an open field, with and without company if possible. Does it become strong when turned towards home? Does it try to stop when turned away from home and give you the feeling it might argue?

Finally, take it up and down the road alone and see if you feel safe and in command. Is it a comfortable ride? Is it reasonably responsive and willing? What sort of condition is it in? It could be very quiet because it is in poor condition or because it has been worked really hard before you came and is now very tired. Does it become tense at the sight of traffic or spook at things in the hedgerow?

Find out how long the horse has been in regular work. How many people have ridden it? A horse that has only ever been ridden by one person can be worried by the feel of a different rider at first. Has it been kept stabled or out at grass or half and half? What has it been fed? Has it any real likes or dislikes? Has it any peculiarities?

If possible, see the horse being loaded and unloaded. If this is not possible it could be safer not to pay for the horse until you have it loaded.

Do you like the horse and feel confident when handling and riding it?

Remember that, as a general rule, most Thoroughbred or hot-blooded horses are quick-thinking, quick-reacting, more sensitive and more excitable than commoner horses. A horse that is less well bred, slower thinking, slower reacting, less sensitive and calmer in temperament may be more suitable for you.

If you buy a horse that has already been partly broken and backed, it is a good idea to revert to the early stages of breaking and repeat these yourself. You will then get to know each other gradually and the youngster can learn to respond to a new voice and new actions.

YOUR OWN TEMPERAMENT AND EXPERIENCE

If you are in the least nervous, tense or lacking in confidence when riding or handling horses, then do not buy a young horse. The horse will sense your nervousness or hesitation. It, too, will become jumpy and unsure of itself or else it will realise that it can intimidate you or use its strength to get its own way. Even with a knowledgeable person helping you regularly, you still need the right temperament to succeed with a young horse.

Even if you are very confident, you will need supervision and advice from someone experienced with young horses the first time you take on the breaking and backing of a youngster. If you have the slightest problem, ask for advice immediately or the situation may get worse. A small problem can soon become a big bad habit unless rectified quickly.

WHERE TO BUY YOUR YOUNG HORSE

Many home-bred horses have been given too many titbits and become thoroughly spoiled and pushy, with no manners or discipline and no respect for people. On the other hand, they are often completely unafraid and trusting with people so that they will accept being ridden quite happily. A well-disciplined, confident, calm, home-bred horse would be ideal. To find one, read the advertisements in your local paper with care or ask the advice of other horse owners whom you respect.

Horse sales have the advantage that you can see a young horse in a strange, noisy, frightening environment and get a really good insight as to its temperament.

Look for a horse that is standing quietly watching everything, ears moving slowly backwards and forwards, with a relaxed, normal head carriage and a calm eye.

You do not want the type that is whizzing round the box or pen, digging at the floor with its forelegs, kicking at its neighbours or fighting the halter rope and lifting its forelegs off the ground.

Nearly all sales have warranties (guarantees). The wording of these varies from sale to sale, but when buying an unbroken horse you should look for the word 'sound' in its description. This means it must not be lame or suffering from any defect. Note when the warranty expires − it may be any time from 24 to 48 hours from the time of sale. This is all the time you will have to make sure the horse is sound and apply for redress if it is not.

If you buy from a local horse dealer they will wish the horse to be a success because of their reputation in the area, so most local dealers are unlikely to try to sell you a bad horse. (Of course, they may sell you an unsuitable one if you do not make your requirements and own level of experience clear − but this is your responsibility, not theirs.)

At a dealer's yard you may find more animals to choose from and compare in one place. Some dealers will give you a written guarantee that they will exchange the horse if you cannot get on with it. This could prove very useful to you.

Remember that dealers' horses come and go and may have been through sales, therefore they might carry coughs, colds and other infections into your yard, so any new horse bought from this source should be isolated for at least two weeks to protect your other horses.

Never go alone to look at a horse. Take someone with you who has broken and schooled lots of horses and whom you have seen riding them calmly and successfully. Someone very knowledgeable but who has never dealt with young horses cannot give sufficient guidance.

Ideally, take the person who is going to help and supervise you throughout the time you will be breaking and schooling your young horse. This person

Figure 8.19 *A three-year-old in the sale ring.*

Figure 8.20 *A four-year-old being ridden in the sale ring.*

will be motivated to find something you can make a success of together.

Finally, never buy a horse you do not really like even if you cannot put your finger on the reason for this. On a bad day, when everything is going wrong and you think you own the worst equine juvenile delinquent in the world, only the fact that you really like the horse will make you keep your temper and try again.

THE EFFECT OF CHANGE ON YOUNG HORSES

If you buy a young horse from the place where it was born and reared and take it to a new environment, even a placid type of horse is going to become confused, unsure of itself and apprehensive at first. A nervous horse, that was manageable when you first saw it in its home surroundings, may become very difficult to control in new surroundings. The animals and people it knew and trusted are no longer there. Every sight and sound is different, and the horse may have travelled in a vehicle for the first time.

All of this adds up to a very traumatic experience and unless patience and understanding are shown, the horse's character can change.

If possible, put the horse out straightaway in a field that it cannot jump out of, with a quiet companion of the same sex that is unlikely to bully it, and give it a couple of days to settle. If you must put it in a stable, have a quiet horse or pony nearby, where it can be seen. Give the new horse a small feed and some hay to keep it occupied.

If the youngster starts tearing round the box, threatening to jump out over the door, fix a grill over the top part of the doorway or tie a strong bar in the gap above the bottom door. Position this so that the horse cannot get its head through the gap between this bar and the door. Shutting the top door is not a good idea; it will make the youngster feel claustrophobic and if the horse is unable to see other horses it is unlikely to settle.

Whether in or out, treat the horse as if it is completely unbroken. Start from the very beginning of the training described in the first chapters of this book. Put a headcollar on and lead the horse round the box, saying 'Walk on', 'Whoa' or 'Stand' or whatever are to be your regular words of command.

Let the horse get to know you and your voice. Handle it all over and then leave it alone for an hour or so. (Do not leave it tied up at this stage.) Progress gradually through this early work until you know how the horse will react to everything you want to do. If you discover something that the horse is unsure of or worried about, repeat this action until the horse is calm and confident about it.

All of this will take time but you and the horse will learn a lot about each other and you are much less likely to have trouble than you would if you immediately tried to ride it. This advice still applies even if you have previously seen the horse ridden and going quietly or even if you rode it yourself before buying it. A new environment can completely change a horse's reactions to things it previously accepted in familiar surroundings.

Some horses settle very quickly and you can progress to riding them within two or three days. Others could take a week to settle enough to be ridden again.

An unbroken horse is likely to take longer to break in new surroundings than would have been the case if this had been done in its own home. If possible, turn the horse out in a field for some part of every day even if you cannot keep it out all the time, which would be preferable and is likely to give you a calmer horse to deal with. Some sort of freedom in which to buck and kick, gallop and roll is really essential. A safe cattle yard, a well-fenced outdoor manège or an indoor school could be used to give a taste of freedom each day to relieve any mental tension.

Horses that have lived out most of their lives and drunk only from streams, ponds or water troughs will often adamantly refuse to drink from a bucket in a stable, no matter how clean both it and the water inside it are. They are also likely to be more worried by the restriction of being shut up in a stable.

Instead of an ordinary tall, narrow bucket, you could try putting water in a wide, more shallow feedbowl, but if the horse has drunk nothing at all for twelve hours, lead it out to a trough or to somewhere where it will drink. In time, it will gradually get used to a bucket.

You must be aware of how much your horse is drinking and keep its water fresh and clean. Ignore people who tell you to leave it thirsty if it will not drink on the principle that you must be cruel to be kind. A horse that does not drink enough water can quickly become ill.

Find out how the horse has been fed, if at all. Was it kept in a very poor field that was short of grass or was it in a field with very lush grazing? Has it had any hard feed?

Coming up from very little grass into a very lush field can give a horse colic, but if you have no alternative, put it out for half an hour at a time and make sure it has had a feed of hay first so that it will not quickly gorge on a lot of lush grass on an empty stomach. Gradually increase the time it is allowed out to graze but take into consideration the horse's bodily condition. If it is very fat it will need to have its hours of grazing controlled in any case.

If the horse has come from plenty of lush grass to your field which has very little grass, it may need to be fed hay so that it will not lose too much weight. It is likely to lose weight anyway through anxiety over its change of environment and may lose more weight when you begin to work it. Weight lost in this way can be difficult and slow to put on again, so feed good hay ad lib if you are short of grass.

If the horse is really thin, sugar beet, bran, mollychaff, carrots and horse and pony nuts could be fed, plus a little boiled barley, starting with 450 g (1 lb) per day and gradually building up to 900 g (2 lb) per day (dry weight before cooking), but do not give any form of corn, high protein nuts or energy feeds as these can very quickly change your quiet sensible horse into a strong, lively, difficult-to-control animal.

A thin horse should have a worm count done from its droppings and should in any case be wormed regularly every six weeks. If the worm count does not show a worm problem, and the horse is lethargic and does not put on weight, a blood test should be done. An anaemic horse will not thrive.

Check that the horse is chewing comfortably in a regular rhythm and swallowing without 'mouthing' and spitting out lumps of half-chewed food (quidding). This is a sign that the sharp edges on the outside of the teeth of the top jaw are catching on the inside of the cheeks. These top teeth may need rasping by the vet, or it could be that the horse is teething. The back milk teeth are rather like flat caps; as they loosen they can move sideways and press on the gums and cheeks before they fall out.

Your young horse should never be so thin that you can feel its ribs. Its hindquarters should be round, not hollow with a protruding backbone and hip bones. Feel the horse's ribs, backbone and hip bones with your fingers. When you hold the horse's crest between your fingers and thumb, the neck should feel firm and muscular, not like two pieces of skin with very little between them.

Check your horse's bodily condition in these three ways regularly and notice any changes. This applies particularly during the winter when weight loss can be difficult to replace and can be hidden by a hairy coat.

Figure 8.21   *a) A well-rounded horse in good condition. b) Very poor condition; the backbone is visible, the hips and ribs are sticking out, and there is no neck.*

Figure 8.22 *The neck should feel firm and muscular when examined, not like two pieces of skin with little between them.*

If your horse loses weight it may become lethargic, drag its hind toes or begin to stumble or brush. Possible causes of weight loss are:

- Not enough food for the work the horse is doing.
- Not enough food for the horse's size.
- Poor quality food with little nutritional value.
- Worms.
- Anaemia.
- Difficulty in chewing because of sharp teeth or loose milk teeth.

If your horse loses weight, try to establish and remedy the cause immediately. Ask for expert advice as soon as you notice any unexpected physical or mental change.

Always put your young horse in the same stable so that it begins to think of it as home − a safe place to relax. Use as big a loose box as possible, or even a cattle yard where the horse will have even more freedom to move around.

At first, look after the horse entirely by yourself if possible. Always handle it in exactly the same way, use the same words and tone of voice (most important) and do things in the same order so that the horse begins to learn its routine and knows what is going to happen next. Only when the horse has settled in and is calm and confident should you begin to vary your routine.

If a horse lies down in a new stable, this is a good sign because it shows that the horse feels safe there. In the wild the horse is at its most vulnerable when lying down because flight from danger is its main form of self-preservation and precious seconds could be lost when getting up.

When you approach the horse in its box, do not sneak up silently and throw open the door with a crash, giving the horse heart failure and causing it to flounder to its feet if lying down. Make some sort of noise as you approach the box; call its name or whistle so that it knows you are coming.

┏9┓ ENVIRONMENT

The horse is an intelligent animal with exceptionally sensitive skin (watch its reaction to one small fly on its coat). It is an active animal, constantly grazing, playing, watching and listening and only dozing for short periods. Being shut up in a stable for 23 hours out of 24 is totally unnatural and very frustrating for a horse. Would you like it? Wouldn't you become neurotic and tense and go a bit crazy when you were finally let out of 'prison'? A day off out in the field is fine, but a day off in the stable is a whole day in prison, so at least lead your horse out for a walk and to graze.

To be out in the field as much as possible and in a big yard with free movement and interesting things to watch (people, traffic, other animals or birds) is a far better environment for a young horse. It is not kind to keep a young horse alone all the time.

Figure 9.1 *An ideal yard for young horses which have to be kept in. They have shelter, plenty of room (large enough for company), safe gates, and a view of their surroundings to keep their interest.*

Have you ever noticed how tense, neurotic, slightly hysterical people often have children, horses and dogs that are in much the same state? None of them has the safe feeling of knowing what is going to happen next and that it will happen in a calm, orderly manner, controlled by quiet voices and gentle movements.

You must have noticed how in some households you feel at peace with the world and in others you are soon tense and tired because there is perpetual noise and commotion and you never know what to expect?

Try to create a peaceful, safe life for your young horse. Be calm, consistent and logical. Attempt to put yourself in the horse's place and ask yourself if you would like and understand the treatment and work you are giving your youngster. How would you react? Many problems and accidents with young horses are caused by one thing only — lack of thought — so think first!

FIELDS AND FENCING

A young horse is better turned out in company. When bringing horses in, never leave a youngster in the field until last or it may panic when it finds itself alone. For the same reason, never turn a youngster out first.

Barbed wire is dangerous for all horses, but even if they do not gallop into it, young, unbalanced horses can cut themselves as they gallop past it and lean towards it in turning. They can also catch themselves on it as they stretch their necks out over it to talk to a horse in the next field, or may strike out at another horse getting a foreleg caught in it.

Figure 9.2 *If wire or electric fencing is unavoidable, tie wooden bars to the wire and plastic tape to the electric fence to make them visible.*

Guard rails made of barbed wire attached to another fence, or any loose barbed wire, are lethal. The oblong mesh of pig netting is dangerous, because horses will often strike out with a foreleg at horses in the next field, and, if a hoof goes through the mesh, the horse may be cut above the heel when it tries to pull its foot out. If the horse is shod, the wire can become caught in the heel of the shoe and be pulled tightly between the shoe and the foot. The horse will panic when it finds its foreleg is trapped and may come down or become completely tangled in the fence. Terrible cuts are caused by horses striking out over wire and also by them rolling too close to wire fences of any type, and getting their legs caught in them. Such accidents are very common indeed, so think ahead and avoid them.

A good strong hedge or a sound post and rail fence is ideal but often unavailable. A safe fence that you can put up yourself is an electrified fence. With this method, a dangerous existing fence can be made safe. The posts used to carry the fence can be made of either plastic or special insulated wood. The plastic posts are 90 cm − 1 m (3−3½ ft) high and the wooden ones are higher, at 1.2−1.4 m (4−4½ ft).

Small insulators can also be fixed to the tops of the posts of an existing fence to carry a top line of electric fencing.

The ribbon type of electric fencing wire is best, because horses can see it clearly. Once the horses are used to it, two rows of this ribbon wire can be used to divide up paddocks between groups of horses; the horses will not go near it. If only the standard wire is to be used, strips of plastic bags, tied to the wire at frequent intervals, will ensure that the horses can see the fence.

To introduce horses to an electric fence, put it up 90 cm (3 ft) away from an ordinary fence of any sort. The horses will go up to the ordinary fence, stop and touch the electric fence, snort and gallop away. After two or three days it should be safe to divide up the field with an electric fence only. It is essential to lead the horses round the perimeter of their electrically fenced paddock so that they know where the new boundaries are.

If neighbouring horses have been squealing and striking out at an existing fence, one strand of electric ribbon (in this situation plain electric wire would also be safe) 15−30 cm (6−12 in) directly above the existing fence will stop this behaviour, as will an electric fence 90 cm (3 ft) inside the original fence.

The electric current can either be supplied by a portable unit or from a mains unit run from a house or building. Insulated handles with hooks on them will allow you to open and close your entrance.

When setting up your electric fencing to divide a field, remember that some sort of shelter must be made available to horses, so do not fence this off. The horses should have access to a thick hedge, trees, walls or buildings.

Electric fencing is excellent if you have one horse that kicks others or one fat horse that needs to be kept in a small paddock. It is also ideal for

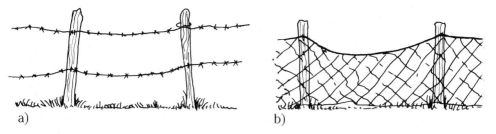

Figure 9.3 *Bad fencing. a) Barbed wire. b) Pig netting.*

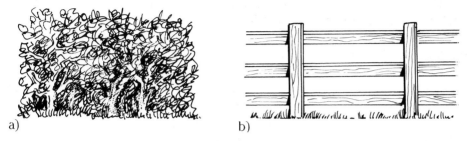

Figure 9.4 *Good fencing. a) A strong hedge. b) Post and rail fencing.*

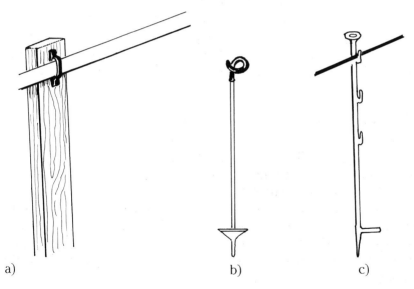

Figure 9.5 *Electric fencing. a) A wooden post with a plastic insulator and wide electric tape. b) A pigtail post; the electric strand is threaded through the plastic pigtail, and the post is metal. c) An all plastic post.*

separating mares and geldings. It is easily moved and can be used for strip grazing, moving the fence over a yard or so each day. It also makes it easy to graze off odd patches of grass and small areas that are not normally used.

GATES

Horses will rub on gates and also strike out at them. They dash through them when they are open and try to open them when they are closed! A big, strong, wooden gate is safest but very expensive. Some metal gates have fairly narrow gaps between the bars in which a foot could get stuck. This often happens where the sloping bars form a V, imprisoning the foot.

Make sure there are no nails, hooks or sharp obtrusions on the gate or gatepost which could cut a horse as it tries to dash through.

A safe catch and a strong padlock and chain (on both ends) of the gate if it could otherwise be lifted off its hinges) are probably necessary wherever you live these days. (Even if your horses live in a field beside your house, they can still be stolen and it is a good idea to have them freeze-branded for their own protection.)

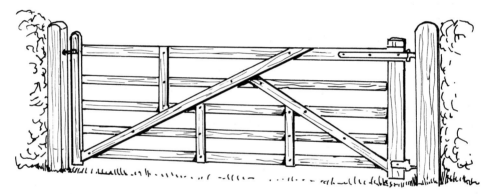

Figure 9.6 *A strong wooden gate is the safest, but most expensive, gate.*

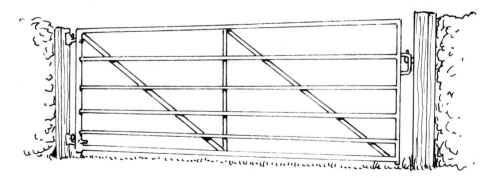

Figure 9.7 *Metal gates with narrow gaps between the bars which can trap hooves are not a good choice.*

WATER

A water trough with a ball cock is a safe, clean watering system. Horses can bang their knees on the sharp edges of old baths, while, if turned out in a head collar, a horse can easily get this caught on a tap. In winter you will need to lag the pipe and also break the ice two or three times a day. The trough will need cleaning out regularly.

A clear, fast-flowing stream with a sound bottom and safe access is fine providing that nothing unpleasant is liable to be dumped in the water further upstream. Unlike a trough, a running stream may not freeze up in the winter.

Check a pond carefully − there may be dangerous debris in it and it may become stagnant or dry up in the summer or become a breeding ground for biting insects. In frosty weather you will have to break the ice regularly.

FIELD COMPANIONS

Never turn one new horse out with a group of others that already know each other. They are almost certain to be jealous and chase, kick and bite it. They may corner the horse and really hurt it or drive it over or through a fence, terrifying it and causing serious injury. Introduce your new horse to one other steady animal over a stable door. Allow them to sniff at each other but stand well clear and out to one side so that you cannot get kicked or struck out at.

When they accept each other, lead them out into their field and take them both all round the perimeter and up to the water supply. Let them both go at the same time and do this near the gate so that they will not gallop back towards it. Turn them to face the gate and you before you release them so that you will not get kicked if they buck as they gallop off. If you have any doubts about being able to catch the young horse, leave it wearing a well-fitting head collar which allows it to chew in comfort. (It is safer, however, not to leave a head collar on in the field, so only do this if it is really necessary.)

If the young horse will have to go out in a large group eventually, try to introduce one extra horse at a time into its field. If possible, always keep mares and geldings in separate fields. If you cannot do this, never put two or more geldings in with just one mare or they are almost certain to fight over her, especially when she is in season which happens for three to four days every three weeks from spring through to autumn.

In time, a group of horses establish a natural 'pecking order'. You must be aware of which horses are the strongest and weakest characters in the group and know your horse's place in this order. If any feeding of hay is done in the field, is your horse getting its fair share? You must always put out several more piles of hay than there are horses in the field or the weaker characters and youngest horses will be chased off and get nothing.

Bucket feeding should never be done when there is a large group of horses in a field. This is just asking for injury from kicks, because fights over hard feed can be really violent. If there are only two or three horses in the field, it is possible to space the food bowls out well and stand there to keep order while the horses eat, but you do run the danger of being 'mugged' while you try to get the arrangement sorted out, or of being kicked if you intervene in a squabble. If you bring one horse only out of the field and bucket feed it away from the group, they may attack it when it returns to the field because they can often smell the food on its mouth, so keep it away for sometime before returning it to the field and sponge off its muzzle before you turn it out again.

SAFETY

Never, ever let children enter a field containing loose horses. This is especially true with young horses which, merely in play, will often trot up to a small child who is wandering about and strike or kick out at it, causing serious injury.

A group of loose horses is even dangerous to adults because, again, in play or out of jealousy, they may kick or strike out at each other and injure a person by mistake.

10 TRAVELLING YOUR YOUNG HORSE

Even if your youngster is not of show standard, travelling in a box or trailer to visit a show will be very good experience.

LOADING

Loading into a Trailer

It is important that you teach a youngster to load calmly and sensibly from the beginning so that you will be able to manage it on your own. Park the trailer against a wall or hedge. Take the partitions out if possible. If this is not possible, move the back of the partition over to make a wider space for the horse to walk into. Open the front, groom's, door to let in more light so that the horse will not feel it is walking into a trap. Put straw on the floor.

Remove the breast bar so that the horse does not see it as a barrier and stop with its hind feet on the ramp. When the ramp is up, quietly replace the breast bar.

If your trailer unloads at the front, drop both ramps, remove the partition and breast bars and put straw in the trailer and on both ramps. If possible, lead a quiet horse, that is well known to your youngster, into the trailer and out again at the front, encouraging the youngster to follow very closely. If this goes well, next time through halt the schoolmaster inside and get the youngster to stand still next to it. Lead the youngster out first, then put the partitions and breast bars in. Now load the older horse, followed by the youngster. Quickly and quietly raise the back ramp. Tie the horses up and quietly close the front ramp.

Practise loading every day until the horse accepts it as part of its daily routine. If the horse still loads reluctantly after a few days, feed it in the trailer so that it associates loading with a pleasant experience. Make sure it is quite happy about being in the trailer before you take it on its first short journey. It really pays to spend time on these early stages as there is nothing more infuriating than a horse that makes a fuss about loading or simply refuses to do it at all.

If possible, travel your youngster with a companion for its first few trips. If travelling the horse alone, it is better to travel without a partition because

269

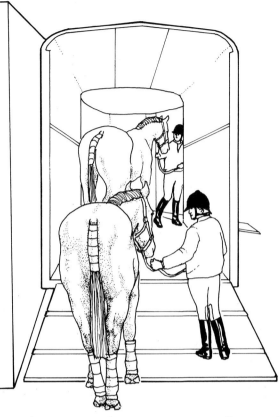

Figure 10.1 *Encouraging a young horse to enter a trailer can be helped by parking the trailer against a wall or hedge to block one exit route, and by letting down both ramps and opening the groom's door to allow as much light into the trailer as possible. If possible, allow the youngster to follow an experienced schoolmaster into the trailer.*

this prevents the horse from leaning on one side, bracing its feet against the other side and scrabbling on corners, possibly coming down, frightening itself and probably becoming difficult to load for the rest of its life.

When travelling a horse alone in a trailer without a partition, always cross-tie it using two ropes, one from each side of the head collar, so that the horse will not try to turn round. Always tie loops of baling twine to the rings at the front of the trailer and put the ropes through these, so that they will break in an emergency. Tie the horse so that if it steps back its hindquarters will touch the back of the trailer just before the rope pulls on the head collar, then it is unlikely to pull back and panic.

When travelling a horse alone in a trailer with the partition in, stand the horse on the side closer to the middle of the road. In this position it will be easier for the horse to keep its balance and, because of the camber of the road, the trailer will be easier to tow. If travelling two horses, put the heavier horse closer to the middle of the road.

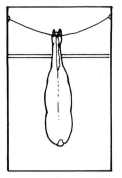

Figure 10.2 *A horse travelling alone in a trailer without a partition should be cross-tied using one rope on each side of the head collar.*

Loading into a Horse Box

When loading into a horse box, again, park close to something solid on one side to form a wall, and drop the ramp onto higher ground so that it is not too steep. Move the partitions to make room inside so that the horse can walk straight forward into an open space. It is too much to expect a young horse to walk up a ramp and immediately turn or move sideways into a stall. If possible, load another horse or pony first so that the youngster can follow.

Unbroken youngsters that have not been handled much are safest travelling loose in a horse box.

Problems with Loading

If your horse is unwilling to load, tempt it in with food, using an assistant to encourage it forward with a hand on its quarters. Never pull on the lead rope or the horse may run back or rear.

If the horse will not go forward, one foreleg may be lifted and put on the ramp, the assistant again encouraging the horse forward.

If this does not work, it may be necessary to have two assistants holding lunge lines attached at one end to the trailer and crossed over just above the horse's hocks.

An older horse that is nappy about loading, but should know better, may be loaded by the use of various, more forceful methods such as a prod from a stable broom, the use of a whip, etc. These methods should never be used when teaching a young horse to load. A youngster is not being naughty just because it is doubtful about entering a box or trailer the first few times; it is being cautious. It is better that the young horse learns to do what you ask through trust rather than punishment. An older horse who has lost that trust, perhaps because of a bad experience, should be reschooled to load with the methods used for youngsters.

Figure 10.3 *Loading a reluctant horse with the help of two assistants holding crossed lunge lines just above the horse's hocks.*

The second the horse has loaded, your assistant must put the ramp up, trying not to bang it too hard. (If the partition cannot be removed, it must be adjusted after the horse is in and the ramp is up.) Any delay will give the horse time to run back, and, once learned, the horse will remember this trick and repeat it.

Never tie a horse up in a trailer until the ramp is up, in case it panics and runs back. For the same reason, when unloading, always untie the horse before you bring down the ramp. If your trailer unloads to the rear, make the horse wait for a few seconds, with an assistant at its quarters, before backing out. If it should rush back, never pull on the lead rope; leave it slack so that the horse will not panic and throw its head up, perhaps banging it on the roof of the trailer as it rushes out.

If you travel an older horse with a haynet, remember to pass the drawstring through the bottom of the haynet and pull it up really tight so that it will not hang down when empty. Tie the net up really high and very securely. If the horse paws when travelling, a foreleg can get caught in a badly tied haynet, pulling its shoulder muscles or causing it to panic, come down and be badly injured.

Do not travel a young horse with a haynet on its first short journeys, wait until it is used to travelling and will not panic or try to rear. Even then, be extremely careful and use a small net tied high enough to avoid these problems.

BANDAGES

Your youngster should wear travelling bandages or boots for protection. You may also feel a poll guard would be sensible. Get your horse totally accustomed to wearing all these things in the stable before it travels in them.

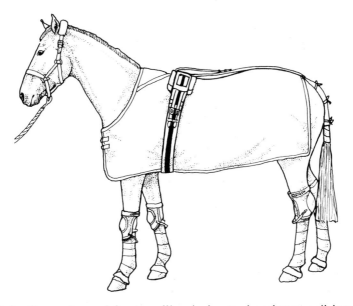

Figure 10.4 *Horse dressed for travelling in boots, bandages, tail bandage and poll guard.*

TRAVELLING ONE HORSE IN A LORRY

If possible, section off the area of the lorry containing the groom's door, or tie the horse well away from this door so that no part of its fore or hind legs can reach it. The door should always be kept clear so that you can have safe and easy access to attend to the horse.

Some horses will constantly kick out behind or bang and paw with a foreleg when travelling; the groom's door may break or buckle under this ceaseless barrage. Many serious accidents are caused by horses getting their legs stuck in damaged grooms' doors so keep your horse safely out of reach of this danger.

Alternatively, use a partition to section off the groom's door. The more solid type of partition should either fit very close to the floor or have a gap of 46−61 cm (18 in−2 ft) so, if the horse falls, there is no possibility of it getting a leg trapped between the partition and the floor.

Horses keep their balance more easily when travelling at an angle and

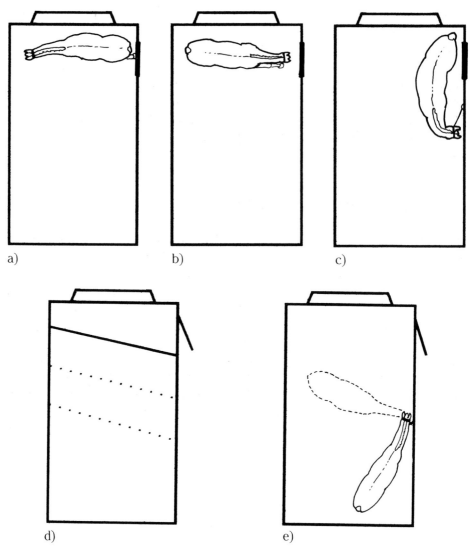

Figure 10.5 *Travelling one horse in a lorry. a) This horse could kick at the groom's door, and should the door open slightly a leg could be trapped. b) The horse could strike out at the groom's door with a foreleg and if the door was opened could try to get out. c) This horse could get trapped in a corner. d) The groom's door partitioned off for safety. The dotted lines show further spaces for other horses. e) No partitions so the horse is tied well away from the groom's door.*

also have a greater length in which to stand, and some prefer a wider stall to stand in. In a stall, as in a trailer, tie the horse so that its hindquarters can touch the side of the lorry before the rope pulls on the headcollar then it is less likely to pull back. When a horse pulls back on the rope its head goes up, its hind legs slip forward and it often falls.

When loading, close the partition then tie the horse up. When unloading, untie the horse before opening up the partition. Horse boxes are often designed so that the horses face directly to the front or rear. They travel well in this position but some may be frightened if the padded stalls are very narrow, and may lean their quarters and shoulders against one side of the division while scrabbling their feet on the floor near the opposite division. At such an angle they often fall and a fear of travelling can develop. Giving them a much wider stall so that they cannot get into this position should cure the problem.

DRIVING THE BOX OR TRAILER

Drive really carefully, starting and stopping very gradually, changing down in good time before corners and turning slowly and smoothly. Remember that the horse cannot anticipate starts, stops or corners and has no hands to hold on with. It has to balance on its feet and must be given time to alter its balance in order to stay upright. Never drive at speeds over 64 kmph (40 mph) and on your first few trips do not exceed 40 kmph (25 mph).

Imagine that you are driving with a bucketful of water in the back and do not want to spill a drop. Reluctance to load, scrabbling and panic are very often caused by experiences of bad driving. If all box or trailer drivers had to travel in the back just once without holding on with their hands, they would be much more considerate when driving horses!

11 RESCHOOLING

RESCHOOLING HORSES

If you have a horse that always rushes and hurries even on the flat, you will not slow it down by holding it back or using a more severe bit. Mark out a school of 20 × 40 m (22 × 44 yd), using cans and cones, and work the horse in this area in rising trot, never going straight, but always turning, circling and changing direction by using an endless pattern of serpentines and circles that are large enough for the horse to keep its balance.

At first stay on the same rein all the time. Because you are constantly circling, you will not need to hold the horse back; later the constant changes of direction will slow it down for you. You may need to do this for a full hour before a fit, strong horse will begin to relax and slow itself down, so you need to be fit too. Repeat this twice a day, stopping within a few minutes of the horse relaxing and slowing down to walk.

Always work in the same area until the horse begins to work quietly, then move about the field or school, still working in the same rhythm of rising trot and still changing direction. If the horse becomes excited or strong, immediately return to your original work area until it has relaxed and become soft in your hand. This really works but may take days, or occasionally weeks, depending on the horse (and rider). Progress to a few steps of canter, then trot again, aiming to keep the rhythm and lightness, and returning to the schooling area for correction when necessary.

By always cantering for only a few steps before returning to trot, you will take the excitement out of the gait. Knowing that it is going to be asked to trot again almost immediately, the horse will not get so much on its forehand and, for this reason, will find the transitions down much easier.

Progress to cantering only on the short sides of the school, using a circle in trot before and after each canter to steady and rebalance the horse if necessary. Next, canter along the long sides and trot on the short ones, using a circle in trot when you feel the horse has become unbalanced or is trying to hurry, and always be ready to go back a stage if things are not going well.

RESCHOOLING PONIES

Ponies are very intelligent and quickly learn how to get their own way, especially when ridden by very small, light children.

Perhaps the commonest trick is napping towards the gate or door of the school, with outside shoulder bulging and so much bend in the neck that the head is round on the rider's knee! The more the rider wants to go left, the more left rein they use, leaving the right rein (which controls the outside shoulder and the bend in the neck) in loops. The pony leads with its right shoulder and uses its near hind leg to push itself to the right. To correct this you must either long-rein the pony without a rider or get a good, lightweight rider to ride the pony forward into a strong contact on the right rein and, by using their right leg, to ride the pony forward in the required direction, thus preventing the neck from bulging out well before the pony tries it on.

If neither of these methods is possible, I would use side reins from the bit to the girth, fitted so that the rein is in a straight line when the pony is standing still with a normal head carriage. Lunge the pony first in the area near the gate so that it can feel the side reins before the rider is put on. Once the rider is on board, keep the lunge rein on at first and teach the rider to use the outside rein and leg for control. Now leave the side reins on and try without the lunge rein. The outside side rein will help to prevent the neck bulging out and will thus give the rider more control.

Lowering the head to gain control is another trick of little ponies whose small riders are easily pulled forward out of the saddle. To break this habit I

Figure 11.1 *To prevent a pony lowering its head and pulling a small rider forward, side reins, coming from the bit, are crossed over the crest of the neck, tied together there, then attached to the front Ds of the saddle on the opposite sides. They are not suitable for jumping.*

again use side reins, but this time I cross them at the withers so that the left rein comes from the bit over the withers and is attached to a D in front of the right side of the saddle, and vice versa. To ensure that the side reins will not 'open up' I tie them together on the crest of the neck where they cross. The tie must be far enough forward on the neck to prevent the head being lowered. The side reins must not come into action with a normal head carriage − only when the head is lowered. Lengths of baling twine can be substituted for side reins, but they must be adjusted very carefully to an equal length.

If the rider needs to have more control when jumping I put the side reins (or twine strings) from the bit up through the loops of the browband, knot them on the crest and fasten them on the front Ds of the saddle. The pony can then stretch its neck out to jump but cannot put its head between its knees or eat grass, the latter being the cause of a lot of trouble in the summer when fat ponies have to be kept short of grass to prevent laminitis.

For ponies that put their heads up to get control, or that nap and whip round, I use a Market Harborough. This looks like a running martingale but the straps continue through the bit and back onto the rein where they are attached by a buckle or clip to Ds on the rein (see page 109). They must be adjusted so that the rein comes into action just before the Market Harborough does in order to have a correcting action, not a forcing one. This action lengthens the pony's top line and can really improve a ewe-necked animal by developing the muscle along the top of the neck. It is safe to jump in a Market Harborough because it allows the horse to stretch forward and

Figure 11.2 *Grass reins will stop a pony perpetually trying to put its head down to eat, but also give it the freedom to stretch its neck forward for jumping. These reins are fitted the same as those in Fig. 11.1 but they pass through the loops of the browband before being attached to the bit.*

down, but make sure the pony is used to the feel of it before jumping in it. (You may not be allowed to use it when competing, so remember to check the rules before entering a competition.)

If the pony behaves it will not even know it is wearing a Market Harborough. I have found this a safe, successful correction for ponies and one that can be used without constant supervision because the single rein is easy for a child to manage. I have also used a Market Harborough to improve the head carriage of young ponies whose riders lack experience. It lengthens the top line of the neck and gives a good outline, without the rather 'set' look that is produced by constant lungeing in tight side reins or riding in the running reins that are used on many show ponies.

A Market Harborough can safely be used out hunting and has enabled many children to enjoy hunting ponies that would otherwise have been too much for them. As with a running martingale, the riders must be warned to be very careful not to let the straps get caught on gates.

Riders must also be warned to push their hands forward and ease the rein immediately if a horse or pony wearing a Market Harborough starts to run back. When worn for the first time, it must be adjusted loosely and used only under the supervision of an experienced person because some animals may not accept it.

A lot of damage can be done by gadgets used incorrectly but there is a correct time and place for many of them, particularly for reschooling when you want to get a result quickly and safely and remain in control. Before using any gadget, ask an expert to advise you, fit it for you and then to check frequently that all is going well. Dispense with it as soon as possible.

TO CALM A VERY EXCITABLE HORSE

If you are really experienced, and can work the horse in a very small paddock or indoor school, you will be amazed at the difference it makes if you take the horse's bit out and attach the reins to the rings of a drop noseband. Lead the horse about for a few minutes without the bit in its mouth. Talk to it, stroke it, gain its confidence.

Now mount but keep your seat out of the saddle, and your weight forward and a little to the inside as you ride on a 20 m (22 yd) circle. Keep both reins in your outside hand and stroke the horse's neck with your free hand. Ask the horse to walk on with your voice, keeping your weight out of the saddle and forward, the reins loose and your free hand stroking.

The horse will be very puzzled, its ears flicking rapidly backwards and forwards, its muscles tense under you. If the horse trots, stay forward. Do not attempt to hold it back, just put one rein in each hand and guide it gently on the circle with your inside rein. Keep your seat out of the saddle and talk quietly.

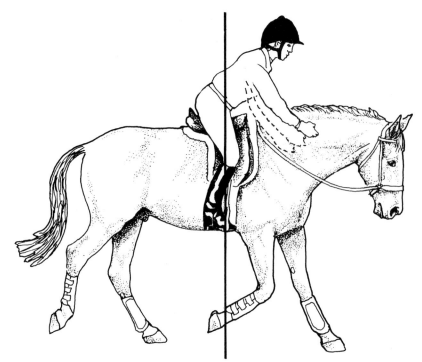

Figure 11.3 *Calming a very excitable horse by removing the bit, attaching the reins to the rings of a drop noseband, taking the weight out of the saddle, putting the reins in one hand, and stroking the horse's neck with the free hand. The line shows that the rider is in balance.*

Change direction without holding the horse back. If it canters, again keep your seat out of the saddle, stay on a big circle, sit in balance and talk to the horse and stroke its neck. When it trots of its own accord, begin to change direction frequently and go on doing this until the horse walks of its own accord.

Depending on the horse (and rider), it will take from ten minutes to half an hour using this method to have a relaxed horse going quietly at the pace you want.

A rider who tightens the reins or gets out of balance with the horse for even a second will hinder the progress.

I have done this myself literally hundreds of times and the results are really spectacular and often instant. I particularly remember once, when I was teaching in Ireland, I had a boy of about twenty in the class, on a very hot chestnut Thoroughbred that was creating havoc and throwing itself about. I took the bit out and rode the horse myself, exactly as described. It honestly went like a lamb and in ten minutes was relaxed and happy. The class were astounded and from then on believed every word I said and treated me with great reverence! The boy rode well enough to carry out the same procedure himself and it worked for him too.

I do exactly the same thing with horses and ponies that hot up and rush in jumping. Work them on the flat until they settle, then introduce jumping stands without poles. Never try to hold these horses back. Change direction to slow them down. When they no longer hurry at all when working between stands, put a pole on the ground and go over that, gradually working up until you have three or four very small cross poles, close together, but not in line, in the schooling area.

Never jump more than one fence at a time. Circle or change direction after each jump and always work in the same rhythm of rising trot. School the horse until it will keep this rhythm of its own accord. Trot away from the schooling area and jump other fences, coming in on a half-circle. Be careful not to go beyond the centre line of the fence in the approach, and follow the curve of the circle on landing. Never jump another fence until you have a calm horse going in the same, even rhythm. If the horse rushes, it must go back to the schooling area until it has completely settled again.

If you do not have a small safe, enclosed area, leave the bit in but put a second pair of reins on the noseband and ride with these, using the bit rein only in an emergency.

Obviously, an older horse that has rushed and been held back all its life will take longer to train, but if the rider is confident and has enough balance and feel, it is surprising how quickly even this sort of horse will improve. It is essential to be able to sit in balance with the horse at all times, and change your weight and rein aids very gradually and with perfect co-ordination. 'Think' what you want and be conscious of the feel and mood of the horse under you. Notice the gradual change from a tense horse with high head carriage, quickly moving ears, stiffness in the back, jerky gaits and noisy 'hard' footfalls to a softer ride with a lower head carriage, calmer ears and quieter, gentler footfalls.

The horse will be mentally and physically happier, more comfortable and calmer to ride, so will be more responsive to your wishes. A tense horse is often so worried that it does not listen to your aids. It then gets punished for its 'disobedience' and soon becomes a mental wreck!

12 FITTING TACK

BITTING

There are no hard and fast rules as to what bit should be used for a young horse. In the early stages of breaking some people use a bit with 'keys' that hang down from the centre of the mouthpiece. These keys lie on the tongue and their purpose is to encourage the horse to play with them, thus causing it to salivate and have a wet mouth. Some horses, however, will play with these keys all the time and will then go on to try to play, or in other words mess about, with any other bit they find in their mouths.

A straight rubber bit is fairly gentle but can give a rather dead feeling, and horses often chew these bits. If you do own one, check that it has a chain running through the middle for safety. Some makes do not and if these are bitten through there could be an accident.

A straight or half-moon metal bit does not give the horse or rider an independent feel on each side of the mouth; if you feel the left rein, the right side of the bit moves forward. It acts more directly on the top of the bars of the mouth and on the tongue. It is not so easy to keep a young horse going forward in a straight line in an unjointed bit.

Jointed bits act on the top and sides of the bars of the mouth, on the corners of the lips and also on the tongue. The two 'arms' can work independently and there is a certain amount of nutcracker action (inward pressure of each arm of the bit on the lower jaw).

Horses may chew a jointed rubber bit.

An eggbutt snaffle with smooth, rounded joints is less likely to rub the corners of the mouth.

A loose-ring snaffle allows the bit to move more freely in the mouth but may pinch the corners of the lips. The wire-ringed type fits more closely into its joints and is less likely to pinch the lips. Rubber 'biscuits' can be fitted to prevent pinching. The eggbutt mouthpiece prevents pinching but allows less movement of the bit.

The double, figure-of-eight-shaped joint of the French snaffle has hardly any nutcracker action. Many young horses go exceptionally well and happily in this bit. There is movement of the bit, there is room for the tongue, and the bit follows the natural shape of the horse's mouth. Each 'arm' can be used

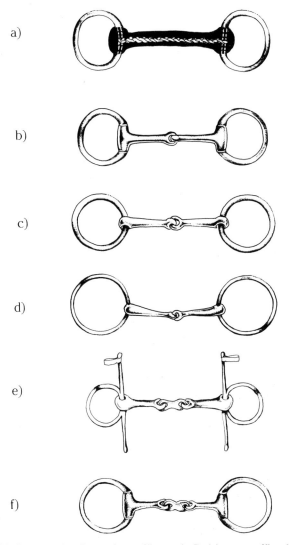

Figure 12.1 *A selection of snaffles. a) Rubber snaffle (with a chain running through it for safety). b) Eggbutt snaffle. c) Loose-ring snaffle. d) Wire ring snaffle. e) French snaffle with cheeks. f) French eggbutt snaffle.*

independently. There is very little to fight or dislike about this bit.

Horses' tongues vary in thickness and a horse with a thick tongue may find a thick bit too much of a mouthful. A double-jointed bit such as the French snaffle will give a thick tongue more room. If you use one with cheeks kept in place by little leather keepers attached to the cheek pieces of the bridle, the keepers will keep the cheeks in line with the bridle, and the cheeks keep the bit raised up in the horse's mouth which a fussy-mouthed or thick-tongued horse may find more comfortable.

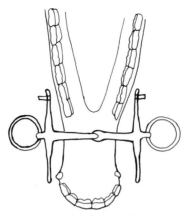

Figure 12.2 *The mouthpiece of a cheek snaffle sits higher in the horse's mouth.*

Figure 12.3 *The different positions in which a cheek snaffle and a ring snaffle hang in a horse's mouth.*

Any form of jointed cheek snaffle must be used correctly, with the keepers in place. This bit hangs at a totally different angle to a jointed ring bit and acts on a different part of the mouth. Its action is a little higher up on the tongue and a little higher up on the bars of the mouth. Because the bit hangs higher and the pressure is higher up on the tongue, the horse is much less likely to try to get its tongue over the bit when first introduced to this new feeling. There is more direct nutcracker action on the lower jaw with the single jointed bit and the cheekpieces help to 'steer' the horse more accurately.

The habit of getting the tongue over the bit must be avoided as, once established, it is very difficult to cure. It is much better to have the bit slightly too high in the mouth at first than to allow the horse to get its tongue over.

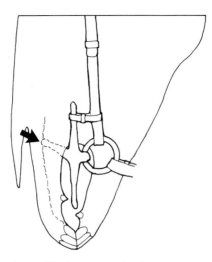

Figure 12.4 *If a cheek snaffle is too wide, it presses on the roof of the mouth when the reins are used (the arrow shows the pressure point). Note the leather keepers correctly attached to the cheekpieces.*

The bit must not be too wide for the horse's mouth or the joint of a jointed ring snaffle will hang down in a low V in the centre of the mouth. The pressure of the bit will then come low down on the tongue and the horse can very easily bring its tongue over the bit. In addition, as you feel on one rein, the bit will slide through the horse's mouth and the centre joint may then press directly on the bars of the mouth on that side.

If a cheek snaffle is too wide, the joint will stick up in a V into the roof of the horse's mouth when you feel on the reins, probably causing the horse to open its mouth and throw its head up.

Well-bred, Thoroughbred-type horses and Arabs have very narrow lower jaws, often no wider than that of a 12 hh pony, so use a bit that is suitable for the width of your horse's jaw. Do not assume that because the horse is 16.2 hh it will automatically require a large bit. A well-fitting bit should protrude about 7 mm (¼ in) on each side of the horse's mouth.

'Mouthy' Horses

Some young horses are very 'mouthy', chewing or manoeuvring the bit in their mouths all the time, moving their tongues all over the place raising, lowering and turning their heads in their efforts to get rid of the bit. It is better not to try to control these horses' heads in any way. After a week of daily lungeing or loose-schooling, they will usually settle down.

Jointed or straight-bar bits, made of metal, nylon, rubber or vulcanite, can be tried to see if one is more acceptable to the horse but this behaviour usually remains the same no matter what bit is in the horse's mouth – the horse just hates the feeling and wants to be rid of it. Sometimes leaving the bridle on in the stable for a few hours each day can work, but you must make quite sure that there is nothing for the bridle or bit rings to get caught up on. Also be aware that the horse may attempt to get rid of the bridle by rubbing it off over its ears. Sometimes a Polo mint tied in the centre of the bit can occupy the horse's mind (see page 197).

If this problem has still not been overcome when you begin to ride the horse, you will have difficulties because the constant head movement unbalances the horse and makes control very difficult. Sometimes removing the bit and riding in a mild bitless bridle or attaching the reins to a drop noseband will enable you to ride the horse, but you should only do this in a small, enclosed area because you will not have much control over a very 'green' horse.

When the horse can be guided by pressure on its nose, try putting the bit in without reins attached to it and continue to use nose pressure alone to guide the horse. Next, attach a second set of reins to the bit in the normal way but continue to use mostly the noseband reins, gradually taking up a little contact on the bit rein as well.

A young horse may have a sore, uncomfortable mouth when teething; the age between three and five causing most trouble. Be patient and aware of how your horse's teeth are developing. If the horse seems really uncomfortable, do not use a bit for a few days. Uncomfortable, sharp teeth or loose milk teeth can be the cause of mouthiness, as can wolf teeth.

Very often, however, this resentment of the bit seems to be a mental problem. Some horses get over it completely but this can take a year or longer. It is no good tying up the horse's head with gadgets, nor getting furious, because this will simply make the horse's tension worse. Patience, and riding on as light a contact as possible, using your weight, voice and legs as aids, but very little rein, may win through eventually. Obviously, such a horse will never go well for someone with heavy or rough hands.

A young horse's soft skin at the corners of the lips often gets rubbed by the bit. Keep the skin greased with Vaseline so that splits will not form. These cause a lot of pain and can become chronic. Rubber rings or 'biscuits' on the bit may help but they can be very fiddly when bridling a young horse.

FITTING A BRIDLE

Before putting on a bridle for the first time, put a head collar on first. Move the horse's quarters into a corner of the box. Let the horse sniff this new thing. If the horse is worried by bridling or tacking up in general and turns away into a corner, presenting its hindquarters to you each time you approach, take a handful of food or a carrot with you to encourage the horse to look forward to your coming.

Remove the noseband from the bridle then hold the bridle up against the horse's head to get a rough idea of fit. Undo all the keepers so that you can quickly readjust the bridle when it is on.

As you lift the bridle with your right hand, keep it well away from the horse's eyes. Use the finger and thumb of your left hand to ease the bit into the mouth, being careful not to bang it against the teeth. Slip the headpiece carefully over the ears (by pointing the ears forward, not folding them in half and tugging them through as so many people do).

Adjust the bridle. Open the mouth a little to see where the joint of the bit is lying. It is better to have it too high than too low to avoid the horse getting its tongue over the bit.

If the horse is afraid of its ears being touched, undo the nearside cheekpiece and remove the browband completely, or slip the nearside loop out so that the headpiece does not have to be passed over the ears.

If you use an ordinary cavesson noseband with the bridle, it should lie two fingers' width below the projecting cheekbone and you should be able to insert two fingers inside the noseband. If you use a drop noseband, it must lie well clear of the nostrils, resting right up on the bony part of the nose, and also be loose enough to insert two fingers.

Make sure the cavesson noseband is fitted high enough so that the corner of the top lip is not pinched between the noseband and the bit when you feel on the reins. This is often only noticeable when you are using the reins, so ask someone to check this for you when you apply the rein. Such pinching can cause sore lips, head tossing or even rearing and often the rider is totally unaware of the cause.

As you take the bridle off over the ears with one hand, keep the other hand on the nose until the bit is safely out of the mouth. This will prevent the horse from throwing up its head, causing the bit to bang against its

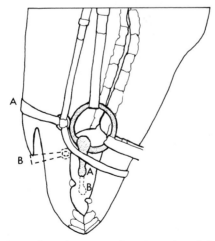

Figure 12.5 *The fitting of a drop noseband and a jointed loose-ring snaffle. Correct fitting (A), and incorrect fitting (B − dotted line).*

teeth and frightening it or even getting caught behind its front teeth, especially the tushes. Incidents like this upset the horse and make it run back. It will also expect pain every time the bridle is removed.

Stand the horse with its hindquarters in a corner as you take its bridle off, so that it cannot run back.

When using a bridle with a lungeing cavesson, put the bridle on first. The cavesson headpiece then goes over the top of the bridle headpiece, but the padded nosepiece of the cavesson should do up inside the bridle cheek-pieces, so that there is a smooth, snug fit. The Wels-type lungeing cavesson is fitted below the bit, just like a drop noseband. With both types, it is easier if you remove the leather noseband from the bridle.

Either take the bridle reins off completely or twist them, one over the other, under the neck until there are no loops hanging down loose, then pass the throatlash through one loop and do it up. This keeps the reins safe and secure and is better than looping them twice round the horse's neck from where they can slip off over the ears if the horse suddenly bucks or lowers its head.

FITTING A SADDLE

Tie the horse up or ask someone to hold it. Let the horse sniff the numnah and then put it on the horse's back and move it about. Use a warm type of numnah rather than one of the 'cold' cloth ones. (It is advisable to use a numnah because a young horse's back is soft and unaccustomed to the pressure of a saddle.)

Let the horse sniff the saddle (with the stirrups removed) which should already have the girth attached on the off side. Place the saddle on the horse's back making sure it easily clears the withers and spine but will not sit up so high that it is unstable. Do not let go of the saddle for a second as the horse may be very frightened if it moves about too much or falls off its back.

Ask an assistant to let the girth down gently on the off side and pass it to you. Hold the girth strap in one hand and the girth in the other and gently let the horse feel the pressure of the girth. If the horse is already used to a roller, there should be no problem, but if this is the first time the horse has felt something tight round its middle it may panic completely when you do the girth up.

The girth must be done up just tight enough for the saddle to stay in place however much the horse bucks. Unlike a roller, which can be tightened gradually and is unlikely to make the horse panic even if it does slip round, the saddle will cause sheer terror, and quite possibly lasting fear, if you do not do the girth up tightly enough to keep it in place and it ends up under the horse's belly.

Figure 12.6 *The saddle's lowest point is too far back (indicated by arrow), and the whole saddle slopes backward. The rider will slide to the back of this saddle.*

Figure 12.7 *This saddle's lowest point is further forward (indicated by arrow), and it sits level on the horse. This saddle will help a rider to sit correctly.*

Tie the horse up and leave the saddle on for half an hour or so in the stable for several days before taking the horse outside in it, unless the horse is very familiar with the feel of a fairly tight roller. (The horse must be tied up otherwise it may roll in the saddle and break the tree or roll over and become cast against the side of the box.) For safety reasons, do not have leathers or stirrups on the saddle at this point in training.

Remember always to place the saddle gently on the horse's back. Do not let the girth clonk against the horse's legs. Be careful not to pinch the skin or pull the hair as you do the girth up and pass your hand between the girth and the horse to be sure it is comfortable.

Checking the Fit of a Saddle

Horses and ponies change shape with age and degrees of fitness in winter and summer, so check the fitting of the saddle regularly. Check the fit without a numnah. You should be able to see daylight right through from pommel to cantle and there should be no inward-pinching pressure just below the withers, a problem that sometimes occurs with very narrow, high-withered animals. When you are mounted, stand in your stirrups and lean forward with your fingers under the front arch of the saddle; they should not get pinched. There should be room for two to three fingers to fit. If in doubt, ask an experienced person to check the fitting.

If the saddle panels feel hard and flat, they need restuffing. Make sure the saddle sits on the horse so that the lowest part is at the centre. If the lowest

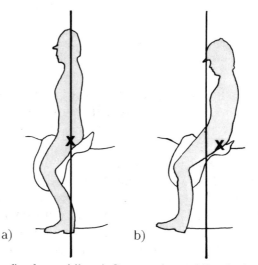

Figure 12.8   *The fit of a saddle. a) Correct: the saddle sits level with the deepest point in the centre (X), and the rider is in balance. b) Incorrect: the saddle slopes backwards with the lowest point at the back (X). The rider's seat slides back and the lower leg comes forward putting the rider behind the movement and out of balance with the horse.*

part is too far back, you will slide to the back of the saddle, with your lower leg forward, and be out of balance with the horse (behind the movement), encouraging it to hollow its back, move with a high head carriage and trail its hind legs.

Make sure the weight is evenly distributed on the saddle panels and carried over a wide area of the back, supported on the muscles that lie on each side of the spine.

If, having been quiet to mount, your horse now becomes fidgety, suspect that the saddle is hurting its back and investigate this by feeling and pressing on the bare back. If, as you lean forward when preparing to dismount, the horse throws up its head, puts its ears back or fidgets and seems apprehensive, the saddle is probably pinching inwards below its withers. Leaning forward to get off would immediately increase the pressure here and should give you an early warning of trouble. When a horse's normal pattern of behaviour changes, uncomfortable equipment is often the cause, so check this very carefully before assuming the horse is just misbehaving.

SAFETY OF SADDLERY

The antics of a young horse can put a lot of strain on your saddlery, so buy the best quality saddlery you can afford from a reputable saddler. Always use stainless-steel bits and stirrup irons for safety. Make sure your stirrup irons are big enough for your feet to slip out of easily in a fall. Nickel bits can break without warning, cutting your horse's mouth and leaving you without any control on a frightened animal. Nickel stirrup irons can break or bend or even close on your foot if the horse falls on a hard surface.

Buy the best quality leather, especially for your stirrup leathers and reins. These days so much imported saddlery is of an inferior quality, and although it is certainly cheaper than British or the better quality foreign leather it may well snap suddenly and cause an accident.

Every time you clean your leatherwork, check the stitching on every part of your saddle and bridle. Look at the girth straps. Have the holes split slightly? Check the webbing that attaches the girth straps to the saddle. There should be three girth straps and two pieces of webbing. One piece of webbing is attached to the front girth strap and the other is attached to the back two girth straps. If you use either the first and second girth straps or the first and third girth straps you have the safety offered by both pieces of webbing, so that if one piece of webbing breaks, your saddle will still not come off. Do not, therefore, attach your girth to the second and third girth straps because, if the webbing breaks, the saddle will come off causing an accident.

Check the buckles and stitching, and the webbing, leather or other material of your girth. Always use either a pair of girths or a girth with two buckles at each end so that if one breaks the remaining buckle will prevent the saddle from coming off.

Keep your girth clean and supple, not only to prevent breakage, but also to protect the horse from rubs and sores.

Check your girth before you mount. A saddle slipping round as you get on can terrify a young horse and may make it difficult to mount for months afterwards. Check your girth while out on a ride and always before jumping. If the girth is loose and the horse shies or swerves, your weight shifting over to one side can make the saddle slip and panic the horse. You could have a bad fall, and if, as a result, the saddle slips round underneath the horse it can be so terrified that it may gallop into a fence and really hurt itself. It is quite likely that the horse will never forget this incident, so be careful.

On the bridle, check the folds in the cheekpieces where the bit hangs, because the leather here can become dry and brittle and rot, as can the leather where the reins are attached to the bit. Check the stud billets and the buckles to see that all the metal parts are strong and unbent and that the leather attaching them is sound. Check the bit to see if it is worn and damaged.

Check your stirrup leathers to see if the holes have split. If they have always been used at the same length, there may be a weak place in the leather where the stirrup iron always hangs. If this is the case, take the leathers to the saddler and have them shortened a few inches so that the iron will hang in a new place.

If the saddle tree breaks, the front arch of your saddle, which previously fitted your horse well, can open out so that the saddle presses down on your horse's withers. This damage to the saddle can be caused by a fall or a structural weakness.

To test a saddle for a broken tree, hold it, seat upwards, with the cantle (back of the saddle) resting against your stomach and one hand at each side of the front arch, thumbs upwards. Try to wiggle the front arch in and out, using all the strength of your hands. If there is any movement or squeaking sounds, the tree is damaged and must be checked by a professional saddler.

After mounting, check regularly the fit of your saddle by putting all the fingers of one hand under the front arch on the horse's backbone. Now stand in your stirrups and lean forward. If your fingers get pinched, the saddle does not fit the horse, will hurt its backbone, and will need restuffing in order to fit the horse correctly and comfortably again. It should be stuffed properly so that there are no ridges sticking into the horse on either side of the withers or at the back of the saddle. If a great deal of stuffing is put in at the front, the saddle may then be uncomfortable for you and tip you backwards, so it is a good idea to get an experienced person to check the

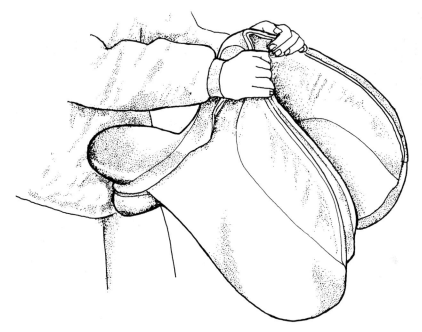

Figure 12.9   *Testing a saddle for a broken tree.*

fit of the saddle on your horse. A saddle cannot be made to fit any horse by restuffing or by the use of a numnah. If it does not fit, you must change it for one that does.

A GOOD SADDLE FOR THE RIDER

When riding a young horse you need a comfortable saddle that you feel secure in. A general purpose saddle with slight knee rolls should prove suitable. Make sure that the lowest part of the saddle is in the centre or slightly nearer to the pommel so that it will be easier for you to sit in balance with the horse and go with it if it shoots forward.

The saddle should distribute your weight evenly over the horse's back. If the saddle sits with the lowest part towards the back, your seat will continually slide backwards to the lowest point, your lower leg will come forward and you will be behind the movement and out of balance with your horse. Your weight will be further back on the horse, making you more difficult and more uncomfortable for the horse to carry. You will find riding much more difficult in this position. If the horse leaps forward or misbehaves, you will be left behind. Your hands will probably go up and you are likely to yank the horse in the mouth, with disastrous results.

13 FEEDING YOUNGSTERS

A VERY GENERAL FEEDING GUIDE

Heating foods
oats
maize
peas
beans
barley
high protein or high performance mixes

Non-heating foods
hay
oat straw
bran
soaked sugar beet
carrots
horse and pony nuts
grass nuts
non-heating mixes

When you first ride your young horse, feed only non-heating foods. If it is lively enough and does not tire easily on these foods, stick to them until you feel the horse does need more energy. Only then should you introduce small amounts (450−900 g [1−2 lb] a day) of the more heating foods and see how the horse behaves for a week or two before slightly increasing the amount.

I am not suggesting that you should keep your horse short of food so that it is quiet enough for you to ride, merely that you do not overfeed it on the wrong type of food so that it becomes difficult to manage.

So many problems are caused by overfeeding and a lack of exercise. A horse that is calm, sensible and obliging when kept out and ridden off grass can become an entirely different animal − bursting with energy and devilment − when kept in a stable and overfed and underexercised. The horse can become unmanageable and the owner frightened.

FEEDING GUIDE FOR YOUNG STOCK

(This guide is very approximate as horses vary enormously in size and temperament.)

If at all possible, and no matter what age your youngster is, try to turn it out every day.

294

Foal to one year old

- Accustom the foal to bucket feeds before weaning.
- The foal is probably best kept in at night for the first winter.
- Start feeding at the end of August — earlier if the grass is poor.
- Feed 900 g (2 lb) a day in one or two feeds for one month, then two feeds a day (total 1.8 kg [4 lb]) or, if using a brand mix, feed according to the makers' recommendations for age and weight.
- Give good quality hay ad lib.
- Give access to a mineral salt lick.
- Clean water must always be available.

One to two years old

- Keep in or out at night according to the breed, the youngster's condition and whether the field is well sheltered or not.
- Start feeding at the end of August (earlier if the grass is poor).
- Feed 900 g–1.4 kg (2–3 lb) a day in two feeds, increasing over time to 2.7 kg (6 lb) a day or, if using a brand mix, feed according to the makers' recommendations for age and weight.
- Give good quality hay ad lib.
- Give access to a mineral salt lick.
- Clean water must always be available.

Two to three years old

- As for one to two years but increasing the feed gradually to 2.7–3.6 kg (6–8 lb) a day or as recommended by the maker of the brand mix you are using.
- Give good quality hay ad lib.
- Give access to a mineral salt lick.
- Clean water must always be available.

Three to four years old

- At this age the amount of hard food that should be given depends on:
  the build of the horse
  temperament (do not overfeed an excitable horse)
  the work the horse is doing
  its bodily condition.
- Give three feeds a day, totalling 1.4–4 kg (3–9 lb) of hard feed, or as recommended by the manufacturer of a brand mix.
- Give good quality hay ad lib unless the horse is very fat when the hay must be rationed but given in four small feeds to prevent boredom.
- Feed a very lively horse sugar beet (soaked), bran and non-heating nuts.
- If the horse is fat and well, it will only need a total of 900 g–1.8 kg (2–4 lb) bucket feed a day to keep condition.
- Give access to a mineral salt lick.
- Clean water must always be available.

Four to six years of age

- Feed according to the horse's build, temperament and the amount of work it is doing.
- Give 1.8–4 kg (4–9 lb) of bucket feed a day, divided into three or four feeds, or the amount recommended by the makers of the brand mix you use, adjusted to suit your own horse. Start with a few kilos and increase the amount gradually. Do not overfeed hard feed to a young horse or it may get out of hand. If you cut down the hard feed, increase the hay. As a very rough guide for a horse in work, give its height in pounds of hay and half its height in pounds of bucket feed (1 lb = 450 g).
- Give good quality hay ad lib unless the horse is too fat.
- Give access to a mineral salt lick.
- Clean water must always be available.

Winter Feeding

This is an enormous subject, but if your young horse is just being hacked out and is not enormously fat, it can have as much good hay as it can eat. This should be offered from early September until the end of April (and even in the summer if there is a real shortage of grass in the field). The youngster may also need two feeds a day. Probably two double handfuls of dry sugar beet pulp which has been soaked for at least twelve hours (sugar beet nuts need 24 hours' soaking), mixed with 900 g (2 lb) of horse and pony nuts and 450 g (1 lb) of bran or Mollichaff fed twice a day will be sufficient. Start with a small amount. An overfed, overfresh horse can soon learn to take advantage of its rider.

To keep the horse in good condition, with no ribs showing, a well-rounded outline and a good neck, – the youngster may need more food. Feed whole barley, boiled until soft and swollen, coarse mix, or any of the many brands of non-heating foods available, up to 1.8–2.7 kg (4–6 lb) a day. A horse that is hunting or doing fast work will need less hay and more hard food, up to 3.6–4.5 kg (8–10 lb). Always remember to increase the amount of hard food very gradually. Feed according to the amount of work the horse is doing, the horse's temperament and your riding ability. A mineral lick and clean water should always be available.

Do not be afraid to ask a knowledgeable person to check your horse's condition and advise you on feeding.

Losing weight

If your horse is losing weight for no apparent reason, you should examine its teeth to see if the horse finds chewing difficult. A horse's top jaw is much wider than its bottom jaw. As it chews with a sideways motion, the outside edges of the top teeth do not get worn down and thus can become

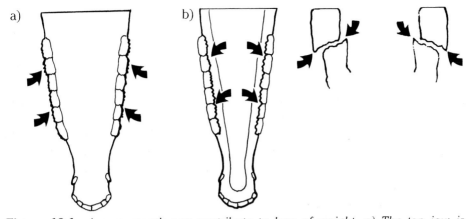

Figure 13.1 *A sore mouth can contribute to loss of weight. a) The top jaw is wider than the lower jaw, and the outside edges of the top teeth do not get worn and may cut the cheeks making chewing uncomfortable. b) Lack of wear on the inside edges of the teeth in the narrower lower jaw may mean the sharp edges cut the tongue. This is not such a common problem as (a). (The arrows indicate the sharp edges on the teeth.)*

sharp, cutting the cheeks and making chewing very uncomfortable. Normally, a horse will chew with an easy, regular rhythm. If it has sharp teeth, however, it will give two or three chews then cross its jaw, half-opening its mouth, and let partly chewed food drop out (quidding) then chew for another few seconds.

Sometimes the inside edges of the bottom teeth can also become sharp so that they cut the tongue, but this is not nearly so common a problem.

A young horse may also find chewing uncomfortable when it has loose incisor or molar milk teeth.

To check the horse's teeth, put on a head collar that is big enough to allow the horse to open its mouth easily. Have an assistant to steady the horse's head by putting a hand on its nose, well above the nostrils. Hold the tongue out to one side with one hand and insert your other hand, flat and palm inwards, into the gap between the top teeth and the cheek on the other side. Push out towards the cheek with your fingers and push your hand back as far as possible to feel for sharp edges. Repeat on the other side. Teeth should be checked every six months and rasped by the vet if necessary.

Mares have 36 teeth; geldings or stallions have 40. The four extra teeth in males, called the tushes, are found between the molars and the incisors. These tushes often collect lumps of tartar which make the gums very sore. The tartar can easily be removed with a hoof pick or small pair of pliers.

Wolf teeth (tiny, extra teeth found in the top jaw just in front of the first molar) can sometimes cause discomfort. They are easily removed by a vet.

Figure 13.2 *Holding the horse's tongue out to one side in order to check for sharp edges on the teeth, with the help of an assistant.*

If you have wormed the horse regularly every six weeks, worms should not be the cause of weight loss, but, to be sure, send a sample of the youngster's droppings to the vet for a worm count. If there is nothing wrong, yet the horse is still losing weight, have a blood test done because the horse may be anaemic and an anaemic horse will not put on weight.

Increasing the amount of boiled barley, bran and Mollichaff, and adding linseed may help. Use one teacupful of raw linseed a day. It *must* be well boiled until it forms a jelly or it can be poisonous. A 14.2 hh pony could need as much as 3.6 kg (8 lb) (dry weight) per day of barley, bran or chaff, nuts and sugar beet pulp, plus 7.25 kg (16 lb) of hay if it is working hard. This total of 10.85 kg (24 lb) is above average but some ponies do need it. If they are looking a bit lightweight, they must be given as much as they can eat if they are working. A horse will need a total of 11.8–13.6 kg (26–30 lb) of food per day, according to type and weight.

Ponies and horses that live out often get lice; lice are bloodsuckers and can very quickly reduce equines to skin and bone. The first lice always seem to appear around the ears and roots of the forelock. Look carefully every week from November until spring for tiny, yellowish-grey, pin-head-size bodies creeping about on the skin between the hairs, or yellowish eggs sticking to the hairs. Even if you only find one or two, treat the horse, because they breed very quickly. Louse powder placed on your hand and rubbed in gently on the forelock, mane, neck, all along the back and roots of the tail will kill them. Shaking the powder on chokes you and frightens

Figure 13.3 *Tartar on the tushes can make the gums sore. The tartar can be removed with careful use of a hoof pick or a small pair of pliers.*

the horse. Repeat the application once a fortnight. Look carefully even if your pony is fat and well and you feel your care of it is excellent. Any pony can get lice but the careful owner finds and treats them in time.

All animals that live out in winter must have a sheltered field with trees, high hedges or walls for protection against wind and weather. If several animals share a field, it is essential that you make sure your animal has its fair share of food. It will probably be necessary to bring it in out of the field and hold it while it eats its bucket feed. Ensure that there are more haynets or piles of hay than the number of horses, or the nervous horse will never get any. (Remember to loop the strings through the bottom of the hay nets and tie them really high so that legs will not get caught in empty haynets.) Watch the horses feeding. If you see that your animal is always being chased away from the food and is getting thinner, you will have to make another plan to ensure it gets its share.

The grass has little food value after August and does not really grow again until May, so your winter feeding will need to start in September and continue until May. Small ponies can live out in a big field all winter and may look fat and well without any hay, other than during a hard frost or snow. Make sure the 'fat' you think you see is not just a big, woolly coat over a skeleton! Monitor the condition of each animal by feeling the crest, ribs and hips regularly and increasing the food as soon as an animal *starts* to lose any weight.

In frosty weather, remember to break the ice on the water trough several times a day or provide buckets of water.

14 ADVICE FOR THE RIDER AND TRAINER

USING YOUR VOICE

Your voice is a most important aid when working with a young horse. Even a foal can learn to obey your vocal commands and to know from the tone of your voice whether you are pleased or cross with it, so talk to your horse as you approach it and when you handle it in the stable. Do not click your tongue as you approach a horse because this will *not* calm it.

When giving vocal commands, you must be absolutely consistent in your use of words and in your tone of voice. 'Whoa!' or 'Stand!' – whichever you prefer to use – must be taught early on. Be really strict in teaching this command, although at first you can only expect to be obeyed for seconds. If possible, work on this every day with your youngster because a horse that will stand still when told to can save both itself and its rider from accidents.

This is particularly important when mounting, a time when you are easily unbalanced and very vulnerable. Do not let your horse move off the minute you sit in the saddle. Make it wait while you check your girth, adjust your stirrup leathers and put your gloves on. If you always do this the horse will learn to relax and wait until it is asked to move off.

Keep your vocal commands to a maximum of three words at a time when lungeing or loose-schooling. If you talk all the time the horse will stop listening to you. A short, sharp reprimand may be necessary if the horse misbehaves while it is moving, then repeat your normal vocal command.

Use a slow, calm, deep voice to decrease pace or gait and a quick, bright, higher tone to increase pace or gait. Precede all vocal commands with the word 'and' to get the horse's attention. Praise the horse when it is at halt out on the track, or go up to it and praise and stroke or scratch it. Do not allow the horse to come in to you or it will always be trying to do so.

When riding your young horse, use exactly the same vocal commands and apply your weight, leg and rein aids in that order after your spoken command so that the horse learns to connect these new aids with the vocal commands it already understands.

If a horse is tense or worried while you are riding it, talk to it in a calm, soothing voice and keep on talking. This will also help you not to tense up or stiffen (and so worry the horse even more) because while you are talking you will be breathing normally and are therefore more relaxed.

When your horse sees something it is frightened of and raises its head, pricks its ears and shortens its stride, repeat your vocal command 'Walk on!, Walk on!' as you use your seat and legs to encourage the youngster to go forward.

A horse that answers to your voice is a pleasant, easy ride and there is no reason why you should not continue to use your voice when riding an older horse. The sound of your voice can give your horse confidence and encouragement, calm it down or wake it up, reward it, warn it to behave or reprimand it when it is being naughty.

Do remember, however, that you will lose marks for using your voice in a dressage test and that it is considered most unprofessional to shout at your horse while jumping in competitions or to click your tongue when riding in company.

SAFE CLOTHING

Always ride in a BSI (British Standards Institution) approved hard hat that is securely fastened. Gloves should be worn to protect your hands when holding the reins and to prevent rope burns when leading. It is also sensible to wear a hard hat when leading, loose-schooling, lungeing, long-reining and loading any horse, but especially youngsters.

Always fasten your coat or anorak before mounting, as a flapping garment can cause an accident. Never ride a young horse in any garment that crackles as you move. Do not carry anything in your pockets that will rattle or that could harm you or the horse in a fall.

Never ride in any form of footwear that does not have a heel. If you fall, your foot could slip right through the stirrup iron and you could be dragged, with fatal consequences. It is best to ride in proper jodhpur boots or riding boots. Wellington boots are too soft and bulky.

THE DOS AND DON'TS OF WORKING WITH YOUNG HORSES

Do:
- Check the fitting of all tack.
- Look for rubs or sore places.
- Note any change in your horse's behaviour in the stable or when ridden or worked.
- Note any change in the horse's eating or drinking habits.
- Note any change in its droppings.
- Notice any change in your horse's bodily condition.

- Worm your horse regularly.
- Ask the farrier to come regularly.
- Feed your horse according to its temperament, the work it is doing and your own riding ability.
- Be prepared to change your plan for the day if the weather is bad — wind, heavy rain or thunder can all upset a horse.
- Avoid riding a thin-skinned horse at a time of day when the flies are very bad.
- Put yourself in the horse's place and try to think as it does.
- Be calm and quiet in handling the horse.
- Make your requests clear and concise.
- Realise that it is usually you who are at fault, not the horse.
- Ask for experienced help and advice the first time anything goes wrong.
- Be prepared to go back a step or more in your training whenever necessary.
- Think of your horse's well being and comfort before your own.
- Work consistently and logically with your horse.
- Be prepared to give your horse several weeks' rest when necessary.
- Be very observant.
- Be a 'thinking' trainer.
- Introduce anything new in the horse's own stable first.
- Practise everything you do on an older horse first.

Don't:
- Lunge, long-rein or ride a young horse if you are in a hurry, cross, tired, tense or pressurised in any way.
- Work a young horse in any way if you are frightened of it.
- Try to progress too quickly.
- Try to find out how high the horse can jump.
- Give other people rides on your horse.
- Have a battle with your horse — it is bigger and stronger than you are.
- Show off on a young horse.
- Gallop a young horse.
- Ever lose your temper.
- Constantly feed titbits.
- Overfeed high-energy foods.
- Use more and more severe bits to try to control your horse.
- Shout at your horse.
- Jab your horse in the mouth — either when riding or leading — because you are cross.
- Hit your horse because things are not going well and you are frustrated or angry.
- Try to open a gate on a young horse if the gate opens towards you. (The horse may dive through and trap your leg in the gate.)

- Pull a gate shut behind you as you go through − it will trap the horse's heels.
- Continue to work a horse that shows signs of tiredness or weakness (dragging toes, brushing, stumbling, loss of weight, clicking/forgeing, lying down a lot).
- Work a horse that is growing and changing shape rapidly (much higher behind than in front, for example).
- Work a young horse in very deep or very unlevel going.
- Hurry when loading a young horse into a lorry or trailer.
- Drive fast when travelling a young horse.
- Try to do something with or on a young horse unless you have done it successfully several times on an older horse first.
- Do anything without thinking − you may regret it afterwards.
- Muck out the stable with a wheelbarrow across the doorway when your horse is loose in the stable.
- Let small children in a field with loose horses.

INDEX